SPHERES OF INFLUENCE

BY SYDNEY MORRELL

I SAW THE CRUCIFIXION: The Story of Munich

SPHERES OF INFLUENCE

SPHERES
OF
INFLUENCE

SYDNEY MORRELL

DUELL, SLOAN AND PEARCE
NEW YORK

940.5
M841s.

PRINTED IN THE UNITED STATES OF AMERICA
BY THE VAIL-BALLOU PRESS, INC., BINGHAMTON, N. Y.

This book is dedicated to the memory of Walter Ludwig Peres, formerly of the European Communist Movement, who lived to see the end of the Russian myth but who fought on for democracy. Beheaded in Prague, May, 1941.

ACKNOWLEDGMENT

THE texts of foreign broadcasts quoted in this book are as given by the former daily monitoring reports of the Federal Communications Commission, now the Foreign Broadcast Intelligence Service of the War Department. My thanks are also due to friends and former colleagues of the United States Office of War Information who discussed with me the many aspects of their work, and to Kathleen Bowker who assisted materially in reading the manuscript.

"Only by taking infinitesimally small units for observation (the differential of history, that is, the individual tendencies of men) and attaining to the art of integrating them (that is, finding the sum of these infinitesimals) can we hope to arrive at the laws of history. . . . We must completely change the subject of our observation, must leave aside kings, ministers, and generals, and study the common, infinitesimally small elements by which the masses are moved."

—TOLSTOY, *War and Peace.*

GLOSSARY

AMG	Anglo-American Military Government in former enemy territory.
AFHQ	Allied Force Headquarters in Italy for the whole southern and southeastern European theatre.
BBC	British Broadcasting Corporation, a monopoly organization operating under Royal Charter and controlled by the British Government.
CHETNIKS	Jugoslav nationalist guerrillas serving under Draja Mihailovitch. Bitterly opposed to the Jugoslav Partisans.
EAM	The National Liberation Movement of Greece, ostensibly an all-party movement.
EDES	Greek nationalist guerrillas serving under General Zervas. Anti-communist in policy and opposed to EAM, which they accused of being controlled by the communists.
ELAS	The army of EAM.
KKE	The Communist Party of Greece. Also possessed its own elite forces in ELAS in much the same way as the NAZI SS preserved its own special military formations and separate identity within the German Army.
OWI	The United States Office of War Information, in charge of psychological warfare on behalf of the United States.
OZNA	The secret police of the Jugoslav Partisans. Patterned on the lines of the Russian OGPU.
PWB	Psychological Warfare Branch, in charge of psychological warfare under the Anglo-American armies. Its personnel comprised officials from OWI, PWE, and technical specialists from the armed forces. Operated only in a theatre of military operations.
PWE	Political Warfare Executive, in charge of psychological warfare on behalf of the British Government. Operated under the joint control of the British Foreign Office and the British Ministry of Information.
TUDEH	Russian-sponsored "Workers' Party" in Iran.
UNRRA	United Nations Relief and Rehabilitation Administration.
USTACHI	Quisling troops of the German puppet state of Croatia.

CONTENTS

xi

CONTENTS

I. INTRODUCTION

"*And I said unto them, Whosoever hath any gold, let them break it off. So they gave it me: then I cast it into the fire, and there came out this calf.*"

—Exodus, 32

INTRODUCTION

I

THIS book is not primarily concerned with events, but with attitudes, and, more specifically, with the attitudes of four different peoples as they have emerged from the war. They have not been chosen at random, for each one of these four nations is important for certain definite reasons in the kind of post-war world in which we now find ourselves.

The people of Iran are important because it was in their country that the crossroads of British, Russian, and American influence first met. It was in Iran that the three great Allies took the first steps towards the post-war machinery that now confronts us and which we now call by a variety of names, such as the spheres-of-influence policy, power politics, and so forth.

The people of Greece are important because the events that have taken place in their country are a direct result of the policy of competitive adjustment agreed to, or tacitly agreed to by lack of agreement, at Tehran. According to the spheres-of-influence policy that took shape after the Tehran Conference, Greece was to be in the British sphere.

Under the same agreement, Jugoslavia was placed within the Russian orbit, and the people of Jugoslavia have increased in importance because it is in their country that we are able to examine most clearly and in terms most understandable to the Western World, the tactics of Russian policy outside the bor-

3

ders of Soviet Russia, and the effects that this policy has on a people when nakedly exposed to Russian control.

The Tehran Conference did not envisage any area of Europe under direct American influence, but subsequent events have decreed otherwise. For a variety of reasons, which I hope will become clear in this book, it has become increasingly necessary for America to take a hand in the direction of affairs in Europe, and, of all the countries on the continent, it is Italy in which America is at present most interested and in whose ultimate destiny she has assumed a responsibility.

An interesting part about the decisions at the Tehran Conference is that they were founded, not upon an accurate analysis of European opinion—for, with most of the continent still under German control, no such analysis could have been attempted—nor even on the basis of European opinion before Europe was occupied, but upon a mid-war estimate of what popular movements were likely to arise after the continent was liberated.

Never at any time in history were the leaders of an alliance faced with such problems, and only when the war in Europe ended nearly eighteen months later was it possible to estimate how right or how wrong they had been at Tehran.

For six years the peoples of the world have been cut off from each other to an extent that few realize, even yet. When the European war broke out in 1939, American civilians were withdrawn from the continent. Interpretation of events and of popular trends in one continent or the other was left in the hands of foreign correspondents. There was in those days no official American short-wave radio organization to explain America to Europe, and although the Axis radio was most vociferous in its explanations of Europe to America, it was notoriously tendentious.

And even the American foreign correspondents in Europe found themselves combating an increasingly restrictive cen-

4

sorship, which, under the excuses of military secrecy, went to great pains to squash any reports on the attitudes of peoples towards the war and towards each other.

The conquest of the continent by the Germans darkened the dim-out. One by one, the lights went out. The chatterings of national voices died away. Newspapers ceased to appear. The radio transmitters of the conquered countries were silent. And then, suddenly, there was noise and light again as the press and radio of quisling governments opened up in a paean of praise of their conquerors. But it was all false, ersatz, unreal. . . . The light was not daylight but the harsh glare of a one-thousand-kilowatt incandescent tube. The noise was the clatter of a machine—well-oiled, efficient, but still a machine, with only one master. Deep down and hidden were the people of Europe, but they had no voice. They were too stunned by defeat to seek one and, when they recovered, the power of the occupier was too strong. It was five years before liberation gave some of them the opportunity to express themselves once more. Some of them still have no voice. . . .

The destruction of communications between peoples did not stop with the German conquest, however; for each nation, as it entered the war, centralized the means of expressing itself to other nations. This was true even of the democratic leaders, America and Britain. The events that were reported by radio, leaflet, or by organized word-of-mouth campaigns, and even the manner in which they were reported, became matters of national policy for which special war agencies were created. In America and Britain, policy meetings were held each week to decide, not what should be told to the world in the week to come, but the manner in which events should be reported. Psychological warfare, the newest weapon of war, began to come into its own.

And year by year censorship regulations became more and more stringent until the American and British press began to complain that a full and frank exchange of public opinions even between two such close Allies had become impossible.

British writers, public speakers, economists, and the like were forbidden exit permits to come to America, if it was feared by some bureaucrat in the British Ministry of Information that their remarks would cause adverse American criticism or lead to some teapot tempest.

And if this stifling of opinions took place between America and Britain, how much more did it occur between America and other countries?

Behind these opaque curtains of control, the attitudes of peoples changed and shifted. Under the strain of hopes, disappointments, fears, and hatreds, they were changed violently in one direction or another; and when the Allied armies entered these countries they found peoples whose attitudes bore little resemblance to those described in the army indoctrination booklets. Just as the peoples themselves saw little resemblance in their liberators to those Americans, Britons, or Russians they had known before the war, or whose pictures had been painted to them during the occupation by the Allied propaganda agencies. The blackout of opinions had been so intense that not even the Allied governments themselves had been able to form any real conception of the extent to which these attitudes had changed during the years of isolation. Had it been otherwise, many of the tragic events that have occurred since the war might have been anticipated and forestalled.

This book has been, therefore, something of an experiment. As I wrote, I was constantly tempted to expand some aspects upon which I had merely touched. Whole chapters could be written, for example, on the treatment of foreign refugees inside Jugoslavia and the consequent opinions of Tito that they took home with them; or upon the development of the United States Office of War Information; or upon the picayune personal and departmental intrigues which did so much to hamstring the psychological warfare efforts of both America and Britain. The birth and growth of the Jugoslav Partisan movement and its degeneration into a communist dictatorship is a book in itself, as is the study of post-war events in any of the four countries about which I have written.

But all these are mere facets of the general problem of the world's peoples in their tragic efforts to get into step with each other. These facets are for the official historian, and the sad fact today is that history is moving too fast for the historian. We have to learn to run ahead of history so that when it catches up with us we can all jump on the bus together. And we have to start running fast, because if there is one lesson to be learned from the last generation of economic crises, with their relentless trend towards state control, it is that unless we keep ahead of history the ghost of a Hitler or some other dictator will be hard on our heels.

This requires some revolutionary thinking, commencing with the realization that this was in all respects a People's War. You remember the title, of course? It was chosen by popular acclaim when the late President Roosevelt asked for suggestions after Pearl Harbor. As the war drew on and we slid down one ethical hill after another, we heard less and less about it, until now we just let it go as World War II, praying that this does not denote another World Series. And that sorry tale would make another good book if somebody could get all the facts and tell how those in control of British policy began to concentrate on getting back their empire as soon as it was safe to do so, instead of expanding the ideals which threw Churchill into power after Dunkirk; how the Russians began to develop imperial ambitions on their own account; and how the great American Ideal drowned in a mess of wishful thinking that there would be a Return to Normalcy, permitting the attainment of such lofty ambitions as the push-button kitchen, run-free nylons, and two cars and a helicopter in every garage.

7

But it was a People's War, just the same. In spite of ignoring its title, we all paid lip service to it—even those professional statesmen, diplomats, and military leaders who fundamentally resented the implications of psychological warfare being devoted to the civilian masses. As Colonel Blimp might have said in one of his more verbose outbursts, "By gad, sir, the opinions of the people are so dashed inconvenient that the government must treat them as if they were important!"

It has been shown by Dr. George Gallup, Mr. Elmo Roper, and other such specialists that the measurement of public opinion in any one country can be carried out along certain precise and scientific lines. But the measurement of international public opinion is a different matter. It is not as simple an affair as adding up the figures of all the national polls on any one issue and calculating the average. For example, a strike in the American steel industry may create one kind of reaction among the American public, or even two or three general kinds of reaction. But it would be interpreted in a different manner by the Russian press and radio, whose public would consequently have another reaction. And public opinion would be even more varied in a European country panting for American steel with which to help in its reconstruction.

To make a simile, the attitudes of the world's nations are like a number of stones poised against each other on a mountainside. Move one, and there will be a change of the whole mass of stones in their relations to each other. Some will roll over; others will move only imperceptibly; others will not change position. Or the smallest motion of the smallest stone may produce an avalanche in which even the largest boulders may be crushed or covered.

And, somehow, we have to get it into our heads that, in our interrelation with the world, we are one of those stones on the mountainside and not an impartial observer on some remote peak!

8

So much has happened since the blackout of opinions descended, that even those who have known a country from before that time find it bewildering to attempt to unravel the threads.

To confine this book to a mere study of propaganda methods by America, or Britain, or Russia, would have been futile. In Iran, for example, American propaganda never really came into operation, and yet there have been great changes of attitudes towards America by the Iranians. And even greater changes in their attitudes towards Britain and Russia.

Therefore, instead of starting in 1939 and trying to follow chronologically the changing attitudes in the countries I visited, it was simpler and less confusing to attempt an appraisal of where we stand today with these peoples and to define the main reasons for their attitudes.

This book does not seek to allocate blame or responsibility to any one individual or organization. No such simplification is possible. The last six years of inside contact with bureaucracy and, within my own limited sphere of operations, with the implementation of war policy, have taught me that what may appear on the outside to be a simple matter of right and wrong reveals itself below the surface to be a desperate tangle of opinions, caused by misinterpretations, crossed communications, individual hopes, ambitions, intrigues, mistakes, inefficiencies, and a thousand other things, all combining to drive the researcher to distraction.

II

Modern man, in the few surviving democracies, is frequently called upon to change his attitude towards events and conditions not so much in a series of mental adjustments as in a rapid sequence of psychological somersaults. Black becomes white and then black again with such velocity that eventually it re-

9

mains fixed in the public mind as a kind of disturbing blur. At one stage of the war in Jugoslavia, everyone was told that General Mihailovitch, leader of the Chetniks, was the savior of his country. Later we were told that Marshal Tito, leader of the Partisans, was the savior of Jugoslavia and that Mihailovitch was not only no good but a traitor as well. Now, apparently, we have reason to be dissatisfied with Tito.

In 1941, when the German attack transformed Russia into an ally of the British, the public was suddenly asked to cease regarding her as a rabid wolf among nations and to look upon her as a sort of ewe lamb, newly welcomed into the Allied fold, a democracy in spite of herself; and we were even given stories about religious freedom to prove it. Since 1941 there have been so many changes of policy towards Russia on our part, and of Russia towards us, that few people are certain whether to regard her as a wolf or a sheep, a wolf in sheep's clothing, or a sheep raucously masquerading as a wolf.

Under these conditions it is not surprising that so-called democratic man is rendered ethically dizzy, cynical, and politically color-blind. Bewildered, because while on the scientific plane he appears to have reached the fulfillment of all his ancestors' wildest dreams, yet each new discovery seems to complicate rather than simplify his problems, and instead of hopeful promise for the future there is only an apparently never-ending succession of mental strains. Cynical, because after a world war against dictatorships, he has only to count on his fingers to realize there are more dictatorships now than there were when the war began. Already, at the end of the second world war to end all wars, he is talking about the next one (which is more than he did in 1918); and not merely talking, but, with the varying assurance of the color-blind, watching his governments planning and preparing for what is apparently accepted as inevitable, unless the precautions they propose are accepted.

In his elected leaders he finds little if any comfort. They have no easy solution to offer, because none exists. Few have had the honesty to tell him in convincing terms that the only solution lies in his own hands, and these few have not told him forcefully and often enough. The rest have nothing but meaningless platitudes to offer. If radio microphones were installed on the floor of Congress so that the proceedings could be broadcast, we would have not only abundant proof of these points but a new Congress at the next election.

In the closing year of the war no less than one hundred and thirty different congressmen paid visits to Europe and the Middle East, all at public expense. It is a matter of record that the frequency of these trips overseas contributed materially to the problems of army morale officers, while not one of the returning members has yet made any material contribution to the cause of world stability. To cover up their own miserable failure to understand the real international responsibilities of America after the war, they devised a series of domestic missions for their travels—to investigate Lend-Lease, for example; to inspect military establishments; or to study UNRRA operations. Nearly all the data gathered on these trips could have been obtained from files in Washington. But their plans, consciously or unconsciously, were not so much to study America's position overseas as to get a free trip, see the world at army (i.e., public) expense, and, incidentally, secure as much vote-catching publicity as possible. On returning home, it was simple enough to dig into the files and raise a public song and dance by "exposing" this or that alleged scandal. Political red herrings of this nature were known as "Safeguarding the Public Interest." Before the end of the year, the congressional junketing had reached such heights that President Truman felt himself compelled to announce that henceforth congressmen would pay for their own foreign travel, since which time remarkably few have felt that the "Safeguarding of the Public

Interest" justified a visit to Europe. The confusion disseminated by these gentlemen at the time, however, has rolled on,
increasing like a snowball. Much of it is based on the twisted
assumption that denunciations make headlines, whereas con-
structive thinking does not. The fashion of Denouncing Something has reached such proportions that even former Allies
are included in the list of victims. Not that allies should not
be criticized; it is the privilege of friends to criticize each other.
But the criticism should be based on a background made in-
telligible to the public, and should not consist merely of violent denunciations with vague mutterings of alarm.

At present—though the fashion changes quickly—Soviet
Russia is the most general choice for criticism. Some of the
false prophets go so far as to seek to prove that Russia is at
the bottom of all post-war troubles. Their line is fairly familiar:
Russia is sabotaging the idea of "United Nations" by seeking
to establish her own empire abroad; the Russians have set up
puppet states and whatever dictatorships exist are their creation; they are sponsoring and supporting terrorist regimes in
every state along their borders; in each of these states they
have separated the communist sheep from the democratic goats,
and the goats are being massacred, or starved out of existence,
or deported to the oblivion of concentration camps.

The Old Testament tells the story of how, while Moses
was on the mountain, the Children of Israel came impatiently
to Aaron. Seeking to divert their attention, he caused them
to bring him their golden ornaments, which he melted in the
fire and fashioned into the shape of a calf for them to worship.
When Moses returned and threatened the idolaters with death,
Aaron strove to find excuses. He admitted that the people had
brought him their gold, then uttered the sentence at the
head of this chapter. "So they gave it me: then I cast it into
the fire, and there came out this calf."

"In fact," said Aaron, washing his hands, "it was the fire and not I who made the calf. *The fire is to blame*."

And so it was with many of those elected into public office. To obtain popularity they joined in the common demand: "Bring the boys back home! They don't like us in Europe, so let's pull out and let them go to hell in their own way." They abolished rationing at a time when the garbage cans of this country were crammed with refuse for which queues would have stood in line for hours in nearly every European city (or what is left of them!). They spouted platitudes about reconversion, about building new homes for heroes to live in (while they opposed federal housing and tried to jockey in legislation permitting unbridled speculation in real estate).

Whenever something goes wrong with the formation of that international post-war world, it is the universal habit to blame somebody else—currently, Russia. It does not do to admit that Russia is more than willing—actually eager!—to assume the world leadership that fell to America during this war, and, perceiving an apparent American reluctance to assume leadership together with its responsibilities, is taking advantage of American shyness here and there, to obtain it. There are more homely ways of putting this, but to admit the simile would be too uncomfortable for ourselves; so we just blame the Russians.

But we made the fire; and if the fire throws up a Byzantine calf before which mankind will prostrate itself, then we shall have only ourselves to blame.

Shirking responsibilities by shifting the blame is political self-deception of the lowest order; and if it was dangerous before the war, in the post-war world it amounts to chattering in the condemned cell. The time when man could afford to be tempted away from his responsibilities to his fellow man by the lure of economic superiority is finished. The spiritual hungers of the world have become clearer and more insistent.

13

Many men, in their reflective moments, are aware of this deep uneasiness. A man needs only half an hour alone with himself to realize that he is down to fundamentals.

The escapist feels how good it would be to turn back the clock and return to things as they used to be . . . how satisfying. . . . Forgetting that just as it was impossible in the early days of the automobile to go back to the comparative peace of the horse-drawn vehicle, so it is now impossible to return to 1939 by a mere formal outlawing of the rocket and the atom bomb. Yet that is what we are trying to do in the economic and political sphere, and time and again the efforts of American statesmen to assume some of the responsibilities of international leadership are thwarted or compromised by this consideration. But this time man has really outgrown himself. This time there are no easy alternatives. Man must either live at peace with his neighbor under new conditions, whether in the next state or in the next continent, or face the probable destruction of himself and his family and the certain destruction of his civilization. When we entered this war, fighter planes had a maximum speed of three hundred miles an hour. In four years we not only doubled this speed but also entered on the creation of missiles which surpass the speed of sound, and reduce oceans to the comparative size of ditches in a medieval free-for-all. As for the atom bomb, the two that were dropped on Hiroshima and Nagasaki are already minor affairs, not merely in size and efficiency but in content. The fission of a higher element such as uranium is one thing, but total annihilation will really begin to have a meaning as the scientists work their way down the atomic scale to the simpler elements, say, oxygen or hydrogen: in other words, the air we breathe. At such a stage as this, the outbreak of another war might easily cause some astronomer on another planet to gaze at and ponder over the sudden destruction of our world, just as our own astronomers have been puzzled by the total disintegration of a star a thousand light years away. When one of our more enlightened leaders remarked that this time it was one world or bust, he was perhaps being much more literal than he realized at the time.

Under these conditions, even sub-average intelligence will realize that if there can be no frontiers in another war, there must be no frontiers in the peace, unless another war is to be rendered inevitable. But—and here is the problem that has not yet been solved—if there are to be no frontiers, how can we live in the same world as other nations whose fundamental principles are different from ours? Since the end of the war, half our international headaches have been due to the discovery that while the Russians may use the same words that we do they have an entirely different sense—the word democracy, for instance. At a conference of foreign ministers in London, Molotov devoted at least one press conference and several sessions of the council to insisting that the Bulgarian and Rumanian governments—both creations of the Russians—were democratic. To the well-indoctrinated Soviet citizen, Russia itself is a true democracy whose constitution, as the Moscow Radio puts it, "is not limited to a formal outlining of the citizens' rights, but assures the citizens the real possibilities of realizing such rights." It matters little at this stage to argue who is right. What does seem to be clear is that there is a difference in the definition of the word and in many other definitions of the intrinsic rights of man. Are we to modify our principles and exchange our definitions for theirs to obtain our frontierless world? Or are we to keep our frontiers, shutting our eyes to what goes on beyond them, hoping for the best, but fearing all the time that the worst is going to happen?

A foreign observer, viewing the three powers through the material available to him in their respective press and radio broadcasts, might draw conclusions along the following general lines:

The United States emerged from the war as the foremost power, but unable or unwilling to accept the responsibilities of world leadership. America had not yet learned the lesson— learned thoroughly and bitterly by the British and the Russians —that the victors remain at their posts after the victory, if only to insure the peace.

America had two faces. She applied one set of principles in Europe and another in the Far East. She was against the seizure of territory in Europe, but unwilling to discuss joint trusteeships of Pacific islands which she wanted for herself.

In the interests of a freer exchange of goods, America was prepared to lend money to bankrupt countries—on condition that they reduced their tariffs. But America was not prepared to reduce her own tariffs, thereby indicating to the suspicious foreigner that America was really interested only in promoting American trade.

The U.S.S.R., to our foreign observer, was at once the communist and imperialist bogey. She had twisted and changed and reversed her ideology and foreign policy so frequently that nobody but the most hidebound communist dialectician could make any sense out of it. She had forfeited her position as the hope of left-wing idealists. The history of her broken pledges made even the most liberal of orthodox diplomats and statesmen regard her with a leery eye.

Although professing to be in favor of international settlements, Russia unilaterally settled the Polish question, the Baltic question, and the question of her western frontiers. In Europe alone she absorbed into her sphere of influence as many people as the whole population of the United States—all by military force and ruthless politics.

She maintained that she was a democracy, whereas our foreign observer always thought she was the reverse of democratic. And she maintained this so stoutly that our foreign observer was beginning to wonder what democracy really meant.

Our foreign observer, now somewhat cynical, found little consolation in his contemplation of Great Britain. If he happened to be afraid of communism, he was depressed by the Socialist victory in the elections, by the utter rout of Churchill and the Conservative Party, and by the plans of the new British Government to nationalize the Bank of England, the coal mines, the railroads, and airlines. If, on the other hand, he was in favor of these things, he was equally depressed by what he regarded as efforts to re-establish empires and obsolete regimes by the use of British troops in Indonesia, Palestine, and Greece.

None of these pictures was necessarily correct. They were, perhaps, a little distorted by distance and oversimplification. But they were at least as correct as the picture which the average American had of conditions overseas and of the position which America enjoyed in the attitudes of other peoples as compared with Russia and Britain.

Like the terms "democracy," "collaborationist," "fascist," "partisan," and "communist," power politics is one of those labels we have come to use glibly without any attempt to define what we mean precisely. There are many such terms in this book, and where they are unaccompanied by any definition they are used in their popular sense—which is not necessarily their real meaning. By a communist is meant a faithful servant of the Kremlin rather than a devotee to the principles of communism as they are understood in America and which happen to be out of fashion this season in Moscow. A Jugoslav partisan is a member of the movement as it has been portrayed to America since its foundation—and not the unthinking slave that Tito now demands in his movement.

A more precise definition is needed in the case of power politics, however; for these are events that affect our daily lives. Just as power politics, at the Congress of Vienna, draw the outlines of Europe after the defeat of Napoleon, so today the victors have fallen back upon them to bring some system of order out of the rubble of war. The modern slogan of power politics is The Big Four. In certain cases, it is The Big Three: and, if the *Chicago Tribune* has its way, it will be The Big Two. The essence of power politics is that it attempts to solve international problems without any particular reference to the peoples in the area under dispute. It is a game conducted behind closed doors between statesmen and diplomats, with or without good intentions, and certainly without a sense of responsibility towards the people they are supposed to represent.

The conditions of the Yalta Agreement, for example, were not known to the American, British, and certainly not to the Russian peoples. The opinions of the latter were scarcely important, either then or now . . . such is the totalitarian nature of the Russian regime. The opinions of the American and British peoples ought to have been regarded as important, but neither Mr. Roosevelt nor Mr. Churchill dared to take a chance on revealing the terms of Yalta at the time—not merely because they could not make public the date of Russia's entry into the Far Eastern war, but also because neither the American nor the British public would have agreed to such conditions as the cession of the Kuriles to Russia or the compulsory return to Russia of anti-Soviet Russians throughout Europe. Accordingly the only way of achieving agreement at Yalta was for Mr. Roosevelt and Mr. Churchill to present their publics at some later date with a *fait accompli*, which is precisely what happened.

The danger of power politics, as far as the American people are concerned, is that statesmen and diplomats may be thought to know better than the people themselves what is good and what is wrong for their country. For a nation accustomed to docile surrender of its political rights, this is a system that can pay quick profits, as the post-war policy of Russia has demonstrated, but it is a system that leads directly, if uncontrolled, to the medieval system of government by an elite. At the Congress of Vienna, where kings and emperors spoke authoritatively for their countries, this was a system that could be counted upon to maintain peace for a reasonable period of time. At the end of a war that was once called The People's War, it cannot be called progress.

The time has come for democracy to search its soul and to discover the reasons for its apparently failing popularity. It is no longer in a majority among the world's different systems. Its position is shaken by new competitors. One of these, founded less than thirty years ago, is already in operation as a large cartel with several smaller subsidiaries; it has more modern and slicker sales techniques and it is determined to drive democracy, as we know it, out of business. It even has people working inside the democratic countries who prefer, or profess to prefer, its way of life to ours.

In commercial life, a business finding itself in such a situation would have the sense to realize it was on the skids and, if it were not too palsied, would do something about it beyond complaining that the public was only doing itself harm by preferring inferior products. To keep abreast of such changes in public attitudes, advertising agencies maintain what they call research divisions, whose functions are to indicate to manufacturers the buying public's opinion of their products—and any sensible manufacturer takes note of their recommendations.

This is ordinary common sense in business, but in international affairs we persist as a nation and as individuals in the attitude that if any other nation appears to prefer some other system to democracy, that is their business and they can stew in their own political juice. We have persisted so long that we have our backs to the wall and do not know it.

It is time we realized this fact. It is time for us to regard ourselves objectively and to look at ourselves as others see us. The others do not regard us objectively either, but perhaps there is a mote in our eye as well as in the other fellow's. Our foreign observer may not see us as we think we are. To us he may even appear slightly crosseyed or myopic. But his opinion is important, for, at a time when we need all the friends we can get, it tells us at least where we stand and how the peoples of the world regard us.

And I hope that as we attempt to find out *where we stand*, we shall never cease asking ourselves the other, equally important, question:—*What do we stand for?*

II. IRAN

"Boy, go from me to the Shah;
Say to him. . . .
Win thou first the poor man's heart,
Then the glass; so know the world."
    —From the Persian of Ḥafiz by Emerson

IRAN

EPICENTER OF THE WORLD

In his book, *Modern Egypt,* the late Earl of Cromer, one of Britain's most accomplished experts on the Middle East, wrote, "The public generally end, though sometimes not till after a considerable lapse of time, in getting a correct idea of the general course of events, and of the cause or effect of any special political incident. But . . . it may be doubted whether even this result is fully justified, save in respect to questions of internal policy. In such matters, a number of competent and well-informed persons take part in the discussions which arise. Inaccuracy of statement is speedily corrected. Fallacies are exposed. In the heat of party warfare the truth may for a time be obscured, but in the end the public will generally lay hold of a tolerably correct appreciation of the facts.

"In dealing with the affairs of a foreign country, more especially if that country be in a semi-civilized condition, these safeguards to historical truth exist in a relatively less degree. Opinion has in such cases to deal with a condition of society with which it is unfamiliar. It is disposed to apply arguments drawn from its own experience to a state of things which does not admit of any such arguments being applied without great qualifications. The number of persons who possess sufficiently accurate information to instruct the public is limited, and amongst those persons it not unfrequently happens that many have some particular cause to advance, or some favorite po-

23

litical theory to defend. Those who are most qualified to speak often occupy some official position, which, for the time being, imposes silence upon them. There is, therefore, no certain guarantee that inaccuracies of statement will be corrected, or that fallacies will be adequately exposed. Thus, even if the general conclusions be correct, there is a risk that an erroneous appreciation in respect to important matters of detail will float down the tide of history. The public often seize on some incident which strikes the popular imagination, or idealize the character of some individual whose action excites sympathy or admiration. It would appear, indeed, that democracy tends to develop rather than to discourage hero-worship. . . .

"No casual visitor can hope to obtain much real insight into the true state of native opinion. Divergence of religion and habits of thought: ignorance of the vernacular language: the reticence of Orientals when speaking to anyone in authority: their tendency to agree with anyone to whom they may be talking: the want of mental symmetry and precision, which is the chief distinguishing feature between the illogical and picturesque East and the logical West, and which lends such peculiar interest to the study of Eastern life and politics: the fact that religion enters to a greater extent . . . into the social life and laws and customs of the people: and the further fact that the European and the Oriental, reasoning from the same premises, will often arrive at diametrically opposite conclusions—all these circumstances place the European at a great disadvantage when he attempts to gauge Eastern opinion."

A bare land. A desolate land, two and a half times as large as Texas, fantastic as the face of the moon; with the land scraped down to the rock; flat pebbly deserts out of which rise conical mountain peaks: bounded on three sides by high mountain ranges, and on the fourth by the hot waters of its southern sea. Peopled, outside its towns, by nomad tribes who ignore the federal laws and maintain their own private armies. Its people living partly on memories of a civilization of four thousand years ago and partly on participation in modern commerce, with a shrewdness that would set the West agape: envying, imitating, inwardly despising Western standards of culture.

This is a surface view of Iran, for a time the world's epicenter on which the future of millions of Americans, British, Russians, Germans, and the rest hung in the balance. To safeguard that future, two armies marched into the land, subdued opposition, and placed the country under military occupation.

When the Allies came to Iran in the summer of 1941, they did so with a rush. A premature Nazi-inspired revolt in Iraq, its neighbor to the west, had disclosed the long-range nature of Germany's plans. America was not yet in the war. To the north, German armies were at the gates of Stalingrad and forging towards the foothills of the Caucasus, where there was nothing to prevent a leapfrog action into Iran. A thousand miles to the west, a British army was preparing a last-stand action in Egypt, with nothing at their backs but the Nile, several thousand Italian residents of Egypt who were preparing to give Rommel a royal reception, and an Egyptian army whose loyalties to the Allied cause were so in doubt that it could not be sent into action.

The revolt in Iraq came so close to success that it is a wonder to this day why the Germans did not go through with it once it had started. Pétain had given them a chain of airfields in Syria for use as paratroop bases. The rebel Iraqi army controlled Baghdad and the nearby RAF base at Habbaniyeh. German paratroops had seized the invaluable oilfields and installations at Mosul in north Iraq. The only pinprick in their flank was the unexpected decision of the British to defend Crete after all the rest of Greece had been lost. While the Germans hesitated, the British rushed troops into Iraq from India and Transjordan, and the Germans, losing their nerve, withdrew, leaving the revolt to collapse. Their oil technicians at Mosul did not even destroy the installations before they fled, thus indicating that they fully expected to return shortly.

It was at this stage that Churchill and Stalin decided that, for once, the Allies and not the Germans would be the first to invade neutral territory. The preservation of a neutral vacuum in Iran was fraught with too many potential dangers. A German breakthrough into the Caucasus on the Russian front would place the enemy behind the British back in Egypt. Similarly, a German breakthrough on the British front would allow the Germans to strike the Russians in the back through the Middle East. With victory on both fronts and the Middle East securely in their hands, the Germans would be within sight of victory. Russia would have been isolated, except for the Murmansk convoy route—much too costly in shipping to carry the American and British supplies which Russia needed and without which the Red Army could not have won its later victories. British imperial communications would have been severed and, with India and Indonesia cut off from all help except from Australia and New Zealand, Japan would have been tempted to enter the war much earlier than she did, probably including a weakened Russia among her victims of attack.

The effect upon America, still neutral at this time, was dubious except for the obvious conclusion that with the Allies in such a pass, the arguments of American isolationists to stop Lend-Lease and retain the supplies for American use—an extension of the theory that a strong America is impregnable, even if isolated—would have been reinforced. As it was, public opinion in America was moving away from the idea of active participation in the war.

Acting simultaneously, the Russian and British armies came from the north and west, crossed the mountain frontiers, and emerged on the high tableland of Iran, whose German-trained army put up only spasmodic and slight resistance. Its ruler,

Reza Khan—an old enemy of Stalin's from revolutionary days —abdicated and was shipped off to South Africa, to be succeeded by his son. A few months later, Japan's attack at Pearl Harbor made America an active ally. An American command was established in Iran to handle the trans-shipment of American supplies for Russia. The Germans were driven back from the Caucasus. Though they were still strong enough to mount one more offensive in Egypt, that offensive was smashed at El Alamein. The war, as far as the Middle East was concerned, was finished. The crisis was over.

The crisis may have been over, but, on the other hand, the test was just beginning. For the first time, the three largest powers among the future victors found themselves together in the country of another ally. Three years were still to go by before the three armies met in any other part of the world and faced similar problems of post-war occupation. Military and economic strategy alone had taught all three the importance of Iran in future world politics and economics. For better or worse, Iran was to be a blueprint for post-war partnership among the three. The machinery they worked out there could be used later in Europe. Their mistakes could be lessons for the future. The Four Freedoms had been affirmed. The Atlantic Charter had been signed by America and Britain and its terms officially approved by Stalin.

THE POWERS AT TEHRAN

One hour out from Baghdad, the plane, still gathering altitude, swung high in the clear air, the flat brown loneliness of the desert seemingly motionless underneath. Shivering under our blankets, we gazed out longingly as men imprisoned in a refrigerator might look upon a summer scene. Suddenly a mountain top, covered in snow, darted close underneath the plane, to be followed by another, and yet another, flashing

27

past and giving us some idea of our real speed. The air became rarefied and some passengers lay down to mitigate its effects. This was the mountain barrier between Iraq and Iran. Soon the plane began to lose height and beneath us, spotted with snow, came the gray, flat landscape of the four-thousand-foot-high Iran plateau. The plane wheeled and gave us a view of Tehran, a tight, tiny collection of buildings, herded in on three sides by the mountains with the stony desert stretching off endlessly to the south, a town dwarfed in size by both the mountains and the desert. The plane grounded and bumped its way over the grit to a hangar; the door opened to let in a gust of icy air. There were no customs or passport formalities, nor were there any Iranian officials of any kind. This was Tehran in the third year of Allied occupation. The Tehran Conference had been over two months.

I had gone to Tehran from work in New York, at the request of the British Government, to edit a daily newspaper for American and British troops. Originally founded for British troops, the paper had acquired a new significance after the entry into the theatre of American troops, who, although the *Tehran Daily News* was the only English-language daily newspaper in the country, had found its contents too insular for their tastes.

There was little hesitation on my part in accepting the British invitation. Three years of traversing Anglo-American bases had left one general and puzzling impression with me. While statesmen on both sides of the Atlantic were talking about Anglo-American partnership, there existed a series of isolated spots, far from battlefronts, each with its American and British garrison; yet those garrisons were living in splendid isolation from each other. On lonely airfields, scores of miles from civilization, American and British troops had separate establishments, lived separate communal lives, carried on the old prejudices. . . . In theatres of war, where the unseen dangers of battle

28

forced one man to rely absolutely on another, there was comradeship—of a kind. But for the great future of the post-war era, the battlefields were false examples, for the incentive of battle would not always exist. And after it had gone—what then? The bases were an example. I had often wondered why, instead of merely talking about "the unbreakable comradeship," the statesmen had not done something about seeing to its existence. The truth, of course, was that the civilian agencies entrusted with spreading international understanding were not allowed to operate in such places because, such is the hierarchical structure of government, the bases were under military control and (such is the nature of the average army commander) the military were interested only in the morale of their own men and not in international morale. I was looking forward to Tehran.

Ten months' residence in Iran gave you a feeling of complete isolation from the world. No other capital city was so cut off from the war, except, perhaps, Lhasa in Thibet. It was impossible to get farther away, for to continue by the plane that brought you from Cairo would take you to Moscow, one of the three world centers. Isolation, however, brought a sense of detachment, as though surveying the world from the stratosphere. Reports of desperate events on the battlefronts clicked their way across the ether and, with the sense of remoteness that they gave, might have described battles on another planet.

Almost each week, through the dusty airport on the Kazvin Road, there passed planes bearing important personages to or from Moscow on issues of high state—diplomats, statesmen, generals, military missions, economic missions. They seldom paused long enough for us to learn of their comings and goings, so closely guarded was the field. But invariably the native bazaar in downtown Tehran knew, just as it had known of the Tehran Conference days before even people in the three embassies had known. The sources of bazaar news and the manner in which it is flashed across the Middle East are mysteries which no one has succeeded in explaining satisfactorily. But bazaar gossip is the most important single influence on native life in the Middle East. It is far more than a stock market fixing the prices of local commodities, although this it does too. It is the center of political gossip, the heart of intrigues and rumors. All bazaar rumors are exaggerated, but none is too exaggerated to be discounted because to the millions in the Middle East the bazaar rumor is an objective truth.

Embassy officials, exchanging the latest official news, would invariably ask each other, "What does the bazaar say today?" or "Have you heard that the bazaar says that old so-and-so (naming some politician) is forming his own party?" Most embassies maintained officials, part of whose duties were to keep in touch with local bazaar gossip, to follow up and attempt to explain each rumor. The countless beggars on the sidewalks, the camel caravans from across the mountains, the merchant whose limousine brought him to the dim entrance gates of the bazaar alleys, whence he had to proceed on foot to his stall; the police agent searching for intrigue—all these added to the teeming life of the bazaar which spreads its tentacles across the Middle East.

In this strange milieu Americans, British, and Russians formed three separate communities. Outside the tightly knit diplomatic colony, there was no mingling of the three. With the Anglo-Russian occupation, nearly three years previously, Iran had been divided into two zones, one under Russian control comprising the whole northern area of the country to a line slightly north of Tehran. The rest of the country, down to the Persian Gulf, was under British control. American troops, when they arrived, were concerned solely with operating the roads and railroads along which supplies flowed from the Gulf to the Russian zone, into which neither American nor British troops were allowed to enter. As a rule, the Red Army took over supplies in Tehran, in whose streets the uniforms of all three armies were to be seen—though never together. The men lived in separate barracks or billets, had separate entertainments to which the others went only on special invitation. In public restaurants or cafes frequented by all three nationalities, there was no mixing. They ate separately, made dates with girls separately, got drunk separately, and were even arrested separately by their own Military Police. Like ghost armies in a spirit world, unable to perceive or touch each other, each army lived its own life, convinced that only its existence was the real substance.

The real admission that post-war comradeship was unattainable came, of course, with the Tehran Conference. In the special declaration on Iran, issued jointly by Roosevelt, Churchill, and Stalin—three months, incidentally, after Iran had officially joined the United Nations—all three powers signified their intention to restore "the independence, sovereignty, and territorial integrity of Iran." The intention, it was clear, was motivated by distrust and alarm. Which power distrusted another first and with what justification it is irrelevant to discuss. The British suspected the Russians intended to retain north Iran under one pretext or another; the Russians suspected that the British realized their post-war position would be weak and were attempting to embroil America in Middle East affairs; the Americans were not yet ready to be embroiled. All three sets of suspicions were there; and the result was an attempt to put back the clock, an announcement of the intention to withdraw the armies from Iran, to put back the frontiers, destroy the zones of influence, restore the Middle East vacuum. How Stalin must have smiled when he signed it! The three statesmen left Tehran "friends in fact, in spirit, and

31

in purpose," and Iran with its foreign garrisons was left to carry on with its jealousies and suspicions.

THE G. I. IN IRAN

Two of my American friends in Tehran were Private James O'Neill and Sergeant Al Hine, correspondents for *Yank*, the Army's weekly magazine for the G.I. They were probably more closely in touch with the rank and file in the American command than any other officer or private, and we used to meet regularly either in town or at my villa in the hills above Tehran. As far as creature comforts were concerned, I was more fortunately situated than they, in so far as I could live as a civilian outside the confines of army camp life.

Invariably talk with them turned to questions of local morale and feelings between the soldiers. I knew, of course, that there was no mixing between American and Russian soldiers but I wanted to find out the American G.I.'s reasons.

"They're fairly simple," said Al once. "First of all, there's the language barrier. With the best will in the world, no ordinary G.I. can strike up a conversation with a Russian in a bar. In any case, most of the boys in the command are outside Tehran and seldom see any Russians. When they get a pass to come up here, they aren't going to spend their three days, or their week or whatever it is, trying to make Russian friends. They come up to meet some buddy in one of the American camps here and to go out on the town and get drunk."

There were other reasons. On one occasion I came across a report that a Russian soldier, picked up by an American M.P. for being drunk and disorderly in the street and later turned over to the Russians, had been subsequently shot. True or not, the rumor got around among American troops, and thereafter I frequently saw American and British M.P.'s pass by drunken Russian troops, rather than pick them up and thus, as the police thought, endanger their lives. There was only one subsequent exception to this that I came across, and in this case the American police held the Russian until he sobered up, and then released him.

Towards the British, there was a general feeling of aloofness and dislike. Curiously enough, this was not for anything that the British troops in Iran had done. In most cases, certainly as far as the G.I. was concerned, this feeling had nothing to do with the British he encountered in Iran.

"Take me, for example," said Jimmy O'Neill when we discussed the situation. "I never met the British until I joined the army. Then they brought us out here on a British troopship. We were at sea for weeks, travelling all over the ocean. The ship was filthy. We were cramped like cattle in a truck. The food was awful. Most of us were sick, and there was so little room that we were sick all over each other. It was a nightmare.

"Our first port of call was Bombay. And when we got there we were only allowed ashore for a few hours. That gave us a glimpse of the British Raj in India. That was enough! Down in the native quarter they had whores squatting in cages like wild animals. You could look them over and decide which one to buy. In the white section there were lovely hotels, but no natives were allowed inside. To most of the boys, that picture represented the British in the Empire.

"It's no good telling them that all of India isn't like that, and it's no good telling them that British troopships are no worse, or are probably better, than American troopships. They'd take it as an insult, and they'd feel worse than ever about the British."

Towards the Iranian, the American felt curiously confused.

"When we arrived," said Jimmy, "we were told this part of the country was under the British, so the boys felt it was just another part of the British Empire. They felt sorry for the native. Then they began to pick up things which showed them

33

this country wasn't part of the British empire, but had been independent. So then they began to feel disgusted about the way things are over here and to ask why they weren't made better. Then they got to the point where they could hardly bear to speak to a native without wanting to give him a kick in the tail.

"I know I shouldn't, but there are times when I feel the same way. We're so used to things the way they are back in the States that we can't understand why they should be this way over here.

"My outfit has been over here for eighteen months. When we first came in, we were all missionaries for America. We wanted to show these people how to make things better for themselves. That's all gone now, and there's not one boy who isn't counting his points so he can get to hell out of here and leave them in their own mess.

"The only thing that puzzles me," Jimmy went on, "is how the British Tommy can take overseas service for so long. After a couple of years, all *we* want is to go home and maybe if we're lucky, we get to go home. The British Tommy is out here for five years, and by the time we're going home he's still got three more years to serve."

Jimmy had hit upon a curious psychological weakness of American overseas forces in wartime. Connected with the feeling of the American public that the only way for an American to serve his country is in the forces, a feeling that amounts at times to hysteria (as witness the difficulty of civilian agencies in retaining their specialized staffs in face of the demands of Selective Service), there goes another feeling that nothing is too good for the boys overseas. A thousand Post Exchanges overseas were stocked with goods that became unobtainable back home. The aim of every American base command in its attempts to preserve morale became to re-create a way of life overseas that as nearly as possible resembled life back home.

34

The American camp Amirabad, outside Tehran, became one of these Little Americas. It had its own weekly newspaper, as well as locally reproduced editions of popular domestic magazines. It had its own radio station which, for eighteen hours a day, played recordings of jive, Bob Hope, Fibber McGee, and the like. In its recreation halls, local beer was not good enough—so canned beer was shipped out from America. Tehran had no water supply except that sold by carriers from the private stream of the British Embassy—so American army engineers developed a special irrigation scheme for the camp.

All these were admirable achievements, but their net effect was to cut off the American soldier from all real contact with life around him. For all practical purposes, he might as well have been serving in the Arizona desert.

In course of time the American G.I. became dissatisfied with the British army term for all Middle East natives—wogs. He called them gooks. The Iranian, who reacts to atmosphere with a sensitivity that only Orientals possess, was fully aware of the scorn. His only contact with Americans until then had been with missionaries. Through the latter, through his newspapers and all other forms of communication, he had come to regard America as the great land to the west, a land of freedom and prosperity anxious to help the oppressed. Now he found 28,000 Americans deposited in his country, railroad men, Diesel engine operators, trucking operators; performing strange and wonderful feats in a wild country which he had long since ceased to fight. They were not at all like the American missionaries he had known. In the bazaars, they were more gullible and lavish with their money than either the British or the Russians; they were inclined to pay without too much bargaining whatever price a rascally trader demanded for some tinselly gewgaw; and if servility denotes friendliness, the Iranian had much friendship for the American G.I. It ran no deeper.

Sour as was the attitude of the American private to his allies, his attitude towards his officers in the command was much worse. This, remember, was not a war theatre where officers perforce had to earn the respect of their men if only to obtain their loyalty. Here, in Iran, officers and men lived separate lives. The American command followed the British example and put certain restaurants and night clubs "off limits" to enlisted men. Most of the good restaurants bore notices: "For officers only," and the American G.I., fresh from home, was not slow to resent this mark of his social inferiority. Strangely enough, he did not blame the British who, being first in the theatre and the originators of the system, had morally compelled the American command either to follow their example or, by ignoring it, to be responsible for inevitable complaints among the British troops.

THE PERSIAN GULF COMMAND

There is grousing in every theatre, of course. No soldier is a completely contented soldier, otherwise he would be a psychological misfit. I have visited many different war theatres and have heard enlisted men make all kinds of complaints, but I have never heard of commanding officers subjected to such unmitigated abuse by their men as in the Persian Gulf Command of Major General Donald H. Connolly. General Connolly is a Texan. He was accused by his men of favoring Texans and preferring Texans on his immediate staff. "Anyone would think this was the god-damned Lone Star State," said one G.I. His officers were accused of behaving like fascists, living like royalty, and ignoring the essential well-being of their men.

One officer at Hamadan, a provincial town in the west, behaved, it was said, like a local Hitler. He had requisitioned a luxurious villa on the outskirts of the town, maintained a stable of hunting horses, and had G.I.'s to wait on his table.

Connolly's officers, of course, were aware of the dissatisfaction of the men, but were genuinely incensed by it. I talked one day with a young captain on Connolly's staff; it was shortly after the opening of a new club for the enlisted men at the Amirabad camp.

"If this doesn't please them," he said, "nothing will. They have the pick of USO shows. They have their own newspapers and magazines, and, surely to God, they have nothing to complain about in the PX. They even have their own radio station, which is more than the troops in Italy have." (At this stage, the Allied invasion of France had not yet taken place.) "We even get letters from the boys in Italy saying they can pick up our short-wave transmissions and telling us how much they enjoy them. We've flown out fishing rods from the United States so they can go fishing in the mountain streams. They've got the best that this man's army has to offer. So what in hell are they bitching about?"

I was reminded of Marie Antoinette's remark: "You say they have no bread? Why don't they eat cake?"

The Office of Technical Information, an extensive division of the Persian Gulf Command, operating directly under Connolly to maintain morale among the men, gave the men cake, but it could not give them bread because it was unable to convey the feeling that officers and men shared each other's loneliness.

The American army in Iran was a discontented army—discontented with its surroundings, discontented within itself. The Iranian did not fail to note this.

American journalists passing through Tehran on their way to Moscow rarely stayed long enough to obtain a picture of affairs in the theatre. Whenever they arrived, they were rushed to a billet at Amirabad outside the town and there they were kept on the alert list so that few of them had an opportunity to prowl around the town itself and investigate conditions. In the ten months I was there, I found only two journalists' entries on the visitors' list at the U.S. Embassy. In each case they were British reporters who, not enjoying the privileges of travel via the U.S. Air Transport Command, were stranded at a downtown Tehran hotel until the Russians in their good time provided air transport.

This was a cause for despair, for only a visiting journalist, possessed of some discernment, could write truly of the situation. Even so, it would have had to be written from outside the country; and, even under such conditions, the obstacles were formidable enough, for under a War Department ruling all stories referring to the theatre, wherever written—whether in Tehran or New York—had to be submitted to Connolly's staff for approval.

My diary bears this entry for April 26 of that year: "Cocktails with General Connolly, four of his staff colonels and one major. Also Hermann of the Associated Press and Oscar Guth of the United Press, both resident correspondents who have just come back from a tour of some of the southern outposts in the command. One of the colonels said he couldn't make out why an Englishman living in the States had come out to edit the local English-language newspaper, under British auspices. He took great pains to point out to the General that I had come over here for the *Tehran Daily News*. Presumably it is the impression that the latter newspaper is the Machiavellian hand of Britain. We had chit-chat about nothing significant, although the party was supposed to be a weekly affair enabling them to keep the Anglo-American press up to date on background developments. Guth inadvertently betrayed a source, an American colonel in one of the outposts who had told him about the American planes being rushed through to the Russians. They blew up and one said the colonel 'ought to

38

have kept his god-damnèd mouth shut.' Then he turned to me and said that all the news at these parties was 'off the record, mind you,' and that if I printed anything, 'absolutely anything,' he'd go around 'denying it up and down the lot.' An unnecessary remark, since he said nothing worth publishing. I received the impression that at least two of the colonels, from their questions and expectant air, sat around with the aim of gathering information and news of the doings among the diplomatic colony. They asked a lot of questions about the American Embassy; obviously there is no love lost between the two installations."

THE OWI IN IRAN

There was, indeed, tension between General Connolly's staff and the local American Embassy. I knew of the control which an American army commander exercises in his theatre in time of war. His power far exceeds that of the local diplomatic representative, even to the point where no American, not even a representative of the State Department, can enter a theatre without the express permission and request of the military commander.

Approximately two years earlier, while in Washington, I had assisted in the preparation of plans by OWI for staffing the Iran theatre. The OWI outpost chief in Tehran at that time was a one-time United Press man, Harold Peters, an American who was interested in the country, cared for its future, and believed that America had a general role to play. Eighteen months later the OWI withdrew Peters, whom I met in Cairo on my way to Tehran. He was full of warnings at the sinister influence of the United States military forces on Iranian affairs, but at the time I was disposed to pay little heed to them, believing that Harold Peters' quarrels were no concern of mine. In withdrawing Peters, however, OWI had been unable to secure official military permission to appoint another man, although the circumstances quoted by General Connolly as reasons for Peters' withdrawal were open to question and dispute.

Shortly after the tragi-comical cocktail party, my telephone rang and a male voice introduced itself as that of Barclay Hudson, the OWI outpost chief in Beirut, Syria. When he came round to my office, Hudson explained that OWI had still been unable to obtain General Connolly's consent to open an outpost in the country, and he had been sent on the thousand-mile trip from Syria in order to investigate the situation.

I gave him my opinion, which is presented at this stage without apology for the fact that it is preceded by no explanation. I felt that the Iranians regarded the war merely as another imperialist struggle between imperialist powers. They had been pro-German, I maintained, because their whole economy had been based on German products, especially machinery sold cheaply on credit through the genius of Dr. Schacht, with the aim of tying down local industry to a continual flow of German spare parts and, incidentally, of industrializing the country in such a way as would suit long-range German expansionist ambitions. I felt that the age-old tradition of the country had been to preserve its integrity by maneuvering a balance of power between the empires of Britain and Russia, that the Iranians still regarded Britain and Russia as imperialistic powers, and, consequently, the war as an imperialist war; and that the only hope for founding a faith in democracy lay in the entrance of America into the field with all the information at its command to show the people that this war—at least—at last!—was different.

I do not know whether Hudson was convinced by my earnestness. I know only that he must have put in a report recommending that an American outpost be established. I saw little of him afterwards for he left the country within two months. My information that he had departed was given in-advertently in the form of a call from an official in the British embassy asking me to visit him. When I entered his office, he toyed around with the papers on his desk for a while, brought the discussion round to Hudson, then asked me point-blank whether I had used my privilege to write to New York via the Embassy pouch in order to secrete private messages from Hudson to his headquarters. I replied that of course I had done no such thing and innocently inquired why Hudson, if he had anything he wished to write to his headquarters, could not do so through the pouch of the American Embassy.

"The American pouches," replied the official, "go back to the States via American Army planes, and Connolly has the right to inspect their contents."

It took some time for the penny to drop. "You mean," I said slowly, "that Connolly suspects Hudson may have been writing comments back home concerning his command, that he does not wish to have reported, and that he suspects Hudson may have been smuggling these reports out through other channels than those which he can supervise? But why pick on me?"

"Well," said the official, "you are known to be close to American government officials. You are a sort of hybrid of-ficial, you know, and you have the right to use channels over which Connolly has no control. At any rate, he thinks you are the guilty person."

"But what right has he to think that Hudson is saying any-thing at all about his command that he doesn't want to have said publicly?" I demanded. "Hudson certainly has made no such request of me. I don't think he would do so, and in any case I think that if he had any criticism, he would take out his own notes when he left."

"He left this morning," said the British official. "He was searched at the airport by security officers and they found nothing on him. That's why they think you must have helped him to smuggle them out."

The upshot was, naturally, farcical. I demanded an official inquiry into the report, but there was no answer from Connolly's headquarters. Learning that General Connolly's request had been based on a report by one of his "security" staff, I placed a request that a military inquiry be held to determine the reasons for such a charge. After the request had reached the Persian Gulf Command through the American Embassy, the officer in question was suddenly transferred back to the United States so that he could not be called upon to testify. On pressing the matter, I received, through the Embassy, an official withdrawal of the allegation. "Connolly dictated the withdrawal but said privately he still believed Hudson had been smuggling out reports on his command and that you were the channel," said the American Embassy Secretary.

There was no point in pursuing the matter further. General Connolly and his staff obviously felt in an insecure position, believed that Hudson had penetrated their defenses, and sought to prevent his information from reaching quarters in Washington. Months later, in Cairo, I met Hudson again and we compared notes.

I told him about my experience, and he was full of apologies. He laughed. By that time it was sufficiently remote for both of us to laugh.

Shortly before Hudson's departure from Iran, and as a direct consequence of his recommendations, a new OWI man appeared from Beirut in the person of James Downward, a former advertising executive on the staff of *Time* magazine. Downward proceeded cautiously. He realized that he had been given a delicate assignment and that his sole mission was to interpret America to the Iranians. Even so, Downward's material for Iranians had to be cleared through the Persian Gulf Command, who, theoretically, had nothing to do with Iranians, being concerned only with delivering supplies to Soviet Russia.

I saw Jim Downward frequently. He had a difficult job and at times was in despair over it. Each week a plane brought him material from the OWI headquarters in New York—articles, pictures, magazines, plastic plates for reproduction of photographs. . . . All of it had to be taken to the Amirabad camp and there, as Jim said, it languished for weeks while the censors of the Persian Gulf Command lingered in their contemplation of its suitability for Iranian consumption. Much of this material was of a topical nature and was useless after a few weeks. The only conclusion that Jim could draw was that a deliberate effort was being made to sabotage his work. Yet he had no recourse. Ambassador Dreyfus had left the country before Jim had arrived; a new ambassador had not yet been appointed and the *chargé d'affaires* was reluctant to make a direct issue with General Connolly pending his arrival. There was no way that Downward could report the situation, for he had every reason to believe, after the experience of Hudson, that his mail was being tapped.

In this confusion of weeds, America's spasmodic efforts to sow the seeds of understanding among the Iranians were stifled before they had a chance to grow.

America's information policy towards Iran was simple enough. It had four principal themes.

First; that America was in the war, that American participation did not come too late, and that America's power was sufficiently great to ensure victory for the United Nations.

Second; OWI proposed to provide a flow of news to Iran that would give the facts about America's contribution to victory and, also, American interpretation of world events.

Third; OWI set out to present the United Nations as the real pattern of Allied war effort. This, it was realized in Washington, was supremely important in the Middle East, where the war tended to be viewed merely as one more struggle between rival powers.

Fourth, and finally; To retain America's stake in popular interest and good will.

The channels by which OWI proposed to carry out this policy in Iran were through the establishment of a news service, through short-wave radio broadcasts from New York, the importation of American films, posters, pamphlets, books, recordings of American music, and, finally, through a series of exhibitions throughout the country.

Downward had an impossible task. All his channels were under the supervision of Connolly. OWI itself was distrusted as a civilian agency, not only in America, where it was subjected to spasmodic attacks by anti-administration congressmen and senators, but also overseas. The army resented it, as the army resents and is mistrustful of all civilians in its theatre; career officials of the State Department resented the entry of civilians from commercial life who, at one bound, outranked them in posts they had taken years to achieve.

And for every story, picture, or pamphlet which Downward issued to support the thesis that America was actively interested in the United Nations, the Iranians had 28,000 examples to the contrary, in the American troops of the command.

AMERICAN MISSIONS TO THE IRANIAN GOVERNMENT

There were, however, some factors working in America's favor. In Iran, more than in any other single country in the world, some Americans were giving tangible evidence of their good will. Five different missions, staffed and led by Americans, were working as servants of the Iranian Government to modernize its army and gendarmerie, to restore the economic system shattered by lack of supplies, to reorganize health facilities and the agricultural system. All of these American advisers were men who either knew the Middle East and its peoples intimately or who were skilled in their professions. One of the latter was Colonel Norman Schwartzkopf, of New Jersey, who was in charge of reorganizing the gendarmerie force—a difficult task in many respects, not the least important of which was the fact that Schwartzkopf's territory took in the Russian zone, a fact which made the Russians regard him with some suspicion.

The head of the American financial and economic mission, Dr. A. C. Millspaugh, was a man who had lived and worked in Iran for many years. He knew the cunning and greed of the merchant class, the poverty of the peasants, the independence and power of the nomad tribes and their scorn of the townspeople.

When Millspaugh accepted the request of the Iranian Government to bring in an American financial mission, the economy of the country was in a chaotic state. The rich and fertile lands of the north, where most of Iran's rice and wheat was grown, were in the hands of the Russians, who were not only refusing to allow the produce to enter the rest of the country but were also, it was suspected with good reason, confiscating the rice and wheat for use in Soviet Russia itself. A few token tons of food were occasionally allowed out of the Russian zone, but invariably with a great blare of propaganda-trumpets, as a gift from the Russian people to the people of Iran.

The industrial machinery of the country had run down. Most of it was of German origin, purchased during the Hitler regime through the cheap Reichsmark system established by Schacht. The Germans, as we have seen, had had two objectives in selling industrial equipment to Iran at bargain prices. One was to secure for Germany a never-ending stream of replacement orders, a theory based on the correct assumption that the inhabitant of the Middle East regards a piece of machinery as he does his donkey—to be driven until it can go no further and then replaced. The other objective was to plan the industrialization of the country in such a way as to fit in with a German army's ultimate drive to the East. Thus, iron foundries were established on the northward approaches to Tehran. Wheat silos, with a capacity for three times the 15,000,000 population of Iran, had been built in the barren desert lands of the south, through which a German army would have to pass on its way to India. Elaborate German printing equipment in the German-built National Bank in Tehran had been installed to function as the production center for the Nazi Braunhaus just up the street. And, of course, the country, like every other in the German economic sphere, was flooded with German drugs, effectively shutting out other competition and compelling chemists to rely on Germany for fresh stocks.

Three years of Anglo-Soviet occupation had wiped out almost all the results of the previous twenty years of industrialization. The magnificent presses stood idle for want of a few spare parts which were obtainable only in Germany. The electric-power plants and telephone systems broke down periodically and were only kept functioning by continual improvisatory repairs. Imported goods were reduced to a trickle, for road and railroad traffic was devoted almost entirely to supplies for Russia.

BLACK MARKETS, MONOPOLIES, GRAFT

Under circumstances such as these, the extreme contrasts of Iran were exaggerated still further. Historic and accepted customs, graft and corruption, were carried to fantastic lengths. In a country where nearly every essential of life, and certainly every luxury, was in short supply, it was comparatively easy for the wealthy merchants to establish monopolies and so control the prices at inflated levels. There were controlled prices for everything, of course, but they had as little contact with reality as my opium-smoking servant at the height of a smoking jag. With a serious wheat shortage, the Iranian Government forbade the manufacture of white bread—yet every baker's shop had white loaves in its windows, at the black-market price. Butter was four dollars a pound. Oranges were twenty-five cents each. Saucepans (made from old gasoline cans) were seven dollars each. Primus stoves—there were no gas stoves in Iran—were forty dollars each; a pair of shoes sixty dollars. An automobile tire five hundred dollars. A friend of mine sold his ten-year-old Buick for twelve thousand dollars. The purchaser was an Iranian who reckoned he could make ten thousand dollars a year by using it to run black-market goods from Tehran to some of the surrounding villages.

The only way in which an Iranian could possibly live with these prices was by graft. House servants grafted off their masters, and it was customary for Americans or Europeans to allow their servants to make about ten per cent on the week's shopping bills. Civil servants of all kinds grafted, as did the police, army politicians, cabinet ministers, and prime ministers. On the fall of a government, it was customary for the newspapers to launch a campaign demanding an investigation into the graft of the former administration, but when the bazaar whispered that premier So-and-so had made only ten million *rials*, or about thirty-five thousand dollars during his term of office, it was the general consensus of opinion that he had been very inefficient indeed! The raising of salaries, a possible solution that would occur at once to Occidentals, aggravated rather than solved the problem, for, by a species of logic which to him is irrefutable, the Iranian reasons that the higher salary a man obtains, the more responsible and authoritative is his position; hence his opportunities, and obligation, to graft are correspondingly greater.

47

For example, the colonel of an Iranian regiment receives a monthly pay which varies from forty to fifty dollars a month, depending on his station. In addition to his salary, however, the colonel collects so much from each of his junior officers who, in return, thereby receive his tacit assent to make up their subscriptions and a little more by grafting off their men. The amount collected by the colonel depends on the nature of the countryside in which he is stationed. In a fertile agricultural section, the amount is highest because the regiment can steal more from the countryside. It is thus an established practice for officers to pay bribes to the officials at the War Ministry in Tehran or to commanding generals, in order to be appointed to lucrative districts.

Junior officers collect from their men, not so much in money as in withholding a proportion of the rice and meat rations, for sale on the black market. In cavalry regiments, it is customary for officers to withhold part of the free issue of fodder, which is also sold on the black market.

It was to bring order out of this financial chaos, with every factor of local human behavior against him, that Millspaugh brought his mission of American advisers into the country. He proposed not only to set up a system of price control, but so to direct internal transport that distribution of supplies would be equitable; and to control the customs department, one of the largest centers of graft by the monopolists who wish to prevent imports reaching the public market and thus threatening their prices. In addition, Millspaugh proposed a far-reaching income-tax system which would have stripped the monopolists and racketeers of some of their war-time wealth. He also proposed to supervise the collection of the harvests so that a maximum of domestic supplies could be distributed throughout the nation.

That he did not succeed, that he was subjected to unscrupulous intrigue and opposition, that his position was undermined, and that he was finally compelled to withdraw as Administrator General of Iranian Finances can be attributed more to power politics than to the antagonism of established Iranian wealth.

RUSSIAN TACTICS

My diary has this entry for April 23, 1944: "The Russians are playing a devious game. It is now perfectly plain here that after the war they intend to go their own way, the way of Russian imperialism, and are already doing so. The Iranian press functions under the orders of a joint Anglo-Soviet censorship. There are supposed to be joint directives so that the Soviet Union and Britain can present the appearance of a joint policy. The British censor and the Soviet censor share the same office, and it is agreed that if the Soviet censor vetoes a story the British censor will not release it—and vice versa. In practice, however, the Russians do what they please. The Soviet censor automatically vetoes most of the stories issued by the Polish Government in London, but okays any story emanating from the 'Polish Patriots' Union,' which is a puppet organization founded by the Russians in Moscow and obviously being groomed as the new Polish Government. He refuses to pass any stories of the Polish army fighting in Italy, but releases stories alleging that Poles are being imprisoned in Palestine under sentences imposed by Polish courts-martial for wishing to enlist with the Polish Patriots in Russia. The British censor vetoed the latter stories, whereupon the Russians issued them locally through Tass. Having its headquarters in the Russian Embassy, Tass claims, and is given, immunity from censorship on the grounds that it is an official agency of the Russian Government.

"An amusing incident occurred the other day, I was told by the British censor. A story came in from America reporting that a Soviet official had resigned from the Russian Purchasing Commission in Washington and had denounced the Soviet regime. The British censor wondered what attitude his Russian colleague would take since no objection could be taken to the story on grounds of military security. When the Russian read the story, he went poker-faced, as Russians invariably do on finding themselves in an unexpected situation; after a minute's thought, he requested that the story be 'held temporarily.' That was some days ago, and the story is still being held up. Of course the idea is to hold it up until the news is too stale to use."

April 25: "The Russian censor asked for a 'stop' on a Reuters story that the Rumanians, suing for peace, had sent an envoy named Prince Barbu Stirbey to Cairo. The British censor accordingly banned the story from publication in Iran. Two days later, Tass issued it and the local Russian Embassy paper published it. The assumption of the Iranian, reading a Tass story from an Anglo-American theatre of war that was not also carried by American or British news agencies, is that the Russians have uncovered a secret attempt of the Anglo-Americans to conclude a separate peace with Rumanian reactionaries."

April 26: "The British released the story as carried originally by Reuters. This is going from bad to worse. It only confirms the Iranians' original impression that the British and Americans have been flirting separately with the Rumanians. It also gives Tass a reputation for accuracy and objectivity, which is not fully deserved."

These diary entries indicate how cleverly—and cynically— the Russians used inter-Allied machinery as a weapon against the Western democracies. I believe Iran was the first country where, being in close contact with the Western powers, the Russians evolved the new tactics of attempting to work through the machinery and institutions of the former and eventually of adopting the slogans of democracy and working in the name of democracy itself. Previously—before the war—communists in all countries had been zealous to preserve their separate identity from all other parties and institutions. From now on, the Russian program was to be—Infiltrate! Proclaim your democratic intentions, enter the inter-Allied organizations but render them so ineffective as to destroy faith in them! In their disillusion, the people will turn to us.

The process was already under way in other countries, where the communists had established themselves solidly at the center of the liberation movements, as in Jugoslavia or Greece, but I was not aware until this time of any such attempts to enter British or American agencies.

FLATTERY AND INTIMIDATION

The two most effective approaches to the Iranian—effective in the sense of producing immediate results—are through flattery and intimidation. The Russians made effective use of both approaches.

The Red Army was used for purposes of demonstrating Russian ruthlessness. From Tabriz, the capital of Azerbaijan in the Russian zone, there came regular reports of the brutality of the Red Army troops in their handling of the Iranians. A British friend from Tabriz, having occasion to make an official visit to Tehran (for which, nevertheless, a travel permit had to be obtained from the Russian military authorities), decided to drive the journey in the automobile of an Iranian friend. On their way they were involved in a collision with a vehicle driven by a Red Army officer. The Iranian chauffeur stopped his car and walked back along the road to expostulate with the Russian, who had been driving at an excessive speed. My friend heard a shot and, looking out of the car, saw the chauffeur crumple up on the road while the Russian came striding towards the car with an automatic in his hand, threatening in Russian to shoot all the occupants. It took the production of official British documents and several minutes of expostulation to dissuade the Russian, and my friend reached Tehran congratulating himself on a fortunate escape. In the Russian zone, all things were possible. The death of a British official, officially ascribed to a road accident, would have given rise to no inquiry, especially if that inquiry might lead to an unfortunate fracas between two Allies.

I mention this incident because it was one of many that occurred in the Russian zone and one of which I had credible evidence.

Or take this incident in Tehran:

May 28: "An Indian merchant, who has been living in Iran for the last fifteen years, burst into the British Consulate today in great terror, seeking protection. It appeared from his story, as he hurriedly stammered it out to one of the viceconsuls, that he had just been involved in a collision between his automobile and one of the innumerable jeeps in which the Russian civilians and troops ride about the town (much to the annoyance of every other Allied official who is continually being told about the shortage of transport and warned to safeguard tires). The jeep in this case was driven by a Russian officer, who got out and ordered the Indian, mistaking him for a Tehrani, to drive ahead of him to the Russian Embassy where they could settle who was responsible for the collision. There have been many rumors about people being shot out of hand within the mud-walled compound of the Russian Embassy. Correct or not, these rumors were evidently known to the Indian, who was terrified, but he remembered that the British Embassy was next door to the Russian Embassy, so as they turned their automobiles into the side street, he quickly swung to the right through the gates of the British Embassy, jumped out at the first building he saw, which happened to

52

be the British Consulate, and burst into the office of the British vice-consul. He had hardly finished his story, when the Russian officer strode in and demanded that the man be turned over to him as an Iranian who had committed an offence against the Red Army. The British official pointed out that the man was not an Iranian but an Indian, and therefore a British subject and, as such, was fully entitled to be on British territory. The Russian was momentarily disconcerted, but picked up his argument where he had left off and went away, threatening to have his Embassy make an official protest. The British are now waiting to see what is going to happen."

Naturally, nothing did happen. The Russian Embassy neither made a protest nor even mentioned the matter thereafter. The Indian was privately advised by the British Embassy to check in each day to assure them he was still in the land of the living and that he had not been shanghaied by the Russian secret police.

The latter statement reminds me that allegations of such occurrences may be received with lifted eyebrows by the reader who, having been born, educated, and brought up in a society where the right of habeas corpus is one of the fundamentals, is disinclined to picture to himself and realize the implications of a world where the individual has literally no protection from the unlimited power of a secret police.

Tehran possessed a large population of Georgians and Armenians who had fled from Russia during or shortly after the Bolshevik revolution. Unable to wend their way to the outside world, they had settled in Iran, and, passportless, denaturalized, had gradually reconciled themselves to accepting the degrading life of the Middle East, for themselves and their children.

When the Red Army marched into Iran and began to round them up for deportation to Russia, these people could look to nobody for protection. They had no American passports and so could not turn to the U.S. Embassy. Unlike the Indian, they could not seek refuge in the British Embassy. They were not Iranians, and hence could invoke no protection from the Iranian Government—whatever that was worth. Like rabbits pursued by ferrets, they could only crouch and wait passively for the leap.

Month by month, the arrests went on. Husbands and their wives just disappeared—whether they were shot inside the grounds of the Russian Embassy or whether they were shipped back to the Soviet Union no one knew, because they vanished without a trace. On only two occasions within my own experience, did the victims have friends who were sufficiently powerful and persistent to insist on official inquiries. In each case, the Russians eventually admitted that the persons concerned had been "arrested." But they were never released, nor ever heard of again.

Two years later I read in my New York newspaper that Armenians and Georgians were queueing up outside the Soviet Embassy in Tehran to volunteer for return to the Soviet Union. Let this be their advocate and epitaph to the democracies— from whom at no time they received help or spiritual sustenance—that they had the final realism to accept their disillusionment, the courage to accept the inevitable and to march forth to their own Nirvana.

The advantage of a totalitarian regime is that it can be all things to all people simultaneously—at least until it is ready to engulf them. This was an advantage notably enjoyed by the Hitler regime during its heyday. Hitler's disadvantage was that in being all things to all peoples, he had to take precautions lest the peoples get together and compare notes. He could tell the British, for example, that they were fighting to preserve a world for Americans to enjoy, while at the same time he could tell Americans that they were the tools of British imperialism. His only risk was that the one might perchance learn what he was saying to the other. Russia enjoys the same advantages as Hitler, but is not hampered to the same extent by the same restrictions. Contradictions in the pronouncements of Russia for foreign consumption are, by the peculiar logic of dialectics, deemed to be justifiable on the grounds of expediency. If this is true in the Western world, it is even more true in the Middle East, where logic is definable more in emotional than scientific terms.

To the Iranian there is no illogicality in Russia presenting herself as the epitome of ruthless autocracy on the one hand and of kindly benevolence on the other. The respect that each commands separately is increased if both are mixed together in judicious proportions. The Iranian was not bewildered at being embraced one day by the Russian as a sharer in common cultural achievements and being kicked into the gutter the next day by a Red Army officer. All mysteries belong to God and who was he to fathom their depth.

"Dear Listeners," the Moscow radio broadcast to Iran on November 30, 1945, when the Red Army was organizing and supporting the armed rebellion in north Iran, "you are, of course, fully aware that German imperialism had some evil designs on Iran. In the aggressive plans of Hitler's Supreme Command, there was an important part assigned to Iran. The Hitlerites intended to acquaint Iran with their so-called humanitarianism. It was only the Red Army which saved Iran from a horrible fate. The great Soviet warriors fulfilled their mission on behalf of Iran as well. Centuries will elapse, but the magnanimity and abnegation of the Soviet soldier will not fade out of the memory of mankind, including the peoples of the East."

In their cultural propaganda the Russians sought to prove that the revolution had not interfered with the development of the arts in the Soviet Union, that modern Russian literature and music had their roots deep in Russian history. As a sign that Russia had forsaken the doctrine of internationalism and was falling back on the formerly despised bourgeois emotion of patriotism, this was interesting. Thus my diary:

June 9: "The Russians are holding an exhibition of paintings by Alexander Gerassimov. At the opening ceremony, one of the local university professors stressed the lead that Russia has given the world in 'this most universal of arts.' Said the only art which was understood by all peoples and had an international language was painting; therefore, a painter was the only craftsman who belonged to entire mankind. Further demonstration of this fact had been given by the Iranians themselves in their development of the art of miniatures. Iran and the Soviet Union could boast of close ties in this, the most expressive of the arts." And this:

July 16: "I went today to a reception held by the Irano-Soviet Cultural Relations Society at the National Teachers' Training College. The occasion was the fortieth anniversary of the death of Anton Chekhov. The Soviet Ambassador, Mikhail Alexeivitch Maximov, spoke in Russian on the life of Chekhov and the extensiveness of Soviet literature and culture. It was Maximov's first public appearance since his promotion from counsellor to ambassador following the so-far unexplained failure of the former ambassador, Mikhailov, to return to his post. After his speech had been translated into Iranian, Maximov introduced the Russian composer, Leon Knipper, who had just arrived from Moscow on a cultural mission. Knipper comes from the family of Chekhov and made a speech containing reminiscences on the latter."

A few days later I met Knipper and his vivacious young wife at the house of a friend, a refugee Hungarian engineer. The invitation to dinner was accompanied by the urgent request not to mention it to anyone else as the eyes and ears of the OGPU were everywhere and Knipper would certainly get into trouble if it became known to his officials that he was meeting "foreigners." Apparently Knipper had a reputation with the OGPU of deriving too much enjoyment from his trips to "capitalist" countries and this was the first occasion for some time that he had been allowed to leave the Soviet Union.

Whether these whispered confidences were true or not I have no way of knowing. I noticed, however, that Knipper flashed me a suspicious look on our introduction, and I received the impression that he fancied he had been tricked into meeting an unexpected and possibly embarrassing fellow guest.

During the evening his wife, a Caucasian girl who could speak only Russian and Caucasian, chattered excitedly to our hostess about the variety of goods to be purchased in the shops and how good it was to see a town where one could actually buy things. To a Westerner, accustomed to regard Tehran as a city of extreme shortages, this was an interesting reaction. Knipper was quick to perceive the trend of conversation and explained hurriedly in German, our only common language, that the shortages in Moscow were due only to the war. He then launched into the by-now familiar Russian thesis that Russia alone was carrying the burden of the war.

There followed a dissertation on the favorite Russian complaint that America and England had delayed opening a second front and had only done so after the Red Army had destroyed the Reichswehr. I pointed out that at that very time the German army was showing unexpected reserves of strength in its counter-offensive in France.

He shook his head knowingly. "You're being too soft with the Germans," he said. "The reactionaries in America and Britain still want to preserve Germany as a strong power. You don't realize that the only good German is a dead German."

At this I protested. "After all," I pointed out, "Russia agrees with America and Britain in saying she does not hate the German people—only the Nazis. And so far, Russia is the only

57

one of the three to come out with a 'Free German Committee!'"

"Just our propaganda," he scoffed.

"Talking of your propaganda," I asked, "why does your radio always refer to the Germans in the mass as Hitlerites and not as Nazis? Is it because the term National-Socialism is too similar to the new Stalinist slogan Socialist-Nationalism?"

At this point our hostess changed the subject and the Knippers left shortly afterwards.

THE POLISH PRISONERS

Directly north of Tehran, on the other side of the gaunt Elburz mountains, there lies the largest inland sea in the world, the Caspian. Larger than the state of Arizona, the Caspian is, however, dwindling in size; for although it is fed by such great rivers as the Oxus, which rises in the mysterious hinterland of Afghanistan and wanders across Kazakhstan to empty its silt into the tideless sea, continual evaporation and drainage are emptying the Caspian faster than it is being fed. Over the centuries, the silt that has been drained down into the sea is cast up along its shores to form a series of weirdly shaped lagoons, along whose inner banks numerous towns and villages have sprung up, their inhabitants fishermen, or commercial mariners who have never seen any other ocean.

The Caspian has more than once borne on its breast the miniature fleets of invading armies. Genghis Khan traversed it when he burst out of the east to defeat and annihilate the once-great Persian empire. Red Army troops camped along its shores in 1920 while pursuing counter-revolutionary troops into the northern Iran province of Ghilan. On that occasion, the Red troops stayed a year in Ghilan at the instigation, it is said, of Stalin, who, being an expansionist and a Georgian, wished to see Georgia's nearby province of Ghilan become a Soviet Republic.*

Stalin's puppet in those days was a Ghilan chieftain named Kuchik Khan. An Iranian army colonel, Reza Khan Pahlevi, who had just installed himself as ruler of Iran, seized Kuchik Khan, beheaded him, and displayed the head in Tehran with the sneering remark, "This is the Kuchik Khan that Russia sent against me!" The remark had a double connotation, for Kuchik in Iranian means "little." Lenin, rebuking Stalin, withdrew his troops and signed a treaty of friendship with Reza Khan, who proclaimed himself Emperor of Iran. As Emperor, he ruled without opposition for twenty years, and in general behaved like a dictator, until in 1941 Stalin, this time with the cooperation of the British, sent his army into Iran and deposed him.† His name, however, lives on in the town of Pahlevi which he built on one of the Caspian lagoons.

Twelve months after the Anglo-Russian invasion which led to Reza Khan's abdication, this same little town of Pahlevi was subjected to another kind of invasion. Across the Caspian there came Russian oil tankers, their decks and superstructures choked with a frightening collection of human beings, a ragged, diseased, half-starving army of men, women, and children. They were Poles being released by the Soviet authorities.

In 1939, the Red Army attacked Poland shortly after the German invasion. In the subsequent Russo-German treaty, Russia obtained possession of the eastern and southern half of the country, incorporating the two sections into the existing

---

* See *Men and Politics*, by Louis Fischer, p. 135, for an account of this abortive attempt.

† Dictators the world over dislike admitting failures. Twenty-five years later (November 25, 1945, to be precise), during the Red Army's second, and this time successful, attempt to lop off Azerbaijan from Iran, the Moscow Radio broadcast the following in its Iranian program: "The Iranian nation . . . as a result of their *twenty-seven-year experience* of friendship with the U.S.S.R. . . . was convinced that the Soviet Union would not leave it in the lurch." The Kuchik Khan putsch, the Iranian nation's first experience of Stalin's friendship, was thus conveniently ignored.

White Russian and Ukrainian Soviet Republics. To solve once and for all the minority question, the Polish inhabitants were moved out in a series of mass evacuations. In 1940 and 1941 it is estimated that between one-and-a-half million to two million Polish civilians, each with no more personal possessions than he was able to carry, had left the homeland and disappeared into the recesses of the Soviet Union where no sightseer is allowed—such remote and primitive provinces as Kazakhstan or inner Siberia.

There was no general rule as to who should be deported. This depended on the activity of informers, the whim of the various Russian secret police authorities, and on other local circumstances. But in general the first to be deported were the Polish veterans of the 1919–1920 Russo-Polish war who had been settled in the frontier districts, state forestry service employees, and government servants. Others were deported because they possessed land or property in greater measure than seemed equitable to the Soviet authorities. The land of these bourgeois and kulaks was parcelled among the poorer peasants who were frequently induced to accept these gifts only under threat, and who eventually found themselves deported also because they had themselves involuntarily become bourgeois and kulaks.

There exists no accurate information in the possession of any authority other than the Soviet Government on the number of Poles deported in each flight, but it is known that the deportation of June 25–30, 1940, was the largest.

The method of carrying out the deportations was almost the same in each case. Russian secret police called at pre-selected houses usually between 2 A.M. and 4 A.M., and, according to their humor, gave the occupants from fifteen minutes to two hours to collect some of their belongings, after which they loaded them onto trucks and took them to the nearest railroad station. After a wait of anything from a few hours to a few days at the station, the deportees were packed into trains in which they travelled to various parts of the U.S.S.R., the journeys lasting anything from two or three days to a month. No excuse of illness was of any avail in preventing the deportation of anyone who had been marked down, and infirm old men and women, some of them seriously ill, were deported together with the hale and hearty.

Came 1941 and the German attack on Russia; the British, promising aid, asked the Soviet Union to release the Polish prisoners of war for service in the Polish army, then in Egypt. After lengthy negotiations, the ragged army that debouched onto the shores of Pahlevi represented the Soviet Union's gesture of good faith. They had been travelling like cattle for days with no idea where they were going or what was to happen to them. After two years of living like serfs in miserable mud huts on the endless plains of Kazakhstan, scratching the soil and bartering their clothes for food, many of them had ceased to care. All they knew was that after an eternity of exile, army trucks had come to collect them, had carried them to the nearest railhead, from where they had been taken to the Caspian.

Their clothes were in rags; all of them were verminous. Some were in the last stages of typhus and died a few hours after they landed on their Caspian beachhead.

To be fair to the Russians, they had treated the Poles no worse than their own political exiles. They had merely poured them down the sink and forgotten them. Conditions of travel to the Russian port on the Caspian were easily explicable, Russian transportation facilities then being taxed to their uttermost by the war.

The nature of the Polish evacuations from Russia illustrated the peculiar spurts and starts, the sudden variations from apparent friendship to apparent Oriental deceit and suspicion, which seem to characterize Soviet actions in the eyes of the Western observer.

It had taken painstaking negotiations lasting over twelve months to induce the Russian Government to part with its Polish exiles. It is possible, of course, that what was apparently Russian reluctance was really a genuine difficulty in tracing the Poles in the far-flung places to which they had been deported. At the end of the twelve months, the Soviet authorities acceded to the Allied request and warned the British army authorities in Iran to be ready to receive them at the rate of 1,500 men a week. Nevertheless, the Russians refused to allow the British to send an advance party into the Russian zone to look for camp-sites for the refugees. Then, forty-eight hours before the event actually took place, the Russian authorities in Iran informed the British that there had been a change in plans, that the Poles would not arrive at the rate of 1,500 a week, but that the first shipment alone would comprise a total of 48,000 men, women, and children.

It was undoubtedly a humanitarian gesture of the Russians to release the families along with the men. But what was the reason for the change in plans? Was it due to lack of co-ordination between the Soviet authorities at the Caspian port and the Soviet authorities in Iran? Or was it a sly attempt to embarrass the British with what appeared to be a sudden administrative problem of indescribable proportions?

Whatever the reason, the operation passed off without much mishap. The Middle East was scoured for supplies of all kinds that had not already been provided, from children's clothes to sanitary napkins. It was decided to clothe women in army uniforms after they had been disinfested. "Now, men," said a prosaic British sergeant in charge of one of the disinfestation units at Pahlevi, "this is no time to stand on ceremony. If you're married, it won't be anything new to see a naked woman. If you're not, you're going to be sick of the idea in the next seven days!"

Provision was made for hospital cases, and the local hospital at Pahlevi, whose facilities were at first refused by the Russians, was hastily evacuated by the latter when, on the orders of a British officer, the corpses of the late typhus victims were placed in the street outside its gates. A few Polish officers who refused to clip off all their hair—on the somewhat irrelevant grounds that a Polish officer is never lousy, even after two years in Kazakhstan—were brought to reason when they emerged from the disinfestation units to find that their clean trousers and underpants had been confiscated until they submitted.

From Pahlevi the refugees were moved to camps in the British zone round Tehran and Isfahan. Here, the men departed to join the Polish forces in the Middle East. Most of the women and children were moved across country by the British to the Persian Gulf, and thence departed to more permanent camps in British East African colonies.

Then, suddenly, without explanation, the flow of refugees from Russia was cut off. Negotiations began again, and, twelve months later, another batch was released, bringing the two years' total to 116,000. In the fall of 1943 the frontiers were closed again by the Russians, and this time they remained closed as far as the Poles were concerned. At the lowest estimate, more than a million of these unhappy Poles were still left within Russia.

Several thousand Polish women and children from the two token shipments are still living in camps in Iran, while their status and future is being debated. In the best of surroundings, life in a refugee camp is degrading. The restrictive atmosphere, the deadly boredom of day following day in routine monotony, the restraints on movement outside the camp, the feeling of utter helplessness—all these factors combine to induce in the refugees a feeling of lassitude and despondency, a state of mind which is aided and abetted by conditions of life in the Middle East. *Maleesh*—a single expressive Arabic word, meaning "It doesn't matter," "To hell with it"—was part of the vocabulary of every American and British soldier serving in the Middle East. The Polish refugees developed a hyper-*maleesh* psychology.

Would they see their husbands again? Who knows? *Maleesh!* Would Poland be revived after the war? They hoped so, but—*maleesh!* Occasionally, some of them were offered outside work as a means of supplementing the remittances they received through the Polish Government in London. But *maleesh!*

They reached a depth where they preferred to stay inside the camps.

But one emotion remained unimpaired in its intensity and ferocity—a deep and abiding hatred of all things Russian. Nothing that Russia did was justifiable in their eyes. They hated Russia as their captor and they hated her now as their official ally. They would even have preferred to see Russia fighting on the German side, though such an assumption would have compelled them logically to accept the fact that they would still, in that event, have been languishing in Kazakhstan. Hatred is a dry and bitter root for a human being to feed on, but the Polish refugees in Iran preferred it to any other kind of emotional sustenance. They nursed it jealously and were untiring in their efforts to portray the Russians as devils and beasts. The very violence of their efforts did not fail to impress the Iranians with whom they came in contact. Every gesture of the Russians was interpreted as having an ulterior motive.

On one occasion local agents of the Polish Patriots' Union, formed by the Russians in Moscow, asked those refugees who still had relatives in former Poland or in the Soviet Union to volunteer names and, wherever possible, addresses so that contact between families could be re-established. "You see!" said the Poles to each other and to the Iranians, "The Russians want us to betray our friends so they can clap them into prison or use them to blackmail us into going back. You cannot trust the Russians an inch."

They were a continual thorn in the side of the Russians, and a frequent embarrassment to the British, who were acting as caretakers for the Polish Government-in-Exile in London. With the best will in the world, it was impossible for the British to do anything for the Poles without arousing the suspicions of the Russians in Iran who, by this time, had doubtless come to regard all Poles as incurable Russophobes. In fact, the Russians' decision to stop all further evacuation of Poles from Russia during the war may have been due to their ultimate conviction that to free a Pole was to set at liberty an inveterate and irreconcilable enemy of their country.*

THE TUDEH—OR WORKERS'—PARTY

June 28, 1944: "The Russians have opened large consulates in Isfahan and Kermanshah, outside the Russian zone. There are no Russian residents in these areas, except for a few White Russian refugees from the old Bolshevik days. There are—at present—no Russian commercial interests in these areas, but the Russians are setting about establishing themselves in Iran very thoroughly. Their consular staff in Isfahan alone numbers more than thirty, which is reminiscent of the familiar

---

* The seriousness with which Russia regards the potential opposition of nationals escaping from territory incorporated into the Soviet Union is not confined to the Poles. The little-publicized fracas between Russia and Sweden at the end of 1945 is an example. The incident arose over the Russian insistence that Sweden turn over to Russia some 2,700 German army adherents who had escaped from the Baltic countries after the German collapse. Among these were some 157 Balts. That Russia was more interested in the Balts than in the Germans was shown by the urgency of their demands (at a time when they were informing the Norwegians, who were extremely anxious to get rid of some 20,000 German soldiers belonging to that part of Germany occupied by Russia, that the Red Army could not take over any more Germans from Norway). The Russians sent a special ship to collect the internees from Sweden.

German tactics in the Balkans just after the outbreak of this war.

"Another disturbing factor for the future is the number of Red Army officers who are travelling about the countryside on what are officially described as 'sightseeing tours.' They are most numerous in the Qum area, between Tehran and Isfahan. A possible reason for the opening of the consulate in Isfahan is the fact that the Tudeh Party has just decided to open a branch there."

There are no further references in my diary to either of the new Soviet consulates. I received no reports on their activities and could not spare the time to make a personal journey to the two towns. As far as I am aware, there was no reason why the Soviet government should not open two, or twenty-two, consulates throughout Iran if it felt the expense was justified. What was interesting, however, was the Soviet decision to open these consulates at a time when there were signs of American interest in Iran and when the recently formed Tudeh Party was putting on a recruiting campaign.

The Tudeh (or Workers') Party had been formed a few months previously and received most of its support, financial and otherwise, from the Russians. It professed to be, not communist, but "democratic." (Here again is evidence of that decision to promote "democracy" rather than communism.) Its case, briefly, was that Iran had been governed by dictators and corrupt politicians who were willing tools of foreign interests. Ergo, the solution was to expel the foreign interests and to purge the political hierarchy.

Operating in the British zone, it was comparatively easy for Tudeh to convince the miserable Iranian lower classes that most of their poverty and hardship was due to the military occupation. As far as the Iranians were concerned, the culprits were the military they could see in their immediate vicinity, namely Americans and British. The Russians were not simi-

66

larly embarrassed by Tudeh because the latter never operated in the Russian zone.

From the start, Tudeh spearheaded the attacks on the economic and financial mission of Dr. Millspaugh. This in itself was an anomaly, for if there was one section of the Iranian people which the Millspaugh mission aimed to help, it was that section whose interests Tudeh professed to represent. The abolition of monopolies, the establishment of an income-tax law which would deprive the very wealthy—and wealthy Iranians were generally very wealthy—of eighty per cent of their incomes, the supervision of wheat collection and distribution, all these were measures designed to help the poverty-stricken Iranians who formed ninety per cent of the population of every town and village in the country.

Nevertheless, the Tudehists joined hands with the monopolists in a vicious attack on all the Millspaugh mission's affairs and activities. Their tactics, based on the doctrine defined by Hitler that the greater the lie the more credulously it will be received, were to vilify every American member of the mission. The Americans were accused of inefficiency, of accepting bribes to issue import permits, of receiving exorbitantly high salaries from the Iranian Treasury, of using their official positions to live under luxurious conditions. Each day the rumors were specific. By the early summer, nearly all the American members of the mission had handed in their resignations. At the request of the Iranian Government, they withdrew them temporarily, whereupon the Tudeh campaign was resumed. By the end of the year, the mission resigned again—this time permanently.

Why did Tudeh, the so-called "democratic" Iranian party, join hands with the wealthy monopolists in this campaign against Millspaugh? Why did the Russians permit, or instigate, the Tudeh campaign?

The reason was simple. The war was over in the Middle

East and the Russians felt free to play their own game. They had their eyes on Iran; they felt sufficiently strong to deal with British competition, but they were determined to forestall American entry into the game while there was still time. They could not afford to allow the Millspaugh mission to succeed. Therefore they used the Tudeh.

What was the Russian game in Iran? In late 1945, the newspapers reported the revolt in Azerbaijan and nobody seemed to have any doubt that the rebels had the active support of the Russians, who refused to allow Iranian troops to enter the zone. Azerbaijan, it appeared, wished to obtain autonomy, although the rebels were careful not to come out with their full program for incorporation as a Soviet republic.

The tactics of the communist dialectician are usually to deny that Soviet Russia is interfering in any other country's affairs, but, in cases where Soviet interference is clearly indisputable, the dialectician has a second line of defence, which he adopts without prejudice to his first line. In such cases, the revolt is portrayed as a genuine expression of popular resentment against a local tyranny, as breaking out spontaneously, without the premeditation or instigation of the Soviets; thus, Russian participation is merely to localize the conflict.

Was the Azerbaijan revolt of December, 1945 a spontaneous affair, as Molotov claimed at the time? I have the following entry for June 5, 1944, eighteen months previously:

"Certain Parliamentary deputies from Azerbaijan, in the Russian zone, have joined with members of the 'democratic' group, headed by the Tudeh Party. They have formed a new group in the Majlis (the Iranian Parliament) and agree to vote solidly on all issues. Their total membership is about thirty, which gives them considerable power in a Parliament so hopelessly divided on almost every issue. They have also given themselves a new name—the Liberty Group."

And on October 14: "The Russians obviously will not leave

northern Iran. The papers today gave news of the Soviet Trade Delegation in Tehran and said it had finished its negotiations for trade (including oil) concessions in Northern Iran. The details now go to the Majlis for consideration. If the concessions are granted, it will give a lawful appearance to the continued Russian occupation of the north. If they are not granted by the Majlis, the Russians will just stay anyway and the north will declare its autonomy from Tehran. Either way, the Iranians don't have much choice. With world politics in their present stage of ultra-sophistication, the Iranians might be well advised to accept the position and get whatever payment they can out of Moscow. The trouble is, of course, that they realize matters would not stop there. The more they concede to the Russians; the more impelled the British will feel to strengthen their position in southern Iran, where they have their oilfields."

BRITISH PROPAGANDA EFFORTS

The British contemplated these events with uneasiness. Two hundred years of running an empire in India had convinced them that they could not afford to have a strong aggressive power sitting in Iran athwart their imperial communications. The preservation of the country as a vacuum between Russia and Britain had worked, after a fashion. They were aware that, by breaking down the vacuum in 1941 and installing a joint Anglo-Russian occupation, they had started a chain of events which could never lead back full circle to the situation as it had existed before. Exactly what the situation would be, there was no way of telling. Certainly the British realized that Soviet influence in north Iran, once established during the wartime occupation, would be strengthened rather than diminished.

They themselves lost no time and spared no money in their

69

efforts to consolidate their position in their own zone. Their propaganda organization in Iran was much larger than that maintained by the Russians. (I was about to say, larger than the Russian and American combined—but this would have been misleading, since there was never at any time more than one Office of War Information official stationed in Iran.) By 1944—after three years of occupation had given the British time to reflect on the shape of things to come and to reach the conclusion that Russia had gone imperialist—the Public Relations Bureau had become by far the largest section of the British Embassy. So large, in fact, that the Embassy could not provide sufficient office space and the Bureau established itself, appropriately enough, in the former Nazi Braunhaus from which the Germans had conducted their efficient propaganda until 1941. It had nearly one hundred people on its payroll in Tehran, was divided into separate sections dealing with films, radio, visual publicity, and exhibitions; printed its own magazines and newspapers; sent mobile film units into the outlying villages and towns where no movie halls existed; and otherwise conducted regular propaganda campaigns through the British consulates in the provinces—except those in the Russian zone.

The British directives were similar to those I have listed for OWI. They took into account, however, the fact that Britain had long-standing commercial interests in Iran, such as the Anglo-Iranian Oil Corporation, and stressed the necessity for emphasizing a community of interest between Iran and Britain.

Automatically, in British directives for all countries at that time (as in American directives), there was a treatise on inter-Allied relations, especially relations between Britain, America, and the Soviet Union. At all costs, the British stressed, there must exist no trend in British propaganda which would appear to show Iranians a difference of views between the three leading Allies. Praiseworthy though this was, it left the British tongue-tied on all local Anglo-Russian issues. The reticence of local Russian officials, the fact that even if they had not been so reticent, they were obviously powerless to make decisions on any problem without reference to Moscow, made it impossible for local problems to be settled by local consultation. The result was not only to leave the problems unsettled, but to widen still further the gulf between the Allies.

If the Russians were feared, the British were no less suspected by the Iranians, and their military occupation of two-thirds of the country did nothing to lessen the suspicion.

The planners in OWI in Washington had correctly surmised the situation by saying that the Iranian tended to view the war merely as one more struggle between great powers with the lesser powers being used as pawns. They had, if anything, underemphasized the situation. The Iranian did not merely tend to such an attitude; he was firmly rooted in it. There was no point in describing to him the evils of the Nazi regime. The ex-Shah Reza's twenty-year-old policy of flirting with the Germans in order to maintain a balance of power between the Russians and the British could not be undone in a few months. The cruelties of the Nazi leaders made no impression except, perhaps, to increase the feeling of respect; the Oriental associates cruelty with power. The fact that Hitler beheaded his opponents counted for nothing in a country whose former despotic ruler had made a practice of having his doctors inject air bubbles into the veins of his victims. The only result of citing German atrocities was to strengthen the Iranian in his fatalistic, cynical belief that all rulers were the same, and that a change of regimes meant nothing more than a change of tyrants on top.

Under such circumstances as these, British propaganda in Iran made no positive headway. Its officials were skilled, they knew their territory, and they knew their media; but the tragic fact was that they had nothing to sell because they themselves felt that Iran was indeed destined to be a pawn in power politics, and they did not know what its precise future would be. There was little use in playing up the line of future Iranian independence because the withdrawal of British troops depended directly upon the future Russian willingness to withdraw their troops simultaneously. The British were by no means willing to commit themselves to a military evacuation without good reason to believe that the country would in reality be left undisturbed by the Russians.

By midsummer of 1944 the British propaganda organization in Iran had already received instructions from London to soft-pedal the terms of the Atlantic Charter and to confine itself to the Four Freedoms declaration. The former spoke in too specific terms of the Allies' intention to seek no territorial aggrandisement and to guarantee the independence of all nations. The latter dealt conveniently with the generalities of human existence; fundamental though they were, they were open to different interpretations in different countries.

Diplomatic life in a foreign capital usually tends to resolve itself into a series of cliques. The rules of protocol, the restrictions of language, and, most important, the professional snobbishness of the ordinary career diplomat place the personnel of embassies or legations in a sort of separate community from the people of the country to which they are accredited. These conditions apply to an extreme degree in an Oriental capital where the population is divided into rigidly separated social classes, and where, moreover, the Occidental finds himself enclosed in a comparatively small community of human beings with the same tastes and languages as himself. Communal life for the American or European in a capital such as Tehran consists of a series of parties, often two or three in the same evening, where he meets the same people, discusses the same people, and—fortunately, for his health the next day—is given the same sort of cocktails.

I attended many of the parties and receptions given by the British and was impressed by one fact—that, in addition to the usual mass attendance from the Anglo-American colony, the Iranians who attended were not only the same on each occasion, but were residents of Tehran who were known to be pro-British or pro-American.

Since these receptions were used as an opportunity to present some piece of Allied propaganda—to witness, for example, the private exhibition of an Allied war film such as *Tunisian Victory* or to celebrate the capitulation of Italy or some other Allied victory—the whole purpose of these receptions was defeated. For the British were preaching to the converted, to those very Iranians who, as they had proved by enduring the restraints and persecutions of the Reza Shah regime, had already demonstrated that they were adherents of the British cause. The whole purpose of propaganda is that it should sell an idea to those who are not already convinced. Who, therefore, were the unconverted in Iran—from the British point of view?

There were the pro-Russians. I think enough has been written, and the world has suffered sufficient experiences, for one to realize by this time that the professional pro-Russian in every country has so drowned his logic, his emotions, and his conscience in a flood of dialetics, as to be impervious to all outside influences. The pro-Russian Iranians differed from their fellow-travellers in other countries only in the respect that they were geographically closer to the country they admired.

There were the pro-German upper classes. By this obnoxious term is meant the monopolists who utilized Iran's economic shortages to increase their wealth; the merchants whose German machinery was running to a standstill and who

73

were living for the day when they could renew their orders for spare parts, convinced that Germany, even though defeated, would survive the war as an industrial country; and, finally, those civil servants who were known by their past activities to be pro-German. The British had sufficient sense to realize that all these people, representing only a part of the tiny upper crust, insulated from being a permanent influence in Iranian life—both socially and economically—were unimportant to their long-term interests. First buyable by the Germans, they were now buyable by the British, but could be purchased again tomorrow by the highest bidder.

There were the peasants and poverty-stricken workers of the towns. The gulf between these people and the British was so wide as to be unbridgeable. The Iranian poor in the towns and agricultural vicinities live like dogs, and to the British—not merely the British, but to most Occidentals—they have the manners and cowardice of outcast mongrel dogs such as infest every city in the land. They showed no courage in pressing for reforms. In their corruptibility, they differed only in degree from the "upper classes." They were as yet unorganized, but the Russians were tackling that problem through the Tudeh Party.

THE TRIBES

Finally, there were the tribes. The most important social group in the country, the tribes control the destiny of Iran. Nomadic in their existence, moving each season from one grazing ground to another, during the previous several years they had built up private armies which could defy the official army of their country. Independent in thought and economy, they retain a contempt for the townspeople, poor and rich alike, which can only be compared with the old American contempt for a "dago."

74

Between Isfahan and Ahwaz, south of Tehran, live the Bakhtiaris, the wealthiest of all the tribes, whose leaders had been kidnapped and murdered repeatedly by the ex-Shah Reza and whose consequent suspicions of the Iranian Government are only equalled by, say, the Polish refugees' suspicions of Moscow. Still further south, between Shiraz and Bandar Abbas on the Persian Gulf, is Qashgai territory—the Qashgais whose chief is Nassa Khan Qashgai, a brilliant tribal leader who had drilled his men into an army which, on one occasion, defeated and made prisoners of an entire Iranian army corps sent down to disarm them. In the southeast, near the frontier of India, there are the Baluchis. Near Busheir, on the Persian Gulf, are the Tengistanis; between Shiraz and Isfahan, are the Boir Ahmedis, who have a reputation as robbers and who have had continual fights with the Qashgai. There are the Lurs, the Shahsevens, the Kurds, and many others. . . . No student of Iran can ignore them. They are a continual worry to the government, which is ever fearful that a tribal leader will arise to conquer the country. Their influence cannot be discounted by any power, and it was certainly not discounted by the British during their occupation.

Twenty-eight years previously, during the First World War, a German agent named Wassmuss had made his way secretly to south Iran and, by deft intrigue among the tribes, had kept considerable numbers of British troops engaged in a search for him and had even occasioned some unrest in the government of India itself. Wassmuss left Iran after the tribes, in whose welfare he took a genuine interest, turned against him, wrecked his model farm, and left its modern agricultural implements to rust among the ruins. He died some years ago, but the British took the lesson to heart in World War II. Promptly, on their occupation of Iran, they stationed British army liaison officers with each of the principal tribes.

The reason given to the Iranian Government in Tehran was

that it was most important to prevent tribal feuds arising over seasonal grazing grounds, a frequent cause of unrest. It was vital, the British explained, with food supplies being so scarce the world over and shipping even scarcer, that Iran should remain in a stable condition so as to make the best use of her own resources. A reason not made public was that it was equally vital for the British to anticipate German attempts to send their agents into tribal territory.

The British anticipation was an intelligent one, for the Nazis, whose colony in Iran had been captured intact by the British and Russians in 1941, did attempt to fly agents into the country. They were at first handicapped by the lengthy flying distances, but, as the German eastern advance into Russia continued, they found themselves in a more favorable position. The capture of the Crimea gave them admirable flying bases from which to conduct operations into Iran and in 1943, after two attempts that proved abortive because of bad weather, a Luftwaffe plane, taking off from Simferol, succeeded in crossing the Black Sea and, traversing the mountain barrier and the high plateau, dropped four German agents into Qashgai territory. They came with messages from two relatives of Nassa Khan Qashgai, who were at that time in German-occupied Europe and who were presumably being held as hostages by the Germans.

The four agents established contact with the Qashgai and at once began a series of operations, which consisted chiefly of raiding the American-operated railroad carrying supplies to Russia and conducting an elaborate rumor campaign against the British in Iran. The rumors had a practical form and took advantage of the shortage of those supplies which the tribesmen were feeling most acutely at the time. A common specimen ran as follows: "Don't accept drugs from the government. They are imported from the British and Americans, and they are bewitched." To a tribesman, accustomed to believ-

76

ing that an aspirin tablet is a cure for his malaria because it relieves his headache, the latter statement was by no means preposterous.

A British army captain named Jackson was at that time the liaison officer with the Qashgai. He was in regular contact with Nassa Khan Qashgai and knew that the four German agents were working with the tribe. He even knew with which particular section of the tribe the four men were located, though he had never met them. It should be pointed out at this stage that the Iran tribes, although preserving a tribal entity, consist of a series of roving communities which are often scores of miles apart. Any reader familiar with the history of, say, the Sioux Indians, will appreciate the difficulty of keeping in touch with the daily events of any one tribe and the delicacy that must accompany every negotiation.

Having discovered the arrival and whereabouts of the agents, Jackson then set about negotiating with Nassa Khan for their imprisonment. At first this was difficult because of the two Qashgai hostages in Europe, but after nine months Nassa Khan persuaded his unwelcome German guests to send a message to the Reich through their portable radio transmitter requesting the release of the two Qashgais. When they arrived by train on neutral Turkish territory, the British Embassy in Istambul flashed a message to Tehran, whence it was relayed to Jackson, and the trap was sprung.

The Germans were invited to a tribal festival, in the course of which they momentarily relinquished their sub-machine guns. They were immediately pounced on by the tribesmen and overpowered. Three of them, obviously weary of the whole game, gave in at once, but the fourth, a typical tough young Nazi, fought like a cat and had to be bound. They were brought down to Busheir on the coast and were handed over to the British. Jackson was called to Tehran to receive the

77

special congratulations of his government through the British Ambassador, Sir Reader Bullard.

In their work with the tribes, the British liaison officers had no propaganda motives. They were under the orders of the British War Office, not of the British Ministry of Information. Nevertheless, their work in establishing and maintaining good will is an illustration of the fact, only dimly perceived by the politicians who ran the war, that in a struggle involving whole civilian populations as well as armed forces, the attitudes of the former are affected and swayed one way or another by many events other than those conceived of by the agencies officially entrusted with propaganda, psychological warfare, information, and the like.

Much of the British liaison officers' work was taken up in listening to the complaints of the tribes against the towns. The enmity between town and countryside exists to a far larger degree in Iran than in most other countries. The average Iranian tribesman had seen no sugar or tea for months, yet he knew that unlimited quantities of both were to be had in the bazaar of the nearest town—at black-market prices. "A horse, a gun, and tea are the three essentials of life," says the tribesman; and there were times when he threatened to raid the towns for the third essential. He was already raiding Allied convoys for the second, and with every precaution in the world, it was impossible for American or British sentries to prevent both rifles and ammunition from being stolen. Tribesmen walked unmolested about the streets of some of the southern ports, where the supplies were unloaded, carrying American rifles and 1944 ammunition stolen from freight cars upcountry.

It was the duty of the liaison officer with each tribe to report on the state of the tribe, the condition of the grazing grounds, and the amount of food supplies the tribesmen were able to buy from the merchants. A summer drought might precipitate a tribal war by compelling one tribe to move into the grazing grounds of another. If commodities were not forthcoming from the merchants, except at exorbitant prices, it might result in one of those threatened raids upon the towns.

Each officer, on his regular visits to the tribe to which he was attached, customarily took a supply of drugs to supplement those already on hand. Invariably they were pills of one kind or another, for the Iranian, believing that the seat of all ills and emotions is in the stomach, has a profound belief in pills and an equally profound scepticism about the effectiveness of inoculations. Stricken with a cold, he will say, "I have eaten cold." Terrified, he will say, "I have eaten fear." This, in part, is the foundation of his implicit belief in the miraculous powers of aspirin. Malaria and venereal diseases are endemic among large sections of the population, but the tribesmen believe that aspirin is a cure for both. This belief explains why the merchants established and maintained a monopoly on all the aspirin in Iran. The price of aspirin was twenty-five cents a tablet. At one time twenty million aspirin tablets were lying in the customs house in Tehran, together with sufficient powder for another twenty million, but were prevented from reaching the public market by the wholesale bribing of customs officials. (This was one of the bottlenecks that Millspaugh attempted, and failed, to break.) If the tribes had known of the situation, there would inevitably have been real trouble.

On one occasion, one of the British liaison officers with the Qashgai tribe went up into the hills to keep a rendezvous with Nassa Khan, whose movements were always kept secret to prevent any kidnapping attempt by the Iranian Government. A band of armed tribesmen met the soldier and led him by devious mountain trails to their chief's encampment. Later, squatting on the carpets inside Nassa Khan's tent, the officer produced the supply of drugs he had brought with him as a gift. There were the usual supplies of aspirin, empirin, laxatives (another miracle worker), atabrine, and, finally, a sample supply of sulfanilamide.

"This," he explained, with the customary awe-inspiring preliminary, "is the latest miracle drug. It is the drug that cured Mr. Churchill when he was taken ill on his way home from the conference in Tehran."

Nassa Khan nodded his head solemnly. "In that event," he pronounced, "we'll name it the Churchill Drug."

The officer then went on to explain that the drug was also an effective cure for certain forms of venereal disease.

The gnarled old chieftain looked blank. Then his face cleared evilly. "Aie!" he ejaculated understandingly. "Poor Mr. Churchill. I suppose he caught it from those dirty Tehranis!"

His reaction expressed completely how deeply Iran was divided.

BRITISH AGENCIES

British propaganda agencies during the war were divided into three sections. To deal with enemy, or enemy-occupied countries, or such enemy satellites as Hungary and Bulgaria, there functioned an agency known as the Political Warfare Executive (known by its initials PWE) which, for a time, cooperated with OWI in a joint Anglo-American agency under the military, the Psychological Warfare Branch. Since Iran was a neutral and, later, an Allied country, PWE never functioned in the country, although it took careful note of German-inspired rumors as noted and reported back to Britain by the British Public Relations Bureau.

The latter was the agency of the British Ministry of Information, a department which had sprung up at the outbreak of war but which it was not proposed to extend after the war ended.

The Ministry of Information was concerned exclusively with neutral or Allied countries. In the former it compared most unfavorably with the German propaganda bureaus. In the Allied countries, especially the smaller countries, who were looking to the Big Three for leadership, the Ministry of Information was fundamentally helpless because it was unable to indicate what kind of a lead Britain proposed to take.

But as the war progressed, the Ministry of Information increased in efficiency. Its administration in Britain and overseas countries was purged repeatedly under the pressure of public criticism. The field directors were given increased responsibility while the London headquarters were relegated to a sort of warehouse with the main function of supplying the kind of material requested by the field bureaus; previously, regional directors in London had attempted to run field operations in all matters, even in the selection of the material they thought should be used.

In spite of the improvements, however, the field missions were handicapped by rigidity in policy. Fundamentally, as far as Iran was concerned, they were tied down to the generalities of the Atlantic Charter and, later, to the even more ambiguous generalities of the Four Freedoms.

That is why, in spite of its large staff and output, the British Public Relations Bureau in Tehran found itself preaching to the converted.

This dearth of inspiration was in no small measure the personal responsibility of Mr. Churchill, who saw the war in terms of military and naval operations, had little time or use for propaganda, and was never persuaded to concede that the latter had changed the nature of warfare just as surely as the invention of the long bow and the discovery of gunpowder had changed it centuries ago. The shortcomings of propaganda went even deeper than Churchill, however; they could be traced to the failure of the Conservative-dominated British Government to

81

evolve anything like that human creed for which the world hungered, and is still hungry. On fundamental issues, the British remained silent, and to the peoples of the occupied countries, this very silence was a confession of failure. They drew the appropriate conclusions. To the peoples of the smaller Allies, the silence was depressing and alarming.

The third of the British propaganda agencies was the British Council, an organization formed some years before the war and operating under a Royal Charter in the same manner as the British Broadcasting Corporation.

The Council was unembarrassed by lack of clear directives, for it had long-term objectives of forming cultural ties. Its methods in Iran, as in most other neutral countries, were to open a series of British Institutes at which the Iranians could learn English, read British books, study British paintings and music. It facilitated the importation of British books and films, arranged English university scholarships for a quota of Iranian students, directed Iranian actors and actresses in productions of plays by Shakespeare and Shaw.

Curiously enough, the more leisurely manners of the British Council were surprisingly successful. The collapse of France had destroyed French as the second language of the Middle East, and as the coming defeat of Germany became more apparent the whole commercial profession of Iran began to realize that there would be faint hope of buying German industrial products for many years to come and that it might be sound business sense to start learning sufficient English to enable them to study the American and British trade catalogues.

By 1944 the British Council had three institutes in Iran—one in Tehran, another in Isfahan, the third in Shiraz—all of them with long waiting lists for their English-language classes.

They were not so lucky, however, in other respects. Unlike the Public Relations Bureau, they did not enjoy the privileges of being a government organization. Therefore, much of their material had to reach them via the ordinary mail and not through the inviolate embassy pouch. For months the British Council headquarters in Iran cabled urgently to London demanding the expedition of certain stocks of British books, receiving each time the reassurance that the books had been dispatched. There followed other cables and inter-ministerial communications as the consignments were traced to Cairo and there found to have been forwarded to Tehran by rail. The customs shed at Tehran was searched but revealed no trace of the books, nor even of their arrival. At this point, a bright British censor decided to query his Russian colleague, and discovered that the books had arrived some months earlier and had been seized by the Russian censors. The Russians refused to release them until they had read them all and approved their contents.

When I left Iran in the fall of 1944, they were still in the hands of the Russian censors.

ANGLO-AMERICAN OIL NEGOTIATIONS

The laws of least resistance that govern the boundaries of empires are at present working to the disadvantage of the British. Try as they will, the British cannot disguise the fact that they are on the defensive, this time against a much more serious form of pressure than that exerted by Nazi Germany. Whereas Germany could act only in terms of a direct frontal assault upon the center of the British Empire, the huge, sprawling, but energetic Soviet Union can exert its pressure at a dozen different points. It is inevitable that this pressure should first be exerted at those points where British resistance will be the least, notably the Middle East.

Two years of joint Anglo-Russian occupation in Iran convinced the British that Russia had gone imperialist, and that Russia would emerge strengthened from the war, whereas they themselves would be infinitely weaker in material resources. The only Iranian politicians on whom Britain had any political influence were a section of the wealthy intellectuals or wealthy nationalists. The tendency of the British was to rely primarily on the latter, and in the midsummer of 1944, shortly after the merger between the pro-Russian Tudeh Party and the Azerbaijan "democrats," the British sponsored the appearance of a party named the Party of National Will. Headed by a former exile, Sa'ed Zia Uddin—one of the men who organized the 1921 coup which brought Reza Shah to power—the party was naturally pro-British in its policy. However, the British policy of not allowing any Anglo-American-Russian problems to come into the open in Iran, prevented the National Will Party from taking an openly anti-Russian line; it was confined in this respect to criticizing the Tudeh Party or, as was more often the case, to answering the anti-British charges of Tudeh. Like its British backer, the National Will Party was on the defensive.

By 1944, the British began to look around for some partner to help them hold the wall. They turned, naturally, to America.

Whatever may be said about their politics, British governments are generally composed of realists. In attempting to persuade America to participate in the Middle East after the war, the Churchill government had the sense to realize that appeals to sentimentality would not work and arguments about world strategy and its responsibilities would alarm rather than inspire an American public, conditioned from childhood against foreign entanglements.

There were two ways, the British reasoned, to lure America into the Middle East. One was to take advantage of Anglo-American cooperation during the war to insure that American officials were given key positions of authority and responsibility, thus arousing the benevolent interest of the American administration. This, and not any concern for the prosperity of Iran as such, was mainly why the British continually supported the American missions that trained the Iranian army, reorganized the gendarmerie, and advised the Iranian Ministry of Health. This was why the British took the lead in supporting the Millspaugh financial and economic mission. Incidentally, it was also why the Russians, through their Iranian organizations, conspired against the American missions to offer America a share in the most important single source of exportable wealth that Iran had to offer—oil. Now the American administration was by no means playing the role of innocent victim in these moves. Roosevelt was fully aware that after the war America could not afford to withdraw from world affairs. He was well informed on the strategic and commercial importance of the Middle East. At the same time, he knew of the deep American instinct against any overseas commitments, and that any commitment would need a strong flavor of clever American horsetrading.

The British oil concessions on the island of Abadan in the south of Iran date from 1901, when they were bought by an English prospector named D'Arcy. The world had such a low opinion of the importance of oil in those days, however, that eight years later D'Arcy sold his concessions as a failure. They were ultimately bought by the Anglo-Iranian Oil Company, in which the British Government had shrewdly bought nearly half the shares. By 1940, the company had become the most important single producer in the Middle East. World production in that year was 283 million tons. America produced some sixty per cent of the world's supplies; another fifteen per cent came from the other oilfields to the south in Mexico, Colombia, Venezuela, and the West Indies. Thus, some seventy-five per cent of the world's oil came from the area running from the United States round the great horseshoe that encloses the Caribbean.

The remaining quarter of the world's production was more evenly divided. The Soviet Union produced about ten per cent, mainly from the fields around Baku and from the Polish oilfields near the Carpathians, now Soviet territory. The Middle East oilfields, running from Egypt through Arabia and Iraq to Iran, produced another six-and-a-half per cent, but were capable of producing much more. Finally, there were the Dutch East Indies with three per cent of world production, the dwindling Rumanian oilfields with two per cent, and some newer but smaller oilfields in Hungary and Austria. It appeared certain that with the close of the war, all European oilfields would either be inside the future Soviet frontiers or would lie in countries dominated by the Soviets. This has turned out to be the case.

But the United States, though the largest producer, was not a proportionately large world supplier. Nine-tenths of her oil she used herself. Russia, too, with her enormous wheat-lands and tractor-driven agriculture, had used up her own supplies and would require much more after the war.

Anglo-American oil talks started in Washington in the middle of April, 1944, and were concluded two weeks later. A short public communique, carefully worded so as not to arouse the suspicions of the Soviet Union, announced that the two groups had "explored the full range of both countries' interest in oil on a basis of broad principles and looking to the orderly, long-range development of abundant oil supplies."

Iran was carefully not mentioned; questions were discussed "relating to oil production, particularly in the Middle East, the proposed trans-Arabian pipe-line, the Iraq Petroleum Company's project for an additional pipe-line from Kirkuk to Haifa." The two groups shared the view that peacetime aspects of such matters should be resolved as between the two governments, and there was reason to believe that if American interests decided to go through with the proposal to build a pipe-line from the Saudi Arabian oilfields, no British opposition would be offered.

The latter was an understatement. The British were hugging themselves. Opposition when it came was from entirely different quarters.

Three days after the preliminary oil talks had ended in Washington, the British Ministry of Information issued a long quotation from the *London Times* on the oil situation in the Middle East. Praising the talks, it pointed out that no one of the Middle East oilfields was an exclusive field for either American or British exploitation, that the Iraq Petroleum Company and its subsidiaries included the interests of two powerful American companies as well as British companies.

The proposals, the statement continued, were that the Iraq Petroleum Company wished to build one more pipe-line from Hasa Province on the Persian Gulf to the Mediterranean. This would make a final total of three pipe-lines, two of them being concerned with Anglo-American interests, the third with American interests.

It concluded with the usual reference to the Atlantic Charter. "The governments, supported by an enlightened public opinion on either side, will be able to initiate wider consultation with the United Nations also concerned, leading to agreements faithfully executing the clause of the Atlantic Charter which provides for access on equal terms to the trade and raw material of the world."

The appearance of the statement coincided with the return to Moscow of the Soviet Ambassador in Iran. Was Moscow insulted at not being included in the talks? Or was she disturbed at the prospect of being faced in the Middle East by a strong American-British partnership?

There followed three months of comparative silence during which time Washington and London attempted without success to discover Moscow's reactions. Although Anglo-American statements, referring to the oil talks, said that Russia was being kept informed, the latter was noncommittal.

On July 24, 1944, the American delegation to the oil talks, which were being resumed in Britain, announced their arrival in London. They were headed by Cordell Hull, Secretary of State, and Harold L. Ickes, Secretary of the Interior.

On the same day, the arrival of two American oil experts in Tehran was announced locally. They lost no time in getting in touch with the offices of the Iranian premier, foreign minister, and finance minister.

On August 8, the Anglo-American oil conference was announced to have reached an agreement in setting up a joint petroleum council for "establishing a set of rules in the international oil trade and providing for cooperation and consultation between Britain and the United States along lines of certain broad principles." These principles were not announced, but Reuters, the British news agency, said it was understood that Britain and the U.S. "have agreed in an endeavor to insure: First, that oil will be available in world trade in adequate volume at fair prices and without discrimination; second, that development shall be planned with a view to ensuring that oil will be available to the U.S. and the United Kingdom in times of emergency and to all peace-loving nations in accordance with whatever collective security arrangements are inaugurated; third, that oil areas not now under concession will be subject to an 'open door' principle; fourth, that the present valid concessions will be respected; and fifth, that production, refining, transportation and distribution of petroleum shall not be hampered by unilateral restrictions imposed by either government inconsistent with the broad purposes of the agreement."

There was still no mention of Russia, but the reference to a future "emergency" and to "peace-loving nations" had an ominous ring.

The next day, on August 9, it was announced in Washington that the Anglo-American oil agreement "is welcomed by those working here on the international pattern of the postwar world, as a first step towards guaranteeing a free flow of oil to satisfy the economic and strategical needs of peace-loving nations."

This reference to "peace-loving nations" gave rise to speculation regarding the possibility of oil sanctions being provided for in the scheme of international security which was to come up for discussion at the end of that month by representatives of Russia, the United States, and Britain.

The next day, August 10, it was announced in Tehran by the Iranian Government that a commission, consisting of the prime minister and representatives from his office, the two American oil experts, one American from the Millspaugh mission, and Iranian engineers, had been established and had met at the summer offices of the foreign minister "to discuss matters relating to oil."

The next month the Soviet Government threw a bomb into the whole deal by officially requesting the Iranian Government to grant it concessions to exploit the oil reserves in northern Iran.

It was a bomb because no Iranian Government in its senses would dare give the Russians concessions which would amount to perpetuating the Russian occupation of their north zone indefinitely; it amounted to cession of the whole northern section of the country. It wrecked the American deal because the Iranian Government could not grant, nor could Britain and America press for, oil concessions to the Western powers if a similar request from Soviet Russia were refused. Such an act would have called attention to the flimsy and transitional framework on which the Anglo-American-Soviet alliance was based. It astounded both Britain and America—although why both powers failed to foresee that Russia would stop at nothing to prevent the foundation of American political and strategic interests in the Middle East is beyond my comprehension.

On top of this, the Russians received support from an altogether unexpected quarter. Either unaware, or contemptuous, of the long-range issues involved, the large American oil companies saw in the proposed deal—and spared neither time nor expense in publicizing their opinion—an unwarranted interference by the American administration with private enterprise. The Ickes talks had been based on the announced assumption that American oil reserves were dwindling and that America, entering a future in which her domestically produced oil would be insufficient, must look elsewhere for supplies. The oil companies produced a wealth of detail to illustrate that this assumption was incorrect, while, halfway round the world, the Iranian Majlis refused to grant concessions to any of the three powers.

PRESENT AND FUTURE OF THE POWERS IN IRAN

It is possible now to make an appraisal of the present status in Iran of each of the three powers, of their present policies, and from these to trace at least an outline of the general trend for the immediate future.

The idea of post-war cooperation between America, Britain, and Russia had its first trial in Iran while their armies were still fighting as Allies elsewhere in the world. All three war leaders knew that the military occupation of Iran, one of the vital spheres of the world, presented long-range political and economic problems which would be duplicated later in Europe and the Far East. By deciding to postpone their solution until after the war, America and Britain were outmaneuvered by Russia.

Later, when the expansionist aims of Russia became apparent, and resulted in a drawing together of America and

Britain for mutual solution of the situation, the stage was set for the old game of power politics, with Iran as the football. Once more, Russia so handled herself as to defeat the combination and prevent the entry of America into the Middle East field. Here again, this set the stage for the European and Far Eastern theatres. Power politics, and not collaboration, were to be the rule, with Russia maneuvering to separate America and Britain and to effect the withdrawal of America from the field.

America's position in Iran remains negligible. With the exception of three spasmodic and abortive forays, by the OWI, no attempt was made by America to establish deep-seated ties with the Iranian people. The latter, who had a more sincere regard for America than for any other great power—principally because they realized America had no ideas of territorial conquest that affected them—were severely disillusioned in the hopes they had had in looking to America for help, when they first came into mass contact with Americans through the establishment of the Persian Gulf Command.

Later, the new imperialism of Russia became apparent in Iran—but nowhere else, because it was cloaked by military censorship in the country and because, after the end of the war in the Middle East, the public tendency in America and Britain was to regard Iran as a faraway theatre of no ultimate importance. When Roosevelt and Churchill became concerned, they had no solution to offer other than to propose a return to the *status quo ante*, through the eventual evacuation of the country (as was laid down in the three powers' declaration on Iran at the Tehran Conference), and, knowing that this would be disregarded by Russia, to work meantime for Anglo-American partnership in Iran after the war. The attempt to achieve the latter under the guise of oil concessions was sabotaged by Russia. By relinquishing control of the Iranian State Railways on July 10, 1945, and by speeding up the withdrawal of her troops during the Russian-instigated revolt in Azerbaijan at the end of the year, America demonstrated that she was not yet ready to take any direct issue with the Soviets.

The British position in Iran, although ostensibly stronger than the American, is built on a number of weak props. The fall of the Churchill government saw the rise to power of the Left-wing movement in Britain, whose members were determined to follow a policy of friendship with Russia. Therefore, much as the Labor Cabinet could see eye to eye with Churchill on the dangers of the Iran situation, its opinions on the desirability of maintaining British military occupation of the south of the country, because of the continued Soviet control of the north, were weakened by this public attitude.

The continuity of British policy in the past, however, has conditioned the Iranians to suspect all British governments as potential threats to the independence of their country. Even though it is realized that in this instance Russian provocation occurred first—and the Russian-sponsored "democratic" party sees to it that public opinion in the British zone is confused on this point—this will only intensify the Iranian fear of continued British occupation.

The Churchill desire to maintain Iran as a political and strategic vacuum between Britain and Russia carried with it as a corollary a deliberate British decision to abstain from running the internal affairs of their zone. The British thereby condoned the activities of the monopolists and the corrupt civil service and could take no active interest in the rise of a really democratic movement. To have done so would have meant imposing a virtual British tutelage of the country, which would have been designated as a breach of the Atlantic Charter.

The Russians were hampered by no such material or moral restrictions. Their own domestic population was so subjugated as to be capable of bringing no pressure on its government and was by this time conditioned into a docile acceptance of every twist and turn of Russian foreign policy. Abroad, the populations of the democracies were being conditioned to accept their new Russian ally as a democracy, faithfully adhering to the terms of all agreements. Criticism of Russia was condemned as being against the war effort through undermining the unity of the three Allies—even though that unity existed only in the military conduct of the war, and not even in all aspects of that.

The Russians cheerfully signed the Declaration on Iran, committing themselves to evacuate their zone after the war, because they knew it gave them time to arrange matters in Azerbaijan in such a way that the Red Army could evacuate the region while leaving it completely under the domination of Moscow. The resolution called for the "independence" of Iran, but, as we now know, Russian interpretations of such words differ from those of the Western powers. In Russian eyes, the puppet regimes of, say, Rumania, Bulgaria, and Jugoslavia are both democratic and independent. They had already made provisional plans for Azerbaijan in any case. The Tudeh Party had been formed long before the Tehran Conference. The northern zone had already been sealed off from the rest of the country, and behind the impassable demarcation line the creation of an autonomist movement went on unhampered.

The only thing the Russians feared was the coming-of-age of America and her entry into the Middle East. They therefore devoted their efforts—both indirectly through their Iranian organizations, as in the case of the campaigns against the American missions, and directly, as in the case of the oil negotiations—to prevent this from happening.

In the north of Iran, Russia was thus undisputed master. In the rest of the country, she was both feared and respected.

The immediate future is not difficult to foresee, for the struggle for influence in Iran carries with it far wider implications than spheres of influence in Iran itself.

American troops who were briefed for their term of duty in the country were given a booklet informing them that the great quadrangle bounded by the cities of Astrakhan in Russia, Tehran in Iran, Basra in Iraq, and Aleppo in Syria, was the true strategic or power center of the war, "an area in which a German success would mean the almost certain collapse of Russia and the probable collapse of Great Britain as well." This was why Iran had become the epicenter of the world.

Notice this quadrangle and the territories it contains. These are as follows: most of Turkey, most of Syria and Lebanon, most of Iraq, the western half of Iran, from the north to the south, and that strip of the Soviet Union which lies between the Black Sea and the Caspian and extends to the Caucasus Mountains.

If this quadrangle is indeed "the true strategic or power center of the war," the question for the West is not so much what would happen if it fell into the hands of any one nation, as whether any one nation is making an attempt to obtain possession of it.

In addition to controlling her own section of the quadrangle, Soviet Russia has already, in effect, crossed the Caucasus and established her satrapy in Azerbaijan.

This northern province of Iran contains, in addition to the people from whom it takes its name, two important minorities, the Armenians and the Kurds, both of whom—like the German minorities in the Balkans—are spread over various territories in the Middle East. There is an Armenian Republic in Soviet Russia. There are large Armenian colonies in Turkey, Syria, and Lebanon. There are Kurds in eastern Turkey, and the oilfields district of north Iraq is largely Kurdish in population.

Thus there emerges the possibility that Soviet Russia may

94

use these minorities to acquire still further territory in the strategic quadrangle. Is this the Soviet pattern for world power?

During the war, the church was re-established in Russia. In the fall of 1944, the patriarch of the church in the Soviet Republic of Armenia was given permission to travel throughout the Middle East. He devoted his travels exclusively to the newly established republics of Syria and Lebanon, his ostensible purpose being to investigate the possibility of establishing youth hostels among the Armenians in these two republics. At the same time, the Soviet Government opened relations with both Republics, and the Russian minister to Lebanon announced that "Russia would not tolerate any attack on the Syrian republic." After a tour of the Syrian-Iraq frontier, he said Syria was "free to conclude political and commercial agreements with Russia, as it did with Britain and America."

In Beirut, the Russians established an official Soviet press bureau, staffed by seven local editors—four Armenians, two Moslems, and one Christian Arab.

The Beirut radio, the most powerful transmitter in the Near East, began to take a pro-Soviet line, especially as regards Soviet activities among Armenians.

The Soviet radio began to attack Turkey and was followed by the Beirut radio. When the Turkish statesman, Inonu, attempted to explain that Turkey had followed a pro-Russian policy during the war, he was criticized by the Beirut radio, which supported Russian demands that Turkey cede to the Soviet Union its two eastern provinces of Kars and Ardahan, where there were large Armenian minorities.

Thus, Beirut radio broadcast the following in Armenian to the Near East: "Inonu's speech . . . will not be accepted by the Soviet Union. The Armenian demands (for the return of Kars and Ardahan to Russia) are a minimum which Turkey must fulfill, since they result from several treaties ratified by all the Great Powers on various occasions."

How seriously does Russia intend to press for unification of the Armenians in the Middle East under Soviet control? Here is the Moscow radio in December, 1945: "Recently the newspapers of the Armenian Socialist Soviet Republic published a message of greetings from George IV, the Catholicos of the Armenians, addressed to the Armenian Government and the Party leaders on the occasion of the twenty-fifth anniversary of the establishment of the Soviet regime in Armenia. A group of correspondents of the Central Republican press approached the Catholicos with the request that he should deal in greater detail with some of the questions raised in the message. In particular they asked for his views on how to restore a united Armenian Motherland and consolidate the Armenian people around their mother country, Soviet Armenia.

"The Catholicos stated: 'The hearts of the Armenians, both at home and abroad, are filled with pride and happiness at seeing Soviet Armenia, their Motherland, risen from ashes and ruin and now prospering. With sore hearts we thought of hundreds of thousands of Armenians forcibly torn from their Motherland, scattered over the world, and dreaming of the sacred soil of their forebears on which they had lived for thousands of years. . . .

"Our concern for the fate of the Armenians abroad has prompted us to approach the leaders of the three Great Powers, Stalin, Truman, and Attlee, requesting them to do away with the great historical injustice which has been allowed to befall the long-suffering Armenian people. In our message, we asked that Turkey be deprived of the lands which she forcibly seized, and which are now empty (sic), and that they should be returned to their original owners by being reunited with Soviet Armenia.' "

Does anyone believe that Stalin was surprised on receiving this note from the Catholicos? Or conversely does anyone believe that the note would have been written without Stalin's previous knowledge and consent? Two days previously Stalin had sent a congratulatory message to the Armenian celebration committee and had been elected a member of its presidium.

While using the Armenians to gain territory from Turkey and power in Syria and Lebanon, Russia is using the Kurds as pressure material against the British in Iraq. The early days of the Azerbaijan revolt in northern Iran—next door, so to speak—revealed that the Red Army had organized the Kurdish clans against the Iranians. Having Azerbaijan within its grip, the next step for Russia was to organize disaffection among the Kurds in northern Iraq.

This is not a difficult procedure, for the Iraqis have a reputation for bad treatment of their Kurdish minorities. In the middle of October, 1945, the Kurdish leader in Iraq, Dulla Mustapha, addressed a note to the British Embassy in Baghdad complaining of bad treatment by the Iraqis. The note also accused Britain of responsibility for the military operations carried out by the Iraqi Government against the Kurds.

The pattern thus becomes clear. The only regions of the quadrangle still accessible to the West and not yet directly threatened by Russia are the Mediterranean coastal strip of the Lebanon and half of the western half of Iran. There are British garrisons in each of these territories, although Britain is committed to withdraw them.

Moscow radio, November 30, 1945: "Beirut: Dealing with the question of the evacuation of foreign troops from Syria and Lebanon, the newspaper *Said Ashaa* writes that this is the principal demand of all national demands. The presence of these forces belittles the significance of the independence and national dignity of the country and makes it possible for foreigners to intervene in our domestic and foreign policies, the paper adds."

In this way Russia began to put pressure on the British to

97

withdraw their forces from this area. There is little doubt of what Moscow hopes the foreign policies of the two small republics will be after the British withdrawal.

There remains within the quadrangle only that zone of Iran still under British influence. The establishment of large and active Soviet consulates in this area now begins to assume its real significance, as preparation for the time when the British withdraw from here too.

Every possibility of precautionary moves by America or Britain has been anticipated by Russia. As the Azerbaijan revolt gathered speed, the Russians apparently feared a British *coup d'état* in the rest of Iran. Accordingly, the Moscow radio broadcast a report that the British military attaché in Tehran was plotting the overthrow of the Iranian Government with the collaboration of the then Iranian Chief of Staff. The possibility of American commercial airlines using Iran as a transit base, thereby bringing American commercial interests into the country in a similar manner as the oil concessions would have done, was also anticipated.

Moscow radio to Iran, in Iranian: "According to an Associated Press report *and some current rumors*, (italics mine) negotiations are being conducted between the Iranian and U.S. Governments for acquisition by the latter of the right to use some airdromes in Iran. The American Government requests the right to use Iranian airdromes. The Iranian Foreign Office rejected this request at first, but the Americans insisted and requested that agreement on this point be reached without delay. Apparently in view of this insistence, the Premier and other authorities asked the Foreign Office to comply at once with American wishes."

The deal is thereby pictured as taking place under arbitrary American pressure, against the wishes of the Iranian Government, and therefore as a breach of Iran's sovereignty.

Soon, if they are not already doing so, the American oil

companies in Saudi Arabia may regret having allowed themselves, without considered reflection, to rush into being the unwitting accomplices of Soviet expansion. Whatever the arguments may be about Russia's future intentions, the fact is that the demarcation line between Soviet and Western spheres of interest in the Middle East is no longer on the Caucasus but is moving south towards the Persian Gulf, and west towards the Mediterranean.

The conclusion to be drawn is that there has been a resumption of power politics in the Middle East in which Soviet Russia is on the offensive and Britain on the defensive, with America alternately trying to get into the game and voicing her disapproval of the course it is taking.

In an area which constitutes the crossroads of world power, all three countries have demonstrated to its inhabitants that they are unable to evolve one common purpose for the solution of its problems.

III. GREECE

"Appearances are to us in four ways. For either things appear as they are; or they are not, and do not even appear to be; or they are, and do not appear to be; or they are not, and yet appear to be."

—*Epictetus*

GREECE

EUROPEAN SPHERES OF INTEREST

WHEN I left Tehran in the late fall of 1944 to join the Balkan Mission of UNRRA, the pattern appeared to have been set for Europe. It was too rash an assumption to make at the time, however, for it contained several uncertain factors.

Perhaps the appeasement of Soviet Russia in Iran was only a local phenomenon inspired by American anxiety to bring Russia into the war against Japan. This was certainly the ambition of the American military commanders in Iran—who seemed to have a pathetic belief that Soviet Russia would do something for the *beaux yeux* of the Western democracies.

Naturally, the Kremlin was fully aware of the American hope and dangled it temptingly like a carrot before the nose of a donkey. So, whenever American hopes reached a low ebb and the proponents of a firmer policy towards the Soviet Union seemed to be gaining the upper hand, the Russians would make some gesture as though seeming willing to give serious consideration to the possibility of eventually declaring war on Japan. Stalin would make a speech containing a reference to Japan as the aggressor in the Far East. Or the Russian Government would refuse to renew the Japanese lease on the northern half of Sakhalin Island. Or the Russo-Japanese friendship treaty would be denounced.

Naturally, the Russians would eventually declare war on Japan, but not under conditions which would saddle them with the main land front as the European war had done. Russia's entry into the Far Eastern war would come either when the Americans had opened a main land front in China or when the Japanese were on their last legs.

And if anyone should call this selfishness on Russia's part, Stalin could point to Churchill's refusal to open the Second Front in 1942. . . .

Depressed by the Iranian blueprint of postwar cooperation, the most important question for me was not what future course the Far Eastern war would take but to what extent and with what success had Russian expansionist policy demonstrated itself in Europe?

America and Britain had long ago committed themselves to leaving the Balkan front to the Red Army, thereby abandoning the Balkans to Russian influence if each of the three nations should go back to its old individual policies after the war. In pressing for an Anglo-American invasion of the Balkans while the Red Army was still fighting in the Crimea district hundreds of miles to the east, Churchill had been opposed by Stalin and voted down by Roosevelt, on the grounds that the American public demanded an all-out invasion of Europe through France rather than through a part of the world about which it knew next to nothing.

Rumania, making subsequent peace overtures to America and Britain in the summer of 1944, had been told somewhat brusquely to seek her peace with the Russians, on whom she had declared war. On entering the country, the Red Army had promptly expelled American and British officers who had been working with the Rumanian opposition to the fascist regime.

Bulgaria, who had not declared war on Soviet Russia but who had declared war on America and Britain, sent a peace mission to Cairo. In the middle of the negotiations, Russia suddenly declared war on Bulgaria, ordered the Bulgarian Government to cancel the Cairo mission and to send another to Moscow. Novikov, the Russian Ambassador in Cairo, who had been in touch with the Cairo negotiations, was recalled to Moscow to help conduct the peace talks, which had to start afresh. America and Britain, invited to send signatories, gave way without protest.

In Jugoslavia, America and Britain had been compelled to withdraw their aid to the Serbian nationalists of Mihailovitch and to deal solely with the Russian-sponsored movement of Tito.

Greece had been conceded by Stalin as being a British sphere of interest. So the spheres-of-interest policy applied to Europe also! An ominous beginning for a continent not yet liberated.

THE PWB AND GREECE

The decline of American and British influence in Greece—or, at least, in the affairs of Greece—is in the classic tradition of the Greek tragedy. It seemed predestined from the start. All sorts of occurrences, seemingly unconnected with the central story, played their part and had their appointed effect. The leading players, who apparently had control over their own actions and over Greece's destiny, had no more real significance than pawns; the major roles were played by petty and subordinate individuals. By the time those in authority awoke to the tragedy, it was too late to avert it and the story continued remorselessly to its conclusion. The deflation of British and American prestige was assured before the troops arrived to liberate the country.

I have said before that throughout the war neither Roosevelt nor Churchill understood the full implications and potentialities of psychological warfare, conceiving of it rather as simple propaganda in all its various techniques. I have also said that what appears to be a straightforward problem on the surface often reveals itself below the surface to be a tangle of bureaucratic intrigue and inefficiency. The rise, decline, and disappearance of Anglo-American psychological warfare in Greece is a case in point; and, since it had such disastrous after-effects, it is worth examining.

It was in the summer of 1943 that OWI first entered into the field of conducting operations towards the Balkans from the comparatively nearby headquarters of Cairo. Its British colleague, PWE, had already been established there for twelve months. Whereas the Cairo office of OWI had no Balkan experts, PWE had several. OWI had no radio operation; PWE had its own transmitters in Palestine for broadcasting to the Balkans, and although OWI contributed statements by American leaders and officials for broadcasting over these stations, it never at any time wrote its own programs. PWE had its own organization for producing leaflets to be dropped by the RAF over Greece and other parts of the Balkans. OWI contributed large supplies of paper, good artists for the leaflets, and, later, secured the services of the U.S. 9th Air Force to help the RAF carry the leaflets. Lacking Balkan specialists, however, OWI was in the position of a "poor relation" in the joint Anglo-American propaganda operation carried out towards the Balkans from the Middle East.

Russell Barnes, a capable and level-headed newspaperman from Detroit, who headed the OWI outpost in Cairo, continually asked his New York headquarters to send out specialists, but the New York executives placed such importance on the short-wave broadcasts then being conducted from America towards Europe that it felt its Balkan specialists could not be spared. Eventually, Barnes raised such a rumpus that the New York headquarters of OWI did send out one man, Reuben Markham, formerly Balkan correspondent for the *Christian Science Monitor* and one of the best American experts on the territory.

Once Markham had arrived in Cairo, however, OWI in

New York apparently forgot him. Important decisions were made without his knowledge, often resulting in New York saying one thing to the Greeks, and Cairo saying another. On one occasion, New York recalled the OWI representatives from Istambul and Beirut for a conference on Balkan affairs. Markham, who at that time was struggling to carry out the entire liaison work with PWE for work towards the Balkans, and to supervise the selection of Americans for the propaganda teams due to enter Greece in the Allied invasion then thought to be imminent, was ignored, and first heard of the conference when it was actually being held.

The British, wittingly or otherwise, took full advantage of the situation. They had supported Barnes in his requests for American Balkan specialists. When New York sent none but continued to support the idea of the joint organization in Cairo, the latter remained British by sheer weight of numbers but functioned in the name of both Britain and America.

A thousand miles to the west, operating under the direction of General Eisenhower in Algiers, there was functioning another Anglo-American propaganda organization, the Psychological Warfare Branch, containing officials from both OWI and PWE. Devoted primarily to the softening up of German front-line troops in North Africa and to relaying American short-wave programs to southern Europe, PWB acquired a new significance after the Allied invasion of Italy had placed the powerful transmitters of Bari in the hands of the Allies, not to speak of the Italian airfields, so much more convenient for leaflet operations into Greece and the rest of the Balkan countries. The civilian in charge of PWB under Eisenhower was C. D. Jackson, an American magazine executive who had been sent to Algiers by OWI.

With the capture of southern Italy, Jackson worked out a plan whereby PWB would continue into Italy under Eisenhower, who had assigned Brigadier General McClure as its military head. Jackson's proposal was that all Anglo-American propaganda activities directed towards the Balkans should be centralized in Italy. He proposed that the British head of the Anglo-American organization in Cairo should transfer his headquarters to Italy under McClure.

Now the British, in time of war, have a system whereby civilians, who are working at specialist tasks in conjunction with the armed forces, are given an assimilated army rank commensurate with their responsibilities. Although a civilian, the British propaganda chief in Cairo, Professor Vellacott, enjoyed the assimilated rank of Lieutenant General. After investigating the proposal and finding that he would be called upon to serve under a Brigadier General in the person of McClure, Vellacott declined to transfer himself from Cairo. The matter was taken up with Vellacott's superiors in London with the result that he was instructed to transfer himself to Italy. Vellacott thereupon resigned. Russell Barnes was then transferred from Cairo to this position. PWB was established in Bari, and the Balkans began to receive leaflets from Bari, broadcasts from Cairo.

The shambles was not allowed to end there, however. Although still failing to provide Balkan specialists for the Cairo organization, OWI had begun to feel suspicious about its operations. There had been instances when the organization, wittingly or otherwise, had used the prestige of America for purposes of which OWI did not approve. During the mutiny in the Greek forces in Cairo in the spring of 1944—a mutiny organized by the communist-dominated EAM—RAF planes had dropped leaflets on the mutineers urging them in the name of Britain and America to lay down their arms. The discovery of this incident resulted in U.S. intervention in the affairs of the Cairo organization and the ultimate suspicion with which it was regarded by OWI.

Meanwhile, the Russian offensive through the Balkans had

begun. Field Marshal Wilson, who had replaced Eisenhower as Supreme Allied Commander in the Mediterranean theatre, gave orders to PWB to open up with all the guns in its propaganda barrage in order to harass the Germans in the Balkans. Barnes knew that this meant giving the underground movements the long-awaited order to rise and realized that, in this event, the powerful transmitters in the Middle East would have to cooperate. This meant making Cairo an integral part of PWB. Wilson, on being told about these implications, confirmed his order and a British official in PWB was flown to Cairo, while Barnes prepared the necessary directives calling out the underground. PWB girded itself to go all-out with leaflets and the radio.

In the middle of these preparations, the voice of Washington was suddenly heard. Learning of Wilson's order, Washington felt vaguely it was being committed to something of which it did not fully approve and said so in a cable to the Allied Force Headquarters in Italy. Reading the cable, senior American officers in AFHQ instructed Barnes to draft a similarly strong reply—and then rewrote the draft prepared by Barnes to make it even stronger. Washington was reminded that AFHQ was fighting a war and was not interested in the long-term issues of foreign policy as conceived by the State Department.

With this, the fat was in the fire. OWI's office in Washington ordered the withdrawal from the Balkan PWB of all its representatives, saying that the State Department had decided not to sanction any propaganda work on behalf of America until Greece and the other Balkan countries had been liberated and American diplomatic missions had been established.

The net effect of the whole sad story was that on the eve of the liberation of Greece, America virtually abdicated from the propaganda field. The period was vital. It is in the last few weeks before a military operation that propaganda activities in all their ranges reach their highest and most effective peak. The Greek people had been fed for years on the hope of liberation. For three years, they had been accustomed to think of America and Britain as partners in that liberation. And then, at the last moment, the voice of America was absent from the partnership.

Every move in the process probably had its own justification. Certainly it is not possible to fix responsibility on any one person or set of circumstances. But, whatever the merits of this sorry history, it resulted in the dissolution of Anglo-American cooperation at a time when it was most needed. It was the one thing that the extremists within EAM had hoped and plotted for during the months when they were organizing themselves for revolution and the seizure of power. At the last moment, when it still seemed to be denied them, it was suddenly presented to them on a platter.

GREEK GUERRILLA FORCES

The story of the Greek civil war, of the blunderings of the British in permitting Greek affairs to reach a stage where civil war was inevitable, of the vacillations of American policy, is one for the historian to write. What is important and what can be attempted at this period is to trace the origins of the civil war in so far as they affected American and British public opinion, which in turn influenced American and British policy in Greece to the point where the American and British positions in Greece were concerned.

Throughout the German occupation of Greece, American and British organizations were in close touch with both the nationalist guerrillas of General Zervas and the guerrillas of the National Liberation Front, known by the initials of its Greek title as EAM. Arms, gold, supplies of all kinds were dropped to both sides, but towards the end of the occupation, both the British and the Americans tended to support EAM rather than the Zervas forces. The former claimed to have more supporters than Zervas, and, as far as Britain and America were concerned, this denoted that the Liberation Front was killing more Germans than were the Zervas forces. Only when it was too late to prevent civil war was the falsity of this claim brought home to the British Government, and it dawned upon Churchill that he had been falsely informed by the organization whose function it was to maintain liaison with EAM.

Another British organization had its headquarters in Cairo. Its duties were to smuggle out British, Australian, and New Zealand prisoners of war who had escaped from prison camps inside Greece. It had little or no contact with either of the Greek guerrilla forces, but it was closely in touch with the Greek people.

An Australian or New Zealander, captured during the German conquest of Greece in 1941, and escaping from his camp say two or three years later, had no means of getting in touch with the guerrillas. His only means of escape from the country lay in finding refuge in some private household. It is to the undying credit of the Greeks that the number of collaborators among them was infinitesimal, and during the three years of occupation the British succeeded in building up an intricate network of escape channels, nearly all of which existed entirely outside the organization of EAM or Zervas. Being committed to neither, this organization could look at each with detachment, and at an early stage it reached the conclusion that EAM was not using its arms to fight the Germans, but was reserving them for use after liberation.

But the guerrilla organizations, through their American and British liaison officers, were in a far more powerful position to plead their case. Whereas the one organization was concerned primarily with rescuing the wreckage of war, the guerrillas were an offensive weapon, concerned, at least outwardly, with the active prosecution of the war.

American and British diplomatic officials who had had previous experience of Greek affairs were also handicapped. Their intelligence reports came to them primarily through the American and British organizations entrusted with liaison with the Greek underground organizations, were therefore controlled by the guerrillas at one end, and were subject to the not unbiased interpretations of the liaison officers at the other. And whenever they had serious misgivings over the ultimate outcome of the war in Greece, there was always the unanswerable dictum of the war leaders that the main thing was first to win the war.

More hysterical nonsense has been written either for or against (mostly for) EAM than about any other single political movement of the war. It is the prime cause of public confusion in America today on the real issues of the Greek crisis; for a time it almost permitted a small clique of terrorists to gain control of the whole country under the slogans of "democracy." Most of the nonsense was written by the Anglo-American war correspondents.

Some day one of the responsible and experienced foreign correspondents who worked in Europe before, during, and after the war will take this shabby legend of the war correspondents and blow it apart. Throughout the war, these gallants descended on AFHQ in droves, demanding billets, rations, and, incidentally, stories from the vast Public Relations Branch which had been established to spoon-feed them. At one time, I counted 168 correspondents, two-thirds of them Americans, on the AFHQ list in Rome, where the Public Relations Branch occupied one whole floor. Every morning, at the AFHQ press conference, each correspondent was handed a large envelope containing the day's "releases"—a collection of stories already written for him by the enlisted men in the Public Relations Branch. All the correspondent had to do to insure that his story would not be too similar to the rest, was to rewrite the first paragraph. Occasionally, they were taken "up front" to collect some eye-witness stuff.

With the exception of those writers who had been foreign correspondents before the war, most of them had never been abroad before. More still could speak no foreign language and did not even know the geography of their territory. One summer evening in 1944, I listened to a war correspondent, the representative of a New York newspaper, deliver a lecture at the American Red Cross officers' club in Rome. The lecture was on the difference between the Jugoslav Chetniks and Partisans. He began, "One half of Jugoslavia is bare rocky mountains; the other half is agricultural land. The people who live in the mountains are tough fighters; they are the Serbs. The people who live in the valleys are peasants; they are Croats," and so on *ad nauseam*. When it came to question-time, the officers showed that they knew more about the tragedy of Jugoslavia than the war correspondent, who had just returned from "a seven-day trip" to the country. Nevertheless, his trip qualified him to write as an expert on Jugoslavia —at least as far as his paper's readers were concerned. Some of the correspondents had never even worked on, or for, a newspaper before. They were, in other words, glorified sports writers, dedicated to the task of reporting battles, or of finding local stories about "the boys" for use in local newspapers back home. At that, they may have done a fine job; at any rate, the army was contented. The army did not want its war correspondents to write about political affairs; it wanted them to write about the army. Occasionally there was a fracas—and be it noticed that the men who kicked over the traces were generally those established foreign correspondents who were disgusted at the obsequiousness of this muster of harpies. The conditions under which they lived, even at "the front," were luxurious compared to those of any infantry soldier. Their salaries were many times those of the Public Relations G.I.'s who had to write their stories; and the proportion killed or injured on active service was no larger than the incidence of deaths or injuries in road traffic accidents in America in 1939.

As the Italian campaign took third place to the French and Far Eastern fronts, the war correspondents at AFHQ looked around for fresh sources of news. They brought to Greece an outlook compounded of ignorance, emotionalism, and malevolence. They were blissfully ignorant of the background of the underground movements in Greece and, for the most part, of Greece itself, most of them never having been there in their lives. They were emotional because some of them had accepted the past "hand-outs" on the activities of EAM as signifying unqualified Allied approval of EAM, thereby denoting to their simple minds that EAM were the "good guys," the others were the "bad guys." Some of them were so overcome by the false philosophy of the professional Left that they had drugged themselves into being temperamental world-savers, editorializing rather than reporting on facts, as a study of nearly every newspaper of the last three years will show. They were hysterically malevolent because they saw in the use of British troops in the civil war a deep-seated, reactionary British Machiavellianism rather than a blundering last-minute attempt to retrieve the far worse blunders of the previous twelve months.

During the civil war, it is true, the detailed inside reports from the American and British diplomatic missions in Athens began to reach their respective headquarters in Washington and London. But it was some weeks before these arrived— necessarily so because of the painstaking research into the chronology of events in those confused days, a restriction which by no means hampered the majority of the war correspondents—and it was some days more before these had been digested by the respective administrations. But by that time the damage was done, the reports of the more sober correspondents were drowned by the outpouring of their emotional colleagues, and to this day there remains an uneasy feeling in the minds of both the American and British public that British arms were used to suppress a genuine democratic movement which truly represented the majority of the Greek people. A. C. Sedgwick, Athens correspondent for the *New York Times,* told me of the following incident. At the height of the civil war, a group of American and British war correspondents stood outside the British headquarters in Athens and watched a procession of Greek men and women parading down the street with banners and placards. There were remarks of approval from the correspondents at this demonstration of "democratic courage" taking place under the very guns of the British. "Yes," remarked Sedgwick gently, "but if you could read their placards you would see that they are not supporters of EAM but supporters of EDES, who are anti-EAM." There was a silence and then one of the war correspondents spoke for the rest. "Huh! Fascists!" he said, and with that, the whole group turned back into the British headquarters. This extraordinary agility of outlook, which can regard the same people as either black or white, depending on the banners they carry, is typical of the manner in which the Greek civil war was reported. Had the marchers been members of EAM, the demonstration would have been reported by the majority of the correspondents as a daring exhibition of democratic solidarity. As it was in favor of the EDES army of Zervas, it was termed "fascist" and ignored. Can it be wondered that, as this state of affairs in the American press was reported back to Greece through the short-wave radio, the Greek people imagined themselves victims of some delirious nightmare?

But what was EAM? What was its background, what were its tactics, and what led it to precipitate the civil war? Did it, in fact, precipitate the civil war? Any American who sincerely wishes to make a sober appraisal of his country's position in the minds of the Greek people must be willing, at least within his own mind, to make a fresh appraisal of the political movement which headed one side of the civil war in Greece and to estimate what effect the apparent American support of this movement had on the Greeks as they emerged from the civil war.

Left-wing tendencies were slow to develop in Greece, and though a Socialist Party had been founded before the last war and a Communist Party was founded in 1918, both lacked real popular support. The socialists were largely of a theoretical type, drawn from the professional classes. The communists, as might have been expected, developed mainly in the industrial towns of Athens, Piraeus, and Salonika. Until fascist movements elsewhere presented the Left with a defensive platform and until the Soviet Russian system showed signs of becoming a stable form of government, there was little reason why more than a small section of the people should embrace any form of socialistic theory.

A further check on the growth of communism is derived from the geographical position of Greece as a non-Slav country separated from the rest of Europe by the Slav territories of Bulgaria and Jugoslavia. To a Greek, internationalism implies association with Bulgaria—and a constant principle of Greece's foreign policy has been opposition to Bulgarian claims to Greek territory, or to an outlet to the Aegean Sea. Thus communism, which is regarded by many Greeks as being a Slav policy, the child of Russia, is regarded with suspicion as a movement tending to strengthen the Bulgars. Communism became strongest in the provinces adjacent to Bulgaria, where, incidentally, there were settled thousands of Greek refugees from Asia Minor, who have been Greeks of Greece since only 1923. During the occupation many accusations were made, with or without basis—but with more basis recently, as we shall see when we come to Jugoslavia—that the communists of the North had reached an understanding with the Bulgars and Serbs favoring the creation of a Soviet Union of the Balkans, with Macedonia as an autonomous province.

The spread of dictatorships in Europe during the thirties strengthened the appeal of the Left as defenders of the people's liberties. Under the Greek dictatorship of Metaxas, all forms of political activity were rigorously suppressed. The leaders were exiled or imprisoned, and the former main parties were reduced to an unreal émigré existence in New York, Paris, or Egypt. Only the Communist Party, profiting by the experience of its counterparts in other countries, succeeded in maintaining and increasing its organization, in spite of the secret police system. By the time of the Italian invasion of Greece on October 28, 1940, its influence in the country, especially in the agricultural areas, was greater than it had ever been before.

After the invasion, many of the leaders of the émigré parties were allowed to return, but the war had brought about a degree of national unity which made a return to the old political system impossible, and attempts to restore the old system were largely unsuccessful, until the Germans invaded Greece and conquered the country.

When the German occupation began, the Communist Party was the only political force which possessed any degree of organization. Unlike communist parties in other countries, it had appealed to Greek patriotism by not opposing the war, and when the Germans invaded Russia, two months after the fall of Athens, the Greek communists came to the fore as the leaders of national resistance. Other socialist groups were revived or were established, and on December 27, 1941, the communists took the lead, together with five of these socialist groups, in establishing the National Liberation Front—Ethniko Apeleftherotiko Metopo, better known by its initials as EAM.

The strength of EAM was derived both from the number of people who voluntarily associated themselves with its announced program of resistance to the Germans, and from the stranglehold it gained over the economic, administrative, and military resources of the country. Actually, EAM had established a state within a state in the rural areas before the German withdrawal and rapidly extended its authority to the towns as soon as the Germans retreated. By this time, EAM had set up central and local administrations, backed by its own army, navy, police, youth movement, relief agency, propaganda department, and all the other instruments of modern mass control.

Although the more moderate elements in EAM would have been willing to carry out its undertaking that the Greek Government-in-Exile should return to Greece after its liberation, and administer the country until a plebiscite could be held to determine the form of government desired, the more radical terroristic group, the KKE (Communist Party), which had come to dominate EAM, wished to retain power in its own hands at all costs.

During the occupation, in addition to its own relief organization—EK, the members of which were usually members of EAM, though not always—EAM gained control over almost all the Red Cross distribution committees functioning in areas not directly held by the Germans, principally the remote country districts. In the mountain villages, these committees were usually composed of the schoolmaster (who could generally be depended upon to be a strong Left-winger), the priest, who in the more backward regions was often neither a well-educated nor strictly moral character, and the village mayor, who was an EAM member if he wished to retain his post. In almost all the country areas of Greece, except for the islands, the normal distribution channels were EAM channels, and were used to enlist and control further members.

EAM was designed originally to unite all sections of the Greek people, regardless of their political views, in resistance to the Germans and Italians. It attracted many who were neither communists nor socialist. Nevertheless, there were many others who wished to resist but who were suspicious of the communist control within EAM. For instance, the youth at one of the Athens colleges banded together in a resistance group. When it learned of the development, EAM insisted the group needed the benefit of its advice and experience in underground organization. A Communist Party organizer was detached to work with the group, which, disliking the idea of communist control, disbanded itself a few months later.

Nevertheless, there was no common program which rendered possible the establishment of a single centralized organization of Right-wing tendencies. The result was the formation of a large number of smaller groups of officers or professional men. More than 160 of these groups were recorded at different times during the German occupation, but the only one which achieved any significance or potentiality for armed resistance was the EDES movement of General Zervas. Most of them, Right-wing in tone, were driven through their dislike of EAM into the arms of the Germans. And as time went on, EAM itself, having full faith in an eventual victory of the Allies—who could be depended upon to fight the Germans—tended to conserve the supplies of arms and ammunition dropped to them by American and British planes and to concentrate on the job of liquidating potential post-war political opponents. The Germans, who were well informed on the state of affairs, did all they could to encourage the political hatreds within the country.

The Greek Government-in-Exile, then in Cairo, had little prestige within the country. Its reluctance to condemn the Security Battalions, formed in the fall of 1943 by the collaborationists, increased the distrust felt by EAM. Although the battalions contained a certain number of quislings, they also contained members of the Greek Right who were not collaborationists but who feared an inevitable putsch by EAM. As far as EAM was concerned, the latter were more serious opponents than the traitors, whom the Allies could be relied upon to liquidate.

The result was that by the spring of 1944, nine months before Greece's liberation, internal politics presented a picture of confusion and despair. A stage in their development was reached in March, when EAM set up in the mountains the provisional government known as PEEA (Politiki Epitropi Ethnikis Apeleftheroseos, or Political Committee of National Liberation) in place of the Cairo Government, and extended the scope of its authority to include the Greek forces in the Middle East, many of whom mutinied against the Cairo Government and declared their allegiance to PEEA.

It was only at this stage that America and Britain awoke to the impending tragedy within Greece. The mutiny was suppressed by the British and an attempt was made in May to unite the two opposing groups at the Lebanon Conference. After a four-day meeting, the twenty-five delegates agreed to a National Charter, providing for the entry of a number of EAM delegates into the Greek Government, the return of the government to Greece as soon as possible, the reformation and disciplining of the Greek armed forces in the Middle East, continued planning for and equal distribution of supplies to the guerrillas within Greece, and unification of all the guerrilla armies.

Six weeks later, the EAM headquarters within Greece declined to ratify their signatures and put forward fresh demands, which, if acceded to, would have given them control over all guerrilla forces in Greece and Greek forces abroad. They also demanded an increased number of positions within the government.

In September a further reconciliation attempt was made by America and Britain at Allied Force Headquarters at Caserta, near Naples. Further concessions were made to EAM, including denunciation of the Security Battalions, and EAM agreed to join the government.

Within the country, however, the population was divided into two broad alignments of EAM and anti-EAM. The latter was divided into a small minority whose hatred of EAM drove them into collaboration with the Germans, and a majority who still refused to do so. But it was clear that as soon as the Germans withdrew, these two groups would come together in mutual defense against the threat from the Left. For the first time in history, the Liberals and Populists, Republicans and Royalists, collaborators, and middle-class patriots found themselves welded together as indivisibly as Siamese twins. If one were killed, the other would surely die. At least, this was their belief and, in so being, was to them an objective truth.

When the Germans withdrew from Greece, EAM rapidly gained control of the whole country except for Athens, Epirus, and some of the islands, including Crete. By this time, the Communist Party inside EAM had come out openly in control. Freedom of speech and of the press had ceased to exist in the EAM areas. Levies on produce were imposed for the maintenance of the armed forces, and the authority of the Athens Government—in spite of, or perhaps because of, the presence in it of six EAM members—was weakened and flouted. The EAM National Civil Guard fulfilled the functions of both local police and national gendarmerie.

The determination of the communists never to allow EAM to be disbanded so long as it served as a cloak for their ambitions was among the seeds of the civil war that followed. In November, a few weeks before fighting broke out, some groups within the Socialist Party and the Union of Popular Democracy indicated that they were considering splitting off from EAM, but fear of being accused of forsaking their friends in a crisis, combined with threats against their own personal safety by the gunmen of the communists, deterred them.

EAM AND THE POLITICAL PARTIES

A favorite argument of the apologists for EAM during the heat of the civil war and since its defeat, has been that EAM was not dominated by the communists—that while the Communist Party may have taken the lead in its formation, EAM later developed so rapidly and included such broad sections of the Greek people that, instead of the communists controlling EAM, the reverse was the case. That the Greek people, refusing to be confined to the narrow channels of party politics, had thrown up a mass movement representing a new set of ideals.

It is true that EAM was not so much a political organization as a state within a state. The political parties within the front are worth examining, however, to ascertain where control actually lay.

First, there was the Communist Party, which, since its foundation in 1918, had learned the arts of underground work, of cloaking its activities by creating organizations of various types. An example was its creation of the Greek Seamen's Union, which had its headquarters in Cardiff and a large branch office in New York. The Communist Party took the lead in the creation of EAM and was the largest single constituent party at the time of the liberation. In 1944 it sent three delegates to the May Lebanon Conference between EAM and the Greek Government and, at the September Caserta Conference, was alloted the Ministries of Labor and Agriculture in the enlarged government which EAM finally agreed to enter. Its present policy is to follow the line of communist parties elsewhere in favoring the assumption of power by revolutionary methods if necessary. It attracted not merely professional communists but thugs and criminals who jumped at the chance of legalized lawlessness during the occupation. Typical of these was Aris Velouchiotis, who was political administrator of EAM. During the civil war it was his pleasure to assume personally the task of cutting the throats of the hostages taken by ELAS, the army of EAM. He was subsequently executed by the government for his crimes.

Next in importance was the Socialist Party, occupied in the generation between the wars with trade unions rather than with parliamentary politics. In 1936 they were banned by Metaxas for their connection with the proposed general strike which provided Metaxas with the excuse for his seizure of power. During the German occupation of Greece, they were revived and became one of the constituent parties of EAM. They were represented at the Lebanon Conference, in May, 1944, by their secretary, Dimitrios Stratis.

Third was the Union of Popular Democracy. Founded in the midsummer of 1941 as an underground socialist party, it became one of the founder members of EAM three months later. Its moving spirit was Elias Tsirimokos, Minister of National Economy in the enlarged government that followed the Caserta Conference of September, 1944. Its aim was to attract socialists from the professional classes, whereas the Socialist Party had concentrated on the industrial workers. It was later joined by Professor Svoles, Professor of Constitutional Law at the University of Athens, and later Minister of

Finance in the enlarged government. It was represented at the Lebanon Conference by its secretary, Tsirimokos.

Next, there was the Agrarian Party of Vogiatsis, socialist in its policy but enjoying popular support only in the north of Greece.

There followed a number of groups, all founded and supported by the Communist Party and affiliated to it. The three principal existing groups are the Agrarian Party of Gavrielidis, the United Socialist Party of Greece, and the Republican Party. The significance of these parties lies in the close resemblance of their names to those of the non-communist Left-wing parties of Greece. By founding puppet parties under such names, the communists thus aimed at weakening the other Left-wing parties within Greece by competing for recruits under the same slogans. As a new technique of political warfare, it is not confined to Greece; the Russians have employed it elsewhere, notably in Poland.

These, then, were the constituent parties of EAM. There were the Communist Party, three non-communist parties, only two of which were significant, and a number of others, all directly controlled by the Communist Party. On the voting of delegates alone, therefore, the communists controlled a majority. Even at the Lebanon Conference, supposedly called to iron out the differences between EAM and the Greek Government, the Communist Party alone had three times as many delegates as either of the two principal non-communist parties.

Shortly after the end of the civil war, the two non-communist socialist parties withdrew from EAM and formed a joint Socialist Party, thus robbing EAM of its last pretense at being a movement genuinely representing all sections of Left-wing political thought.

As to the extent to which Russian influence made itself felt through the Greek communists' control of EAM, I have yet to hear of a Communist Party in any country which does not follow implicitly the guidance issued from Moscow.

EAM AGENCIES

There is an old saying in propaganda that policy does not control operations, but operations control policy. By this is meant that, whatever policy directives are laid down by headquarters, they can be implemented in the field in such a way as to defy them. Discovery of this principle, for example, led Mr. Elmer Davis, Director of OWI, to investigate the operations of his New York office, where all short-wave operations to Europe were centralized, and where he found that policy directives from Washington were being virtually ignored.

It was a principle with which the communists in Greece were familiar. Effective as they were in controlling the constituent parties of EAM, they were even more effective in ensuring control of its operations through its various agencies, each one of which was also represented in the governing body of EAM. These agencies are worth examining in some detail because they formed a technique of mass control unsurpassed in its efficiency. The Greeks are not a people given to communism; there is probably no other race in Europe which clings so tenaciously to the idea of individualism as opposed to mass control, and yet in spite of this, and without their knowledge, the communists built up under the façade of EAM an administrative system which had almost the whole of Greece within its grip. It is a lesson for all in the West who say, "It can't happen here."

EAM had its own relief agency, the National Mutual Aid Society, known through its initials as EA (Ethniki Allilengye). Non-political relief agencies were permitted by the Germans to operate only in regions where the population was moderately acquiescent. This left large regions of the country without any organization to help the homeless and hungry —and those regions were most often the ones where German reprisals against the guerrillas had taken place. In such areas, EAM organized relief committees for each town and village to take care of the people in the districts under its control. This was natural. It was equally natural that in these districts the relief agencies should contribute aid only to those who had aided EAM, and not upon the basis of need. The political aspect of EA was most obviously presented by itself, in its own fortnightly news sheet, *Allilengye,* which first appeared in Thessaly in the fall of 1943, and which devoted most of its space to political propaganda rather than welfare.

Better demonstration of the political activities of EA was provided in the period immediately following the liberation of Greece, when supplies shipped in by the Anglo-American military relief agency were divided by EA among local EAM members only, the question of need being omitted altogether.

During the occupation, relief supplies were mainly obtained by levies from the richer non-EAM members of the community, either in cash or in kind, and by subvention from other parts of EAM. Another source during the occupation was the Allied Military Mission, which provided food and medical supplies to areas suffering most from German reprisals. In order to obtain as much as possible from the Allies, EA committees provided well-padded lists, which were generally found to be filled with names of EAM members, until the stage was reached when the Allied Military Mission found it necessary to have the relief distributed by non-partisan committees formed specially for the purpose.

The army of EAM was known as ELAS. Its name was deliberately chosen as a pun upon the Greek name for Greece —Hellas. The full name of ELAS—Ellenikos Laikos Apeleftherotikos Stratos—is not even good Greek, and thus helps to demonstrate what importance the communists now place upon advertising slogans rather than upon ideals.

ELAS guerrilla bands first appeared in Thessaly in the north of Greece in July, 1942, and were at first independent of political control by EAM. In the spring of 1943, war supplies gradually became available through the British Military Mission, and there began that blundering in British policy which led inevitably to the civil war. For the British officers pressed EAM to obtain control of ELAS. Shortly afterwards there occurred an internal crisis within EAM, leading to the resignation of the moderate non-communist secretary general and his replacement by a communist, and this event was immediately followed by an integration of EAM and ELAS. Communist Party members were installed in key, though not necessarily top, positions—generally as political advisers or commissars. Pressure was exerted on men to join ELAS—pressure that often included force as a form. In the later phases of the occupation, ELAS was used primarily to prepare the way for seizure of power by EAM. After the liberation, ELAS took the opportunity to wage open warfare on the nationalist guerrillas of Zervas, in spite of the official truce. But the most significant feature of the civil war in Athens was that most of the fighting was done, not so much by the regular ELAS units —although some were involved—as by the ELAS reserve, as it was known, and which consisted of the elite guard of the Communist Party, drawn from the EAM youth movement, EPON, much in the same way as the German SS elite guard was used within the German army.

EPON had a flamboyant name, which in translation means the United All-Greek Youth Organization. It was founded by EAM in March, 1943, and all boys and girls up to the age of twenty-six were not only invited but pressed to enlist. During the enemy occupation, much of Greek youth was not subject to the ordinary discipline of schools, or to any other form of social restraint. Most of the schools were closed because the buildings were requisitioned by the Germans for other uses, or as a precaution against the spread of disease, or simply because no means existed for the pupils to reach the villages, either through lack of transport or footwear. As schoolmasters were not paid, their number declined greatly. Many were liquidated by EAM, and others joined the movement on the promise of leading local positions. Their influence over the youth changed accordingly, and the young people entered enthusiastically into a life of licensed sabotage and theft. By the end of 1944, they represented the fanatical wing of the Communist Party. They were trained as organizers and sent into the remote villages to organize demonstrations, instruct new groups and teach revolutionary songs and tactics. The older male—and sometimes female—members of EPON were formed into fighting units with ELAS. The girls, however, were mainly used in "welfare" services, such as broadcasting selected news through megaphones to village groups or providing an enthusiastic claque at organized demonstrations.

The commissary of EAM was known as ETA—Epimeliteia ton Antarton. It was responsible for procuring food for ELAS and did so by collecting a production tax in kind, varying from about five to twenty per cent, according to the type of product, and quantity. ETA was used to accumulate large supplies for eventual use in the civil war, and many of the stores stolen from the post-liberation Allied military relief agency disappeared into the hands of ELAS through this organization.

LD, Laiki Dhiafotisis (Popular Enlightenment), was the propaganda section of EAM. It showed great skill; many of its officials had been trained by the British in the Middle East during the honeymoon between the British and EAM. It was entrusted with the task of discrediting the Greek Government before it returned to Greece, and performed its task with great efficiency. It not only controlled newspapers, but spread its doctrine through revolutionary songs and slogans and through the "megaphone broadcasts" in the villages.

EAM had its own navy department, controlled by an agency known as ELAN, although the latter controlled no navy other than the small caique traffic between the coast harbors. It also had its own National Civil Guard, EP, an armed force for the maintenance of law and order in the EAM-controlled areas.

EP was under the control of communist Minister of Interior in PEEA, the shadow government established in 1944, until PEEA was dissolved, and then came under the communist-controlled Central Committee of EAM. In the civil war, EP had control of the several thousand hostages taken by ELAS.

EAM had its own secret police department known as People's Security, and, finally, it had its own strong-arm squads for the execution of political prisoners. Known as OPLA, its full title was the Organization for the Protection of the Common Fighter. OPLA was the armed body which handled the execution of hostages in the civil war. It remained in existence after the civil war.

Constantine Poulos, an American journalist who is one of the most active protagonists of EAM, wrote in an article in *The Nation* twelve months after the civil war, that "to the Greeks, who like to deify, the EAM has taken on an almost mystic form." Mr. Poulos should have known better. The power of EAM, through its organization, agencies, and tactics, was such that twelve months before the civil war had even broken out, it was frequently referred to in whispers not as EAM but as "the organization." Not, however, through any tendency to deify except where this was prompted by fear of death.

NO AMERICAN POLICY

Much of this story on EAM has been written with the gift of hindsight. Neither the British nor the Americans had this advantage at the time. The British found themselves in a situation which was beyond their control and were hurried on from one crisis to another. Before many weeks had passed, they were up to their necks in the sticky internal administration of the country. Agencies that had been planned originally as joint Anglo-American efforts had to be staffed by the British, because of the earlier American decision to withdraw from Balkan affairs until the diplomatic missions had been established.

Foremost among these agencies were those concerned with re-opening the channels of communication between the Greeks and the outside world, of establishing news services, servicing the newspapers and radio stations, of bringing in American and British films, books, newspapers, and magazines. Many months of joint planning had gone into making the preparations, but, a few weeks before final plans were made for the invasion of Greece, OWI had withdrawn. There is no indication that the State Department's decision to withhold information activities until diplomatic missions had been established, was based on a belief that the British policy was too anti-EAM or too lenient towards EAM. Certainly American policy was no more in favor of EAM than in favor of the nationalist guerrillas.

It had been a wise principle in all America's activities in Greece to refrain from supporting one faction more than another. The American policy in all its propaganda through OWI was to praise the guerrillas as a whole, and not to single out any particular organization. In this America differed fundamentally from the British who, at the start, had committed themselves wholeheartedly to EAM and had thus laid the foundations of their disastrous policy. America differed even more markedly from the Russians who had used a policy of intimidation towards the underground movements, prompted, of course, by the pressing anxiety to create as much diversion as possible behind the German lines in order to lessen the pressure on their own front.

Nevertheless, the American policy had its drawbacks. OWI operations were continually handicapped by the necessity of sticking to generalities on every crucial issue. The bitterer these issues became, the vaguer became America's attitude—at least to the listening Greeks—until finally it vanished in the realm of unreality. Seven times a day the people of Greece listened over their radios to the Voice of America program, broadcast by short wave from New York and relayed over the medium wave by transmitters in Algiers and London. They had been deluged with leaflets, bearing the inscription that they came to the Greeks through the RAF and the AAF, consequently denoting—though wrongly—that their contents were approved by America as well as Britain. For in the later stages, the leaflets were prepared by the Allied Army's PWB, from which America had decided to withdraw. The Greeks as a whole did not know of the inter-bureaucratic muddle. Only EAM and the Greek Government knew of the division, and the one was as prepared to utilize it as the other was apprehensive.

OWI went into Greece in early November of 1944. Its Athens office was staffed by eight Americans, all of them trained for special tasks, but restrained by higher policy from taking any definite line in the crisis which was looming ahead. Apart from politics, they found a people who were not only hungry for food and desperately in need of help, but who were also hungry for news of America, and of the part that America intended to play in liberated Greece.

Barclay Hudson, who went to Athens from Beirut, wrote to OWI policy headquarters in Washington, "While at first the people, hungry for many things, would have been delighted with the pretty booklets and instructional pamphlets, they would have experienced severe reaction in face of their real needs. There would have been an inevitable reaction towards America or towards any other nation which lavished intellectual fodder on people so desperately hungry."

OWI in Greece therefore adopted the policy of not going out on a sales campaign among the people but of having the material ready for all who cared to come and collect it. It was a shrewd move under the circumstances. How it would have worked out eventually is hard to imagine, except to say that it must have been based on the hope that eventually American policy would take a definite trend one way or the other. But the policy was given no chance, for next month, the civil war broke out and all the OWI personnel were evacuated to Italy or Egypt.

"In a civil war," wrote Mr. Hudson, "neutrality is too passive a role. It is impossible to be present and inconspicuous if one is a neutral and everybody else is passionately not neutral."

Here was the tragedy of America's position in Greece. EAM continually stressed, through its propaganda organization, that the populations of Britain and America were against the Greek Government, against the use of British arms in Greece, and totally in sympathy with the aims of EAM—and the power of this argument can be understood when it is realized that the Greeks, more than any other nation in Southeastern Europe, look primarily towards America and Britain. The ensuing strife in the British House of Commons reinforced EAM's argument. It was reinforced still further by a hasty statement from Mr. Stettinius, reproaching the British for their part in the civil war and dissociating America from the British attitude. Shortly afterwards, background cables from the American mission in Athens reached the State Department and Mr. Stettinius became noncommittal, but the damage had been done.

But in Athens, where the Greeks looked for tangible evidence of America's attitude, there was none to be found, for the simple reason that no policy existed. From Mr. Hudson's point of view, any policy would have been welcome—either a denunciation of the British and support of EAM, or support of the British and the Greek Government. Either would have helped to finish the civil war within a few days. The effect on both the British Opposition and the Greek people would have been irresistible. But there was no policy—unless an unreal neutrality can be called a policy—because although America was fighting a war in Europe, although America had become the strongest power in the world and the obvious arbiter of people's quarrels, America was not yet ready to assume responsibility in Europe. A firm stand, one way or the other, would have committed America to the responsibility of insuring that her proposals, if put into operation, were given a fair trial not only during the civil war but in the long period of settlement following it, and this America was not prepared to accept.

BRITISH POLICY

The British were feverishly active during the civil war, not only in active warfare but in psychological warfare. The withdrawal of America from PWB in the Balkans had meant that all sections of the organization in Greece had to be non-American, which meant, for the most part, that they had to be British. The cable communications to and from Athens were British-owned, the cable and wireless monopoly being restored after liberation. The British operated the Athens radio station, and although this was captured at one time by ELAS forces, who destroyed some of its equipment when they were forced to surrender, the British immediately flew in spare parts, together with another transmitter for the use of the war correspondents.

The conduct of the British forces during the civil war can be praised or condemned, depending upon whether one is against or for EAM. There is no doubt that the immediate

133

effect on the Greek population was uniformly bad, especially when Spitfires were used to break up the crowds which ELAS forces were marshalling for one of their "spontaneous demonstrations."

But after the fighting ceased, the reaction set in. During January and February, I watched the people of Athens lining up to scan the daily lists of the dead hostages who had been taken by ELAS, later gruesomely executed, and just now identified.

It has been said, in condonation of EAM, that in a civil war both sides commit atrocities. I have neither seen nor read any tangible evidence that the Greek Government committed atrocities during the civil war. It took many thousands of political prisoners after the fighting was over. Many of them stayed in jail for a year, until, by the end of 1945, the government announced its intention to release all except those guilty of murder and other crimes. The taking of hostages, repugnant though it may be, does not constitute an atrocity in the sense in which the word is understood. But ELAS, the army of EAM, did commit atrocities, and the corpses of the hostages were eloquent testimony to the sadistic manner in which they had been murdered. True, the murderers were the extremist thugs of an elite guard within ELAS, but no public is accustomed to making fine distinctions within a movement, and the public reaction, when it began to set in, was against EAM as a whole.

Consequently, within a short space of time, there occurred three distinctly different attitudes of the Greek people towards the British. The honeymoon of welcoming the liberating British army was quickly followed by distrust and hostility in the civil war, and this attitude in turn disappeared as a result of the reaction against EAM, and was replaced by a vague feeling that the British had in fact rescued their country from a dictatorship worse than the German.

The twelve months following the civil war could have been the period in which the British might have made most headway in Greece by demonstrating that they had something to offer the country as a whole. EAM was thoroughly discredited. It had even sunk so low in the public mind as to be blamed for the theft of relief supplies shipped in by the military relief authorities. Wheat, vegetables, clothing, and trucks, captured from the relief authorities, were taken with them by the ELAS extremist leaders when they fled over the border into the safety of Tito territory in Jugoslavia, and later appeared on the black markets in the towns of southern Jugoslavia. To a starving people this was the lowest crime of all.

The British continued to supervise all the main channels of information open to the Greeks. The Athens radio station continued to be controlled by a complex British-Greek Government organization and was so widely recognized as being British that OWI, when it returned to its operations in Greece, had to refrain from using it lest OWI material broadcast over the Athens radio be interpreted by the listeners as evidence of a new joint Anglo-American policy. The cable and wireless monopoly was maintained with cable tolls in favor of British news agencies, and prohibitive to the American agencies, who at one time had hoped to sell their services to the Greek newspapers. The British had also established an internal news agency, known as the Anglo-Hellenic Information Service. Functioning under the local representative of the British Ministry of Information, it gave out whatever news the British Government thought would plead their case. The only other news agency was the Athens Agency, functioning under the Greek Government, which certainly gave out no news unfavorable to the British.

Yet in spite of these obvious advantages, the British position deteriorated rather than improved. Their policy was to build up a stable and self-reliant Greek Government, praying that they would attain it before they were compelled to withdraw their troops. But instead of becoming more independent, the Greek Government, or rather the succession of Greek governments, came to rely more and more heavily upon outside aid. They relied upon the British for political advice, fearing to reject it lest the British leave them to suffer for their mistakes. In their financial and economic chaos, they came to rely more and more heavily upon the mission of UNRRA. UNRRA shipped in large supplies of food and textiles to bolster up the shattered Greek economy, but the main result, for the first six months after the civil war, was to cause the Greek bureaucracy to regard UNRRA as a never-ending source of relief.

In the middle of the year there occurred one of those unforeseen events for which no one was prepared—neither the British nor the Greeks, neither the Americans nor the Russians. At the British general elections the Conservative Party was defeated and a Labor Government came to power in place of Churchill's administration. British policy in Greece came to a standstill until the new administration had time to devise its own; and as it took shape it was clearly not by any means the same as Churchill's policy had been.

For the student of power politics, the results of the British elections form one of the most fascinating studies of our time. Its effects in Greece were far-reaching in the extreme. By no means the least surprised were the Russians, who, having digested the lessons of the civil war and regarding themselves as free of all Allied commitments by the end of the European war, were girding themselves for action in Greece.

RUSSIAN POLICY

The behavior of the Russians in Greece during the civil war was irreproachable. The Russian military delegate in Athens abstained from all contact with EAM except that of an observer during the later peace negotiations. There was no ostensible connection between the Russians and EAM other than the presence in it of the Greek Communist Party, and the suspicious cooperation in the north between the ELAS extremists and the Bulgars, who were under Russian control. The northern revolutionaries were known to be using Bulgarian currency, but since part of this area had been under Bulgarian occupation for three years, this did not necessarily denote that the Russians were financing the revolution through the Bulgars. The Russians in Greece behaved with the correctness that might be expected of observers in the troubled territory of a close ally. But the past publicity which Russia had given to the EAM movement, the vehemence with which it denounced the Security Battalions and EDES alike, made it clear before the civil war that EAM had Moscow's approval. During the civil war in Greece, Moscow radio permitted no direct statements from Russian sources which might betray disapproval of the British. Moscow radio did broadcast reports which were critical of the British, but they were nearly all in the form of quotations from American press reports written by the American war correspondents in Athens. Direct criticism of the British was reserved for Belgrade radio. The fact that the radio station in the Jugoslav capital, recently liberated by the Red Army, was staffed by Russian engineers and otherwise controlled by Russia, was not so well known to the outside world. In other words, whenever Moscow had something bitter it wished to say about the British in Greece, it spoke through Belgrade radio.

The end of the European war brought a stiffening in Russia's attitude. Moscow began to talk more and more openly about the "reactionary tendencies" of the Churchill government. The Bulgars and the Jugoslavs, both of whose governments were under Russian control, were used to put pressure on the Greek Government. The ELAS leaders, who had fled

137

to Jugoslav territory, were used to form the nucleus of an organization demanding an autonomous Macedonia, which would have meant taking in territory from northern Greece. All this was done in the name of democracy and, in anticipation of inevitable counteraction from the British Government, the campaign against the Churchill administration was increased until Belgrade radio was referring to the British as neo-fascists.

At the height of this campaign, however, came the defeat of Churchill at the British elections and the subsequent rise to power of the Labor Government. Obviously not even Moscow radio, which had been using the protests of the Labor opposition against the Churchill government as proof that Churchill was reactionary, could turn around and accuse people like Attlee and Bevin of being fascists—not overnight.

When the war ended there was widespread good will among the people of America and Britain towards Russia and the new Left-wing movements in Europe. In every international issue both publics were generally prepared to give Russia the benefit of the doubt, and there was no doubt that EAM had counted on this good will, almost with complete success, to hamstring the Churchill government while it seized power in Greece. The British public, which had regarded Churchill as an admirable war leader, had for some time before the end of the war been dubious about his merits as a post-war premier. Accusations from Moscow and its puppet propaganda networks that Churchill was a reactionary, especially if those accusations were concerned with events in countries about which the British public was scantily informed, had a good audience in Britain. But when the British public turned around and voted overwhelmingly for a socialist administration, it could hardly be expected to believe statements from Russia that the members of this administration also were reactionaries and neo-fascists, especially since many of its leading members had risen from the ranks of the trade-union movement.

Whenever the Russian official finds himself in an unexpected situation, he puts on his poker face and becomes mute. The effect of the British elections on the Russians was similar to that produced by dropping a very big stone down a very deep well—a protracted silence followed by a dull thud.

The Russians took some hasty and precautionary measures. They quickly strengthened their grasp on those countries under their control, forcing through the farcical elections in Bulgaria and Jugoslavia, and forming a solid Slav bloc by the inclusion of Czechoslovakia and Poland. Communist parties in western Europe were ordered to fight any pacts between their countries and either America and Britain on the grounds that this would form a bloc against the Soviet Union. In the European countries not yet under their influence or where popular opinion was against them, such as Austria, Hungary, and Finland, they set out on a long-term program of destroying the economic and financial systems in the hope that eventually the peoples would become disillusioned with the West and turn to Russia as the only hope. The sudden large increase of reparations demanded from Finland, the seizure of the Austrian oilfields, the deliberate organization of inflation in Hungary, the attempt to wreck Anglo-American reconstruction of Italy, the opposition to the reconstruction of the Ruhr, one of the foundations of European economy, are all cases in point, and each week brought fresh developments of the campaign.

But nothing in all this solved the original problem for the Russians—how to convince the British public that its new government, which would inevitably be opposed to planned Russian activities outside Russia, would be behaving as a fascist government? Indeed unless it solved this problem, Russia could certainly count on increasing opposition from the people of both Britain and America. After the first period of silent reaction, therefore, the Russian propaganda machine began day by day to bring in accusations against the reactionary nature

139

of the new British Government. Very slight at first, they became more and more frequent, until the campaign had taken on an almost undisguised shape.

But a six-months' breather had been gained by the democracies. The fact that the new government made little use of it, primarily because it was committed to cooperation with Russia, is of minor consequence. The major consequences were the effects it had on Russia and the small "target" countries, of which Greece was one. The postponement of Russian all-out expansion, as a result of the sudden appearance of a British Government on its Left when it should have been on its Right, is one of those unforeseen occurrences which continually baffle and confound those prophets who like to base their forecasts of world events on dry statistics of power. Attitudes are more important than rifles nowadays. This is not to say that a determined but unarmed nation can resist an overwhelmingly powerful and cynical adversary—although the war frequently demonstrated that unexpected survivals are possible. But it does mean that the age of scientific analysis is drawing to a close and that the world is waiting for moral and not scientific leadership; that the only thing to prevent the world from destroying itself in another scientific war is not a code, but a creed—not a law forbidding the use of the atom bomb, to which all will pay lip service but disobey when the time comes, but a new social and political faith which the world will embrace and which will render the atom bomb unnecessary. Until that time comes, the three largest nations may devise whole sets of laws and regulations on the atom bomb—but each one will continue to make atom bombs, just to be sure that it will not be destroyed in its sleep.

After the civil war, the Russian attitude towards the government in Greece was one of uncompromising hostility, but it was not without its contradictions. For instance, the Moscow radio criticized the proposals to hold early elections, realizing that the communists, who were held responsible for the crimes committed by EAM, were being pushed aside, and that in the extreme reaction against EAM, the monarchists would win the elections. But when the new British Government, reaching the same conclusion, asked the Greek Government to postpone elections until the electorate had reached a more settled frame of mind, their action was characterized as unwarranted interference in Greek affairs.

For example, Moscow broadcast the following Tass report in Morse to the United States: "Athens: All Greek democratic newspapers published the statement of the leader of the Greek Progressive Party, Kafandaris, concerning the role played by the Regent in the Government crisis. 'If it is believed to be necessary to hold elections in January under any conditions, under pressure of an unlawful clique and its bands, the elections might just as well be held right now. Only the fear of true and free elections compels the agents of fascism to insist on immediate elections,' said Kafandaris."

More than two weeks previously, however, Britain and America had indirectly made it known that they would not welcome early elections in view of the probability that these would show too great a landslide in the emotional reaction against EAM. This, at any rate, was the opinion of the U.S. Government, as reported by the Greek Minister in Washington. A. C. Sedgwick, the well-informed Athens correspondent of the *New York Times*, reported the reaction of the Greek Government towards this trend. "Persons close to the government," he wrote, "report that according to information received from competent observers in Washington and London the continuation of the monarchy in Greece would be frowned on by both capitals, where any decision to bring the King back would inevitably be viewed as reactionary and therefore embarrassing in dealings with Moscow, especially over the question of suitable democratic regimes in states dominated by Russia. . . . Not only royalists but many other persons, frightened lest any swing to the Left inevitably end in communism and a repetition of last winter's civil war, want elections at once. They are opposed by all political groups considering themselves Left of center."

Two days after the Moscow broadcast, a frank exposition of Soviet policy was given by the Prague radio, which, since the liberation of Czechoslovakia, had closely echoed Russian policy. "What is happening in the Mediterranean zone cannot be a matter of indifference to the rest of the world, ourselves included, who have learned so tragically that security is indivisible and collective," said Prague radio in its home service. "The British imperial route to India, the route from the Soviet Black Sea to the Atlantic Ocean (*note the definition of the Black Sea as a Soviet zone, although Turkey, Bulgaria, and Rumania possess two-thirds of its coastline*) the route from France to the French colonies, and finally the route to the oilfields of the Near East, of interest to all three Powers, meet in the Mediterranean.

"Greece especially dominates the links between Europe-Asia and Europe-Africa. A number of airlines cross on Greek soil; Greek islands bar the way to the Dardanelles, dominate access to the Suez Canal, and close the entrance to the Adriatic.

"We reported that a number of Greek political parties had decided not to participate in the elections announced for January 20. The Soviet Union has stated that it cannot regard these elections as democratic, cannot therefore take part in the international supervision. . . . It is impossible to regard the coming elections as expressions of the popular will, as more than 200,000 out of a total of six to seven millions are deprived of their vote by government order."

This broadcast contains two principal points of interest. First, it was the frankest statement of power politics that had yet emanated from the Soviet sphere. It announced that Russia was not content with the possession of all the Balkans, except Greece, nor with control of the Adriatic through Jugoslavia, nor with dominating the Black Sea, nor with access to the oil-fields of the Middle East; she also wanted to expand into the Mediterranean.

The second point of interest was Russia's refusal to participate in international supervision of the Greek elections. Primarily, of course, her refusal was not based upon the alleged undemocratic nature of these elections, because the presence of Soviet observers would have entitled them to criticize any such weaknesses and make recommendations for their improvement—and, in any case, the elections were to be postponed until the anti-EAM reaction had had a chance to die down. Obviously the Russian refusal to participate in the supervision of the Greek elections was based on a desire not to establish a precedent which would have entitled the American and British governments to share in the supervision of the coming elections in Jugoslavia and Bulgaria.

There was, incidentally, a misstatement of fact in the Czech broadcast. At that time the date for the elections had been fixed for February 20, 1946, not January 20. This may have been due to an attempt to prove that the royalists were rushing the elections, and accordingly to bolster the Soviet refusal to take part in their supervision.

The same broadcast gave the number of political prisoners in Greece as 60,000, and was a deliberate attempt to mislead the listeners. Not even EAM claimed anything like such a number. Moscow radio itself mentioned the number as 18,000.

Less than a week after the Czech broadcast, the Soviet maneuvers against Greece were made known, when it was announced in Washington that Russia had asked for military bases in the strategic Dodecanese Islands, which the other major powers wished to reserve for Greece. If Russia had territorial ambitions against post-war Greece, it was obvious that any attempt to be friendly towards any Greek Government would be fruitless, unless that government were willing to accede to Russian demands. The only form of Greek Government which would conceivably give up its claim to the Dodecanese, which had been promised them by America and Britain, would be a Russian-dominated government. For whatever family quarrels the Greeks may have among themselves, they have been united for a generation in their claims to the Dodecanese.

It is difficult to pretend to a nation that, deplorably as they may be oppressed by international reaction, you at least are their friend, and at the same time to raise your voice and tell the rest of the world that this same nation is a nation of fascists and that you want some of its territory. Difficult . . . but it can be done. The following two broadcasts by Belgrade radio show how Russian propaganda masters this difficulty.

The first broadcast was the Morse service of the Jugoslav Telegraph Agency, beamed in English to America and Britain: "Commenting on latest events in Greece, today's (November 15, 1945) issue of the Belgrade newspaper *Borba* says, 'The Greek crisis is not only a cabinet crisis connected with the elections. The resignation of the government, the political situation preceding the formation of a new government, and the creation of the Kanelopoulos Government are expressions of a deep fundamental crisis in the entire Monarcho-Fascist regime in Greece. This crisis has entered upon its most acute phase—the attempt to impose upon the Greek people against its will a regime of the pro-fascist dynasty of Glucksburgs. Monarcho-Fascist Greece is the scene of wild unrestrained activities. In the economic field, the Monarcho-Fascist regime relies exclusively upon those economic quarters which openly collaborated with the forces of occupation. A Reuters correspondent reports that 'pressure in Greece has been exerted by

144

notorious organizations, big industrialists, and enriched collaborators who control production in the country and who regulate the fall and rise of prices according to their political needs.'

" 'Greece is receiving greater help from UNRRA than any other country in Europe. But, despite this, exceptionally difficult economic conditions still exist. UNRRA's help does not reach devastated regions which, under the flag of the EAM, fought for the liberty of their country. The Salonika paper, *Laiki Phoni*, asserts that UNRRA's deliveries are distributed only to Monarcho-Fascists who sell them on the black market.'

"*Borba* stresses that the Greek rulers, headed by Archbishop Damaskinos, despite terrorism against the democratic masses, have not succeeded in separating the broad masses of the Greek people from democracy. The strength of Greek democracy was recognized by Damaskinos himself, who, in an interview with a correspondent of the French Telegraph Agency, expressed his desire that British troops remain in Greece until the elections, calling the Greek people 'a people of rebels and malcontents.'

"The article concludes by stating that Damaskinos through his monarchistic policy, in addition to a small number of his adherents, relies only upon 'thirty thousand gendarmes and seventy thousand traitors and spies'—as was stated by the Greek patriot, Yanis Theodoris, in his article in the Albanian paper, *Perparim*."

Now, quite apart from the final paragraph, which causes one to wonder what a Greek patriot is doing in Albania, which at that time was having frontier troubles with Greece, this broadcast was full of the usual devious twists and turns of totalitarian propaganda.

There was the usual misuse of the word democracy, the attempt to prove that only EAM was democratic and that the Greek government was a government of fascists. The broad-

145

cast, be it emphasized, was not beamed in Greek to the Greeks who would have been able to gauge its accuracy, but to the Western democracies. It carefully steered away from all mention of foreign interference. It did not accuse the British of maintaining an armed rule over Greece, because the British, with their new Labor Government, would have rejected the suggestion. Instead, British troops were being retained in Greece at the suggestion of the Greek Regent, Archbishop Damaskinos, who was also quoted as calling his people "a people of rebels and malcontents." Fascism in Greece was laid at the door of a group of Greek industrialists and "enriched collaborators."

But, the following day, the Belgrade radio broadcast differently phrased extracts from the same article in *Borba*. The broadcast was in Greek to Greece, and this is what it said:

"The Monarchist-Fascist regime's policy towards Greece's neighbors has put Greece in a far from enviable international position. The policy shows to an extreme degree how dangerous to peace and post-war security the remnants of fascism in one country can be, when the decisions of the Crimea and Berlin Conferences are not implemented. The fact that Greece today is the center of intrigues directed against peace in the Balkans can only be explained by the fact that there are anti-democratic and fascist elements supported by international reactionary power.

"It has become obvious that the Monarchist-Fascists have in every sphere of policy come into sharp collision with the majority of the Greek people. It is significant that in the present Greek crisis, Greek leaders under Archbishop Damaskinos have not succeeded in exercising any authority over the Greek people. Neither the reign of terror nor the vesting of extraordinary authority in all those who have shown themselves faithful to the Monarchist-Fascists, nor the fostering of chauvinistic hatred for national minorities and neighboring peoples,

146

nor imperialistic propaganda on behalf of a greater Greece, has succeeded in turning the masses of the Greek people away from the democratic positions which they maintained in the struggle against the invader.

"In the present conditions, the strength of the democratic conscience of the Greek people has been fully demonstrated. The strength of Greek democracy was admitted by the Regent himself when he told a correspondent of the French Telegraph Agency he hoped British troops would remain in Greece until the elections, and called the Greeks a turbulent people."

In this broadcast to Greece, the insults to the country were toned down. A more cautious line was adopted towards the Regent, for, whatever their individual political opinions, all Greeks knew that the Archbishop had amply demonstrated during the occupation that he was a good Greek. So whereas Britain and America were told he had called his people 'a people of rebels and malcontents,' the Greeks were informed merely that he had called them 'a turbulent people,' a phrase of an entirely different, and not uncomplimentary, meaning. Popular Greek reaction against Russian demands for Dodecanese bases, against Jugoslav demands on Greek Macedonia, and against Albanian demands on Greek territory in Epirus was termed chauvinistic hatred inspired by international reaction.

It is also noteworthy that, in the Greek broadcast, the complaint that Greece was receiving more supplies from UNRRA than any other country—an old complaint of the Jugoslavs against the Greeks—was not repeated, nor was the statement that UNRRA supplies were being distributed only to "Monarcho-Fascists." The Greeks knew that the latter statement was not correct, and would not have appreciated the former. However, the first statement was also a falsification of the situation, as UNRRA has repeatedly informed the Jugoslav Government, but for some reason the latter has deliberately set out to allege that Greece is one of the nations receiving too much assistance as compared with herself.

It is part of Russian philosophy nowadays that a free and democratic people, if allowed to vote without pressure being exerted on them in any way, will prefer a republic to a monarchy, and communism to any other social system. Any other result is impossible, in the Russian view. A plebiscite resulting in favor of a monarchy or against the extremes of communism cannot therefore truly reflect the feelings of the people, they reason. The plebiscite must consequently have been fraudulently carried out. It was for this reason that Russia condemned the plebiscite in advance, while carefully refraining from any commitment which might involve her in joint supervision of the elections.

The Greek communists were so certain that the British were intent on restoring a monarchy in Greece that their then leading expert on foreign relations said that his party would change its hostile tactics towards Britain if convinced that British policy genuinely favored setting up a socialist state—even if that state were of Western, rather than a preferred Russian, model.

A week later there arrived in Greece the British Under-Secretary for Foreign Affairs, Mr. Hector McNeil, who proceeded at once to a series of lengthy interviews with Greek political leaders, including leaders of EAM.

At this meeting, according to the Soviet radio's home service, EAM submitted a list of names of the "democrats" killed by Greek Government "terrorists," a list of 129 monarchist bands operating in the provinces, data about arrests and raids on institutions, a list of 18,000 political prisoners, and a list of "traitors" serving in the Greek army and police. "The EAM representatives," said Moscow radio, "concluded by saying

148

that the continuation of anarchy and economic chaos threatens dangerous possibilities and is apt to damage both Greece and Britain, and that EAM is unable to keep the long-suffering people quiet indefinitely."

Now what did this threat by EAM amount to? The Greek Ministry of Public Order announced that between August 1 and October 31, 1945, 140 communist and twelve anti-communist bands were active. Of these, eighty-six communist and eight anti-communist bands were dispersed, exterminated, or arrested by the government by October 31. The remainder were still at large. Of the dispersed communist bands, two escaped across the Serbian frontier. Since the time fixed for the surrender of ELAS equipment on March 1, 1945, the ministry had discovered and seized large stores of ELAS equipment including 119 heavy mortars, 904 heavy machine guns, over four million cartridges, and 1,298 mobile ammunition dumps.

In retaining these arms after the date fixed for their surrender, EAM could have had only one motive, namely the preparation for yet another attempt to seize power by force of arms.

It must have come as a surprise to EAM when McNeil asked the Greek Government to postpone the plebiscite on the King's return to 1948, thus forcing that showdown with the exiled King which the extreme element of EAM had thought improbable. The King himself immediately protested to the Regent, and was supported in the British House of Commons by the Conservative opposition, who maintained that Britain had committed herself to holding the plebiscite as soon as possible after the liberation of Greece. The Regent resigned his office, but the Labor Government won its vote in the House of Commons and pressed the Regent to resume his post. Once more, the British Government had bobbed up far to the Left of where the Communists had expected to find it.

Friends of mine in Greece, Republicans by politics but fearful of communist influence in the country, were alarmed at these moves, and saw in them a new British appeasement of Russia which they were sure could end only in ultimate disaster. I hold a different opinion. If power politics are to be the rule in Europe, the British regard Greece as being in their sphere of influence. As the Prague radio pointed out, Greece is in a position to dominate the British imperial route to India, and in a race for territory the British are no more prepared to release Greece to the possession of a rival power than America is prepared to release the secrets of the atom bomb without first being sure that it will not be misused.

The British are banking everything on being able to fulfill the responsibilities they have assumed in Greece—both political and financial. They are counting on capturing the support of all the moderate Left-wing parties as well as holding the support of those Republicans who, fearing the rise of communism, turned to the extreme Right and the royalists in order to form a bloc against EAM. For that reason, the press is far freer in Greece than in any neighboring country. There were twenty-six newspapers in Athens alone when I was last in that city, and there was no censorship.

In spite of the Russian refusal to assist in the supervision of the elections, America and Britain decided to proceed without her. France accepted her invitation to share in the supervision and announced she would appoint observers. Most important of all, there was evidence that the American and British diplomatic missions were keeping closely in touch with each other, even if they did not see eye to eye on all issues.

About the issue of saving Greece, there was no quarrel. A large UNRRA mission under an American chief was at work in the country and had proved it possible for an international civil service to function without interfering in the political affairs of one of its member governments.

Since my own visits to Greece after its liberation were in the capacity of an UNRRA official, though not attached to the Greek mission, it is possible for me to speak without boasting of the profound effect its work has had on the attitude of the Greek people towards America and Britain.

The early work of UNRRA in Greece was marred by the civil war which prevented the Anglo-American military relief authorities from fulfilling all their promises, and during which, incidentally, ELAS stole large stocks of relief supplies imported for the civilian population. The mission was further handicapped by the bringing forward of the date at which it was agreed UNRRA would assume responsibility for relief.

But within four months the UNRRA machine had established an organization which was primarily responsible for rescuing the Greeks from the starvation added by the civil war to that of the German occupation.

The biggest charge levelled against UNRRA in Greece, especially by the pro-Soviet radio in Belgrade, was that its supplies were being used on the "black market." This was a deliberate travesty of the facts and was based on an entire misconception of the black market as it exists in most of Europe today. For instance, when, in America, the OPA set a price of thirty-nine cents on beef, that was a legal price. If the customer went to market and paid sixty cents, that was black market. But what happens in Greece, and what is happening in nearly every other European country, is different. A Greek is given a ration of, say, chick peas: and does not like chick peas. He takes them to his neighbor and trades for something else. That is not a black market, in the American understanding of the term; it is a free market. Or, in the case of UNRRA meat supplies, which in Greece are mainly soy meal sausages, if a Greek takes his allotted ration of sausages at thirty drachmas a pound and sells his ration at the same price to a merchant because he does not like soy meal sausages, that is a legal transaction. But in saying that the relief supplies were being sold on the black markets of Greece, the propaganda of the professional Left confused the issue by omitting the definition of what the black market was.

Although UNRRA supplies were obtained from a number of countries, including Latin America, the Greeks had the firm impression that they all came from America. And there is no doubt that the work of UNRRA in Greece has done more for the prestige of America than all the organized propaganda work could ever have accomplished. This is not mere cupboard love, so much as a proof that any policy, so long as it takes positive action, is infinitely preferable to the policy of wait-and-see. Greece, with its thousands of people who have relatives in America, its individuality of opinion that makes nearly every Greek a whole political party in himself, feels a natural affinity for America, an affinity which is today the most potent force working in favor of the West against the Byzantine ideas from the East.

In Greece EAM planned to force a revolutionary situation, bringing to a standstill during the civil war all the services and functions of modern civilization, so that in time the mass of the population, finding conditions unbearable, would be forced to take their side, if only to bring the intolerable conditions to an end. The immediate defection of the socialists from EAM as soon as the end of the civil war made it safe, exposed the centralized communist direction of EAM and the terroristic methods by which KKE had, till then, preserved it as a cover for revolutionary activities.

To bring these charges home, of course, only revives the weary challenge from the Left, so frequently heard in Iran, that the West, in spite of the war, was seeking a front with which to shut in Russia. (How repetitious this is of Hitler's "encirclement of Germany" theory with which he justified

German expansion!) This merely provides fresh illustration that power politics have come into their own again, and raises the unanswerable question of "who began it first." There is no doubt in my mind, after the examples of Iran and the Balkans, about who first began imperialist expansion. But to attempt to prove the point, besides trying everybody's temper and patience, would only leave us where we are. The vital point is that the race is on and the problem is how to stop it before the next war comes along.

For let no one doubt that power politics among the so-called Big Three cannot shelve the problem of the next war. The dynamics of nations, big or little, are too powerful to be resisted. Attitudes, not rifles, remember, are now the denominations of world power. There can be no power-politics solution of the Greece problem. If the Soviet Union is really imperialist and expansionist, it must have Greece as an outlet to the Mediterranean and thence to the Atlantic. But a cession of Greece to the Soviet sphere of influence presages a war between Britain and the Soviet Union as surely as the incorporation of Bohemia and Moravia into the German Reich denoted an inevitable war between Britain and Germany. There can be no argument on this score—except between those who still believe the world can be run peacefully on the zones-of-influence system and those who want to see the Soviet Union liquidate the British Empire.

As matters stand at present, the overwhelming mass of the Greek people is passionately in favor of America and Britain—in favor of America rather than Britain, but for either rather than for the Soviet Union. And if anyone doubts this, and doubts the genuine fear and repugnance with which the Greek regards the Byzantine system of the East, let him look at the price which the gold sovereign and the dollar command in Athens today, dictated by the fear of the Greeks that the West will leave them to be engulfed.

They are conscious of our faults, God knows—far more conscious at times than we ourselves are. But we are their only friends and possible saviors.

They lie at the southern tip of half a continent. For hundreds of miles to the north and northeast lies the land-mass of a new and aggressive empire state. The sea that washes their beautiful coast is the vital sea of another imperial power. If power politics are to rule the world, they are the pawn of empires. If they are allowed to have their choice, they will prefer the West rather than the East.

But this will solve nothing for Greece itself, nor for the rest of the world; for the dynamics of empires are continually changing. The problem for the West is how to corner and capture those dynamics and to channel them into a new world creed and organization.

IV. JUGOSLAVIA: PART ONE

"Out of one quarrel, one hundred sins."
—Serbian proverb

A TRIP TO THE DALMATIAN COAST

THE eastern coast of Italy along the Adriatic sea is flat, uninteresting, and unhealthily malarial, even in winter. It is seldom visited even by tourists, except a specialized few who wish to study the Byzantine origin of some of its tiny churches. But across the sea to the east, sometimes discernible on a clear day, there rises the coastline of another country, so different from Italy that it might almost be in another continent. The Jugoslavs—the name means simply South Slavs—have one of the most beautiful countries in Europe and their Dalmatian coast is fairylike in its enchantment.

Six years ago—a generation ago in human thought, or so it seems—the Dalmatian coast was the pleasure ground of the most adventurous of the tourists who had grown tired of the more orthodox spots along the French Riviera. They explored its chain of islands, unspoiled since the days when Venice was a great commercial empire, and were entranced by the tiny ports along the mainland, bathed in year-round sunshine and protected from the wintry east by the high mountain range that rises almost immediately from the water's edge. In winter, a six-hours' run by the little narrow-gauge railroad would climb those mountains and take you out of a land of summer into a barren wintry land where the snow lay deep. For beyond the coastal strip lies a hopeless hinterland of craggy mountains, where only goats can find a blade of grass even in summer and where a guerrilla army can hide out in defiance of the most modern techniques of mechanized warfare.

Little white steamers bustled up and down the coast, stopping at most of the islands and ports, and carrying not only the tourists but the peasant inhabitants as well, together with all their variegated produce and livestock. The gay little steamers were Dalmatia's maritime express buses, for here and there the mountains dropped sheer into the sea, reducing road travel to a perilous crawl along their precipitous sides. From the height of one of these roads, the little white specks on the blue mirror four thousand feet below appeared motionless, but by the time your automobile had hurtled down the hairpin bends to the next town the steamer would be at the dock, already taking on its new crowd of passengers.

My last voyage down the Dalmatian coast had been at the end of April, 1940, when my wife and I sailed from Split to Dubrovnik. It was towards the close of the "phony war" period and there were not many tourists around other than those of the German brand, which had made the species so notorious. Their infestation of Dubrovnik and the nearby naval base at Kotor was one of the things I wanted to write about.

The only people resembling tourists on board the steamer were husband and wife, he a tall man in his early forties. His clipped military mustache, gray flannel trousers, and brown sports jacket gave him the appearance of an Englishman, but in conversation he revealed himself to be an American, although he had that queer accentless accent unconsciously acquired by so many Americans who live for years in Europe without returning home. His wife was a mousy little creature, huddled within herself, who spoke very little. When he heard of my profession, he introduced himself as being also a writer of sorts, principally for geographic magazines in America, and said they lived on the beautiful little island of Korcula, just north of Dubrovnik. He asked me what I thought of American

158

correspondents in Europe and of their reporting. I explained that I knew most of them personally, knew they had had long experience in Europe before the war, and said I felt that they were doing magnificent work.*

In reply, our acquaintance launched into a passionate diatribe against the American press. With the possible exception of one paper in Chicago, he said, it was misrepresenting the facts. Oh, the correspondents were not actually reporting untruths, but by a careful selection of half-truths they were completely distorting the German case. The Germans had a new civilization, he said; in actual fact, National Socialist Germany was far more democratic than America or Britain, and he hoped the British would be defeated before the correspondents had a chance to drag America into the war.

He had spent some years in Europe, it appeared, and he was returning to Korcula after arranging for his money to be transferred from Holland to Switzerland and for his daughter to go to school in Florence.

He left the steamer at Korcula. Later, when we arrived at Dubrovnik, two Jugoslav police officials were waiting at the dock and asked some searching questions about the length of my stay in Jugoslavia. A long-distance telephone call to the head of the press department in the Jugoslav Foreign Office set their suspicions at rest and as they became more expansive, I asked some questions about our travelling companions to which they were quite ready to reply. Our acquaintance was named Douglas Chandler and it appeared that both the Jugoslav authorities and the American Embassy had been attempting without success to persuade him to leave the country. He was

---

* If this seems a contradiction of my observations on most of the war correspondents in Greece, let me reiterate that this conversation took place before Pearl Harbor, at which point many of the most experienced American correspondents felt impelled to join the forces of some specialized government agency, thereby leaving their remaining colleagues in a minority among the new breed of correspondents who flooded into the field.

suspected of being a German agent and it was known that he was on friendly terms with agents whom the Italian Government sent to Dalmatia on the ostensible mission of inspecting the schools for Italian residents. The fact that I had been seen talking to him had aroused official suspicions and had been reported ahead of us.

I thought no more of Chandler until the following month when the Germans suddenly invaded Holland and overran the country. Throughout the war Switzerland remained neutral. Whoever had advised Chandler to transfer his money from Holland to Switzerland had high sources of information on German intentions.

Eighteen months later I heard his voice on the short-wave radio from Germany, exhorting Americans (under the name of Paul Revere) to bring an end to the "senseless war" between Germany and America. Germany was a land of promise, he said, where no one need fear for the future. I wondered if he remembered his own fear of the future and the not-so-perfect trust in Germany that prompted him to transfer his money to neutral Switzerland. I wondered also if he remembered his island home on the Dalmatian coast, now in the hands of the Italians, and the little white steamboats on which he had railed so bitterly against his "fellow correspondents." When the Axis attacked Jugoslavia, some of the steamboats escaped out of the Adriatic and made their way to British ports in the Mediterranean. It was ironic that the same steamboat on which we had met, now painted olive drab, carried me back to the Dalmatian coast on my return to Jugoslavia in the beginning of 1945.

"BEWARE THE JUGOSLAVS!"

A British officer from the liaison mission gave some of the UNRRA staff a very strange briefing before we left the Italian coast. At least it appeared strange to me because it presented a Jugoslavia in no way similar to the country I had known before the war. He did not speak of the tremendous destruction and havoc in the country, for this was something of which we knew more than he, having made a special study of it for months. He talked chiefly of the nature of the people. We would have to behave with extreme care, he warned, as the Jugoslavs were most suspicious of America and Britain, especially after the Greek civil war. In fact, that suspicion was so intense that they had recently compelled Field Marshal Alexander, under whose command the Jugoslav theatre came, to withdraw a British artillery force from the mountains of Montenegro where it was barring the retreat from Greece of a German mechanized army. They thought the British artillery would be used eventually to destroy their Partisan government. They were also suspicious of Americans because America had refused until comparatively recently to withdraw its mission from General Mihailovitch, whom the British officer classified as a quisling. In fact, all the Chetnik forces of Mihailovitch were quislings, said the officer, except those who had deserted Mihailovitch and gone over to the Partisans.

When asked whether by Jugoslav suspicion he meant Partisan suspicion, the officer agreed that this was the case, but he added that Marshal Tito so obviously had the whole country behind him that it was now possible to speak of the Partisans as representing all Jugoslavs. There were, he warned us, several ex-collaborators in the port of Split, for which we were bound. These were the wealthier townspeople, many of whom could speak English, and we would doubtless be approached by them. They would complain about the Partisans, but we must remember that they represented a small and decadent minority in the country. We must be careful not to accept too many invitations to their houses, for the Partisans would notice our Jugoslav friends and judge us accordingly. But Split and Dubrovnik were the only two towns where we would find ex-collaborators in large numbers, we were told, for throughout the rest of the country, the people stood solidly behind Tito.

In those two towns, he emphasized, we would have to be on our guard, for the ex-collaborators were principally those people who had had connections with the West before the war. Superficially, they might appear to share common cultural interests with America and Britain, but we should never forget that while the Partisans had lived a hard life in the forests and mountains, these people had lived comfortably in the towns for the whole of the occupation and had contributed nothing to the war effort.

It was an unfortunate coincidence that their daughters were generally very pretty, much prettier than the average Partisan girl, who looked none too attractive in uniform anyway. There had been a most unhappy incident recently, the British officer told us. The British cruiser Delhi had dropped anchor in Split harbor after having been in action against the Germans a few miles up the coast, where the front line then existed. The Partisan suspicion that the cruiser had arrived to be used against them was in no way allayed by the fact that she had been shelling Germans a few hours previously, and their hostility was augmented by the fact that when the sailors went ashore they invited the daughters of the bourgeoisie to a dance. In the middle of the celebration, Partisan guards entered the building, arrested the girls, and ordered the sailors back to their ship. Only a personal note from the commander of the ship to the Partisan mayor of the town had enabled the dance to take place uninterrupted the following evening.

The British officer then gave a description of the different provinces of Jugoslavia and how they had been affected by the war. In the north and west, Slovenia, Croatia, and Dalmatia were solid Partisan territory, he said, although the Germans had not yet been expelled from Slovenia and part of Croatia, whose capital city, Zagreb, was still in German hands. Serbia was liberated but unfortunately showed traces of Chetnik influence, but that again was because the war profiteers had congregated in Belgrade. Bosnia and Herzegovina had seen some of the bitterest fighting of the war and whole villages had disappeared from the map. Although its capital, Sarajevo, was still in German hands, the Partisan army was fighting at the approaches to the city. Montenegro was liberated and was also solid Partisan territory, as was Macedonia in the far south of the country.

We were then given an outline of the chaotic currency situation; at least eight different currencies were in circulation but none of them had any real value in view of the intense shortages, and barter was the order of the day. One of the greatest problems of the new government would be the introduction of a common currency.

To anyone who had known Jugoslavia before the war, this picture of distrust of America and Britain came as a great surprise. I had never expected Jugoslavia to be the same as I had known it previously. Invasion, guerrilla warfare, and a virtual civil war must have transformed the country. The physical destruction had been enormous; the country's economy was wrecked, and large areas were below starvation level. But to be told that people who were once among our greatest friends had been changed into a nation of doubters, was like being told that a piece of the war had been fought in vain. Somewhere along the line a war aim had gone sour.

True, this particular British officer had never been to Jugoslavia, neither before nor during the war. This, however, from the military point of view, was immaterial, since his function had been to remain at base headquarters and coordinate the reports of those officers who were actually inside Jugoslavia. He knew more about the war in Jugoslavia than any of them; each might have known in immense detail the course of events in the area in which he was stationed, but this man had a picture of the whole situation. He knew the place and date where every battle had been fought. He knew the history of the laborious and abortive attempts to reconcile Tito and Mihailovitch, and he had no hesitation in classifying the latter as a traitor to his country. And he emphasized that the Jugoslavs, meaning the Partisans, distrusted America and Britain.

If all these things were true, democracy had lost yet another friend. And as the little Jugoslav steamer throbbed its way across the Adriatic to Dalmatia, I wondered why.

IMPORTANCE OF THE 1941 REVOLT IN BELGRADE

Probably the most disturbing sign of deterioration among the democracies is their refusal to recognize their friends until they are in danger of losing them, or until they have already lost them. It is a fault not only of the peoples but of their governments as well, though time and again the reckoning has been exacted inexorably in human lives.

I remember discussing this problem with M. W. Fodor, at that time correspondent for the *Chicago Daily News* in Vienna, eighteen months before the European war broke out. It was that spring morning in 1938 when German troops marched into Austria to take over the country, and it was not until that morning that Fodor allowed himself to believe that Austria was doomed.

His reasoning was based on the correct assumption that war between Nazi Germany and Britain was inevitable. In this event, Fodor argued, the countries of Southeastern Europe were vital to the British, not only because their peoples, with the possible exception of the Bulgars, were pro-British and anti-Nazi, but because this area was the most important single source of supply open to Germany. Up to this point Fodor was correct, but here he reasoned that in this case the British would strive to protect their interests in the Balkans and he assumed, in fact, that they were actually doing so, but were losing battle after battle on the diplomatic front.

This was in the days before the term appeasement was used to describe British policy towards Hitler. But appeasement alone was not responsible for the disappearance of country after country in those pre-war months. Appeasement became the policy of the British Government as a direct result of its own failure throughout the preceding years to show the British public where their interests lay. British foreign policy in the Balkans was suffering no defeats at the hands of the Germans, because there was no British policy towards the Balkans. When, after the Austrian Anschluss, the British Government began to wake up to the idea that Germany meant to conquer Europe, British public opinion could not be wakened easily from its lethargy—not until several other countries had disappeared or capitulated.

About that time, the British Minister in Jugoslavia, Neville Henderson, drew a line across the Balkans where he thought it might be possible for British policy to halt German expansion. The line lay north of Budapest in Hungary. But by that time it was too late, as Fodor had seen months before, when he still believed that the British had a policy to save Austria from the Germans. By the time the British realized they had interests in Southeast Europe and that these interests were directly threatened by German expansion, it was too late to defend them.

The bitter lesson of those years before the war is that no nation can afford to remain disinterested in the events of other nations until its own interests are directly involved. The nations are too intimately tied with each other, nowadays, ever to be segregated into different sections.

In a vague way, almost as though settling into a habit, the people of America have come to accept the idea that somehow the Greeks fall logically under the control of the British and the Jugoslavs under the control of the Russians. There is no attempt to question how or why this has come to be so, whether the peoples concerned were consulted, and, if not, what they have done to be so bandied back and forth as schoolboys barter marbles.

The current habit is to regard Jugoslavia's contribution to the war as having been performed through her Partisan army, which at one time was credited with keeping sixteen German divisions tied down in that country when they were desperately needed on the Russian or Italian fronts. In point of fact, her most important contribution and the one that entitles her to most consideration from the West—if only because it demonstrates the prestige of the democracies—was one for which no credit can be claimed by the present leaders of the Partisans. It was made in spite of, and not because of, the men who are at present at the head of affairs in Jugoslavia. What was this contribution?

At the Nuremberg trial of the Nazi war criminals, evidence was offered to show that the German attack on Russia, which took place on June 22, 1941, had originally been set for May 24 of that year but had to be postponed "because of Balkan complications." It was not until April 30 that Adolf Hitler finally called his staff together and said that he had decided to strike at Russia on June 22.

Now what were the "Balkan complications" that caused this sudden postponement? There was the Greek-Italian war, certainly a complication, since Hitler knew he would have to conquer the Greeks and put a stop to the thrashing they were giving Italy in order to have full control of the Balkans for a concentrated attack on Russia. But the Greek-Italian war was not a recent occurrence; the Greeks had been trouncing the Italians all winter.

The only Balkan complication for Hitler was how to get his armies to Greece. Jugoslavia lay in between and commanded the main communications. True, he had Bulgaria in his grasp and Bulgaria also had a common frontier with Greece; but to get to Bulgaria he also had to pass through Jugoslavia or master the bad communications from Hungary through Rumania to the Danube. He had already moved some troops into Bulgaria by this route, but, as a base for operations against Greece, Bulgaria was useless without Jugoslavia.

Jugoslavia appeared to present no difficulties, however. The Regent, Prince Paul, was a weak and vacillating man who would answer to a sharp command. The existing government was most anxious not to offend Germany. And if military pressure were needed, Hitler had more than sufficient at hand. His troops were in Austria, Hungary, Rumania, and Bulgaria, all of which had common frontiers with Jugoslavia. Italy had troops in Albania, jutting into the heart of the country. If Jugoslavia resisted pressure, she would have to face the possibility of attacks from five different directions with no hope of supplies from the Allies.

In the middle of March, Hitler summoned the Jugoslavs to Vienna where on March 25 they signed a pact which would have given German troops passage across Jugoslavia to Greece. Two days later, the people of Belgrade rose in revolt, threw out the government, and tore up the pact. Hitler, realizing that he could not walk through Jugoslavia, decided to fight his way through. The attack was launched on April 6 by the bombing of Belgrade and the helpless country, ill armed and only half mobilized, was liquidated by April 17. There still remained Greece, however, and it was April 27 before German troops hoisted the swastika flag over the Acropolis in Athens. The Germans had conquered the Balkans but they had had to fight their way down the whole peninsula. Furthermore, there were no prospects of a peaceful occupation; troops would be required, troops who would otherwise have been destined for the attack on Russia.

These were the complications that caused Hitler to post-pone his attack on Russia.

The circumstances of the Belgrade revolt were obscured by the fighting that followed and were finally buried by the news of the Russo-German war. This was one of the things I had in mind when I wrote that the democracies forget their real friends too easily. I have with me the magnificent account of the revolt published in the *New York Times* at the time. On my return to Belgrade after its liberation, I had plenty of opportunities to talk with those of my old friends who had survived the war. There is no doubt that it was a popular revolt; the government itself was ousted by pro-Allied elements within the Jugoslav army, but it was the people of Belgrade who rose spontaneously and simultaneously and made the *coup d'état* possible. No revolts were reported anywhere else outside the province of Serbia. The Croats and Slovenes, dissatisfied with the government and with Serbian rule, accepted the German pact—perhaps sullenly, but passively. If there were disorders, they were not reported and played no part in the downfall of the quisling government. It is important to remember that it was primarily the Serbs and the people of Belgrade who overthrew their government.

In a sense, they were strategically well placed. Belgrade was the capital and uprisings in other cities would not have had the same urgent pressure on the government. But the people of Belgrade had no illusions about what would happen to them in tearing up the pact. They may not have anticipated such a sudden collapse of their army, but they knew they could not hold out indefinitely, and they knew they could not expect any help.

The Jugoslav communists played no part in the revolution. Until then, in fact, they had faithfully followed the party line of urging cooperation with Germany, for it was not until after the conquest of Jugoslavia that Soviet Russia finally digested the fact that Germany was preparing to attack and decided to cease the flow of supplies to Germany. None of the other Jugoslav political parties was involved in the uprising, although different politicians took part as individuals. In fact, it was probably the only genuine people's revolution of the war—spelt without the capital P that has made such a mockery of the word.

For this reason, their motives are important. To say that they were anti-Nazi is not sufficient explanation. Every other people in Europe was anti-Nazi, but none produced such an expression of popular will.

Was it love of Britain? Tangye Lean in his well-documented book on the work of BBC during the war, *Voices in The Darkness*, says, "The BBC's best audiences in the Balkans seem to have been Jugoslavia and Greece. There are even well-informed people who claim that it was a broadcast by L. S. Amery that brought about the overthrow of the (Jugoslav) regime which submitted to the Tripartite Pact." Mr. Lean adds that he has found no proof of this, and I agree with his skepticism. Undoubtedly, one of the grounds for the uprising was the abhorrence of the people of any act which would, in effect, place them in the war against the British on the side of the Nazis, but that is not the whole reason. Britain was alone in the war, and no nation commits suicide for the sake of another whose ultimate survival is uncertain.

Was it love of Russia? Obviously not. Russia had declared for neutrality in favor of Germany and at that time showed no sign of changing her attitude. The Jugoslavs are Slavs with a love for Russia, Red or White, but, if love of Russia had been influencing the people at that juncture, they would have acquiesced in the Tripartite Pact.

Was it love of America? On the face of it, this seems unlikely as America also was not yet in the war and no event had occurred to cause the Jugoslavs as a whole to anticipate her entry. But there are some facts that bear examining.

Shortly before the uprising occurred, Colonel (now Major General) William J. Donovan had paid a visit to the Balkans. General Donovan is a passionate and eloquent advocate of democracy and his travels in Southeastern Europe caused the Germans no little anxiety. In Belgrade he talked with many of the politicians in opposition to the government. Exactly what arguments General Donovan used I do not know but he left behind the profound impression that this was the time for Jugoslavia to choose her side.

Some time previously, a radio station in Boston had pioneered the short-wave field in broadcasts from America to Jugoslavia. Whereas the other few existing American short-wave stations, owned by RCA, CBS, and General Electric, had confined themselves to spasmodic news broadcasts to Western Europe, mainly as a method of testing new equipment, this station, WRUL by name, had set out to gain a widespread European audience by a thorough coverage of the field. (This—obviously—was before Pearl Harbor, before all short-wave stations came under the authority of OWI and were devoted entirely to psychological warfare. In the period we are discussing, the short-wave stations were still privately owned and directed.) It had daily broadcasts in their native languages to France, Germany, Jugoslavia, Greece, Turkey, Egypt, Scandinavia, and others. The commentators were men who knew their languages perfectly. Shortly before the Jugoslav crisis, it was broadcasting five times weekly to Jugoslavia, and, during the height of the crisis, these were stepped up to twice daily. Without openly taking the line that American intervention was inevitable, the broadcasts spoke more and more strongly against the Germans and emphasized the increasing American supplies to Britain.

WRUL'S Jugoslav broadcasts were by a former Paris correspondent of the Belgrade *Pravda*, Dr. Svetislav-Sveta Petrovitch. Within a few weeks of his first appearance on the air,
the U.S. State Department was advised by its representative
in Belgrade that Petrovitch not only had a large following in
Jugoslavia but had acquired the power to swing people's opinions. Petrovitch wasted no words in urging his people to take
a stand against German rule over their country.

Since America was still neutral, WRUL had not the same
difficulty as BBC in ascertaining to what extent its broadcasts
were being heard. The mails were still running between
Jugoslavia and America, and WRUL had plenty of evidence
that its broadcasts were being heard extensively throughout
the country. Their effect was beyond exaggeration. Europe
was sick of propaganda broadcasts. Every broadcast on the
ether was automatically damned as propaganda—through what
is known in advertising circles as sales resistance—except that
lone voice heard from the most powerful neutral country in
the world, warning the Jugoslavs in no uncertain tones that
they had reached the crossroads.

OUR DEBT TO THE JUGOSLAVS

This, then, was the background of the Jugoslav uprising.
Their ties of devotion were all to the West; in so far as the war
at that stage was between the Germans and the British, they
were pro-British and anti-German. But, such is the dead weight
of modern government, they lacked that incentive which
would touch off the fiery resentment which nearly all of them
felt towards their government and which would unite individuals in a common movement of protest. That incentive
was supplied by America. The knowledge that the most
powerful democracy had ranged herself unyieldingly on the
side of the British, even though she was not yet in the war, was

all the Jugoslavs needed to throw over their quisling government.

This book is about post-war attitudes, but I have gone into the roots of the Jugoslav rebellion in such detail because it is necessary to uproot the mischievous assertion that the Jugoslavs belong sentimentally to the Russians. If power politics are to be the pattern of the post-war world and nations are to be placed in this or that zone of influence, irrespective of the wishes of their inhabitants, that is a different matter. But do not let us deceive ourselves and justify the abandonment of a people by canting about non-existent affections.

For we have forgotten our real debt to the Jugoslavs. No one has expressed publicly what that uprising accomplished for the three Allies. There is altogether too much talk among the Big Three about which of them won the war. As a contemporary journalist put it, the British believe the turning point of the war came with the defeat of the Luftwaffe in the Battle of Britain; the Americans think they won the war with a little help from other people; the Russians, for their part, know they won the war with no help from anybody else, and are assiduously proclaiming their feat to every small nation in the world. To go into the details of these claims would be invidious, although it is significant that only sixty-five per cent of German casualties were incurred on the Russian front, which saw action four times longer than any other battlefront. As disclosed at the Nuremberg trials.

But if there is any one event which can be claimed to have swung the trend of the war away from the Germans, while its outcome was still in doubt, it is the revolt of the people of Belgrade. Consider its implications. By having to fight his way through Jugoslavia instead of occupying the country peacefully with its rail and road communications intact, Hitler was compelled at the last minute to postpone his attack on Russia by twenty-nine days. Not that this gave the Russians twenty-nine days more in which to prepare for the attack, for they did not accept the inevitability of war until the Balkans had been subjugated. But it did reduce by twenty-nine days the period of summer weather which the German army was counting upon to sweep across Poland and Russia for the capture of Moscow.

As it was, the Germans came very close to reaching their objective before winter set in and forced them to call off their campaign. Russian resistance had been unexpectedly strong, but the striking speed of the German army in those days was such that it is permissible to imagine it reaching Moscow, given another month of good weather for mechanized warfare. No one is entitled to assume that the fall of Moscow would have meant the defeat of Russia, much less the loss of the war; but it would have cut the Russian army into two, one in the north, the other in the south; Hitler's campaign in the south the following year would have been greatly facilitated, and the war's ultimate outcome would have been in doubt. Certainly the loss of Moscow would have prolonged the war immeasurably. Just how much those vanished twenty-nine days meant to the Germans can be gauged by the ferocity with which they handled Jugoslavia after its conquest. Slovenia was absorbed into the Reich; Croatia was split off and made an "independent State." Dalmatia was placed under Italian occupation, Macedonia under Bulgarian occupation, Serbia under a quisling government. Serb minorities in the provinces outside Serbia were massacred.

Our debt to Jugoslavia is that, at a crucial time of the war, she joined the Allied side, knowing she had nothing to expect for an indefinite period but ruthless subjugation. She was the only nation to join the Allied side voluntarily; everybody else was dragged in by virtue of being attacked by Germany.*

* I am ignoring, of course, the token declarations of war by such countries as Egypt and other small countries under British or American influence. These declarations came in the last few weeks of the war and were wangled by the two large powers as a move against the Soviet Union's previous maneuver of

Her entry was prompted entirely by loyalty towards the West and was made in spite of whatever feeling of affection the Jugoslavs as Slavs might have had towards a neutral Russia in the East.

ATTITUDES TOWARD MIHAILOVITCH

Public opinion has been more misled and confused on Jugoslavia, and especially on American and British relations with that country, than on any other country in Europe. The confusion on Greece was a compound caused by the blunderings of British foreign policy and the emotionalism of correspondents whose ambitions were to be editorial writers rather than reporters. But in the case of Jugoslavia, there were no outside influences to disturb the policy of either the American or British Governments—or rather the policies of the military organizations entrusted with organizing resistance inside the country. An ironclad censorship enabled them to operate as they wished without fear of outside criticism. Interdepartmental objections could be, and were, quashed by the organizations with the retort that they were interested only in creating and expanding armed resistance within Jugoslavia. But, inevitably, in the very creation of that resistance, in advising which group to support, they took decisions on policy which ought not to have been within their sphere.

Our first support was given to Mihailovitch and his Serbian Chetniks. The Jugoslav Government-in-Exile raised Mihailovitch from the rank of colonel to that of general and appointed him Minister of War in the government to organize all armed resistance inside the country. Both America and Britain appointed liaison missions which worked with Mihailovitch within the country. Over American and British transmitters

---

whittling herself into a number of separate republics, each with ostensible control over its own foreign policy and consequently entitled to a separate vote in the peace assembly.

Mihailovitch was portrayed to the Jugoslavs as the military leader of their country.

To ourselves and to the people of Jugoslavia, the forces of Tito were condemned as bandits and murderers, but by 1943, some months after Tito had received the official approval of Russia, we sent in liaison officers to work with him.

A few months later, on the advice of their liaison officers, the British withdrew their support from Mihailovitch. Later in 1944, America followed the example of Britain, but, be it remarked, with noticeably more reluctance, and even then only after Tito had refused to allow American officers into his area as long as America continued to maintain a mission with Mihailovitch. By the end of 1944, we—and the people of Jugoslavia—were being told that Mihailovitch was a quisling.

The effect on the American public is naturally to cause it to regard events in Jugoslavia as another case of hopeless Balkan politics, an unfortunate result at a time when there was never a greater and more urgent need for American interest in Jugoslav affairs. The effect on the Jugoslavs was catastrophic.

PARTISANS AND OTHER JUGOSLAVS

The British officer was right when he said there were "collaborationists" quartered in Split. If anything, he had been too lenient. Most of the townspeople, to judge from their complaints against the Partisans, seemed to have been collaborationists.

I decided to go down to Dubrovnik. But before I left, I was again briefed. "You must not put any significance on what you see and hear in Dubrovnik," I was told. "The people in Dubrovnik never took any really active part in the war. There was a lot of collaboration down there, and too many people are complaining about the Partisans. The British liaison officer in Dubrovnik has just had to be withdrawn because he became governed with the obsession that the Partisans are persecuting the Roman Catholics. Ridiculous, of course."

Dubrovnik had a curfew, imposed by the Partisans. Restaurants had to close by 10 P.M. and everybody had to be off the streets by 11 P.M. Permits to stay out longer could be obtained —by American or British officials, but they were valid for one night only. American and British sailors enjoying shore leave from the Liberty ships that had brought arms to the Partisans and relief supplies for civilians were arrested if they were found in the town after curfew hours.

Dubrovnik is a town of mariners, dating back to the days when it was a republic as great as Venice; before the war nearly every family had at least one member somewhere at sea. But now all the vessels that survived out of Jugoslavia's once-extensive merchant marine were in the hands of the Anglo-American shipping pool, being carefully routed to avoid Jugoslav ports lest the Partisans should confiscate them. The only ships held by the Partisans were the remnants of the little Dalmatian steamboat flotilla. Meantime, Dubrovnik's master mariners were used by the Partisans—at best—as clerks or interpreters. They were not allowed to go to sea lest they take the opportunity to sail to an Allied port. The little steamboats were commanded by Partisan seamen, most of whom were not qualified for anything more than coastal shipping. Were the master mariners collaborators? Certainly not as far as their profession was concerned. When the war came and left them stranded as prisoners in an occupied land, they had settled down to endure the occupation. All of them had disdained to sail ships either for the Italians or for the Germans. But they were contacts with a world which the Partisan leaders suspected and towards which they were intensely hostile. Only those approved as being beyond danger of contamination could be trusted to command the ships that sailed between Dalmatia and Italy.

I went up from Dalmatia into the wilds of Montenegro, that rocky and mountainous province on the borders of Albania. It was a journey that involved yet more permits to travel, still more injunctions about listening to "collaborators," and still stronger warnings about keeping to the route laid out for me. If there were "collaborators," I came across none; the Montenegrins had suffered so bitterly from the war that they were too busy repairing their shattered homes to pay any heed to politics. They had been reduced to below the level where political differences can have any significance; a new roof for the coming winter was of more immediate importance than the question of whether the country as a whole should have this or that sort of government.

But the Partisans were hard at work among the Montenegrins, teaching them to shut their minds to the past and look towards the future. A most praiseworthy endeavor in welfare work, but its political connotations required strange feats of color-blindness. The first step was towards creating national pride. It was dinned home that Jugoslavia had saved herself largely by her own efforts, that supplies from America and Britain had been of little significance. This in itself was a difficult assertion since the supplies were there for everybody to see, but this fact paved the way for the second step, which was to identify Jugoslavia more and more closely with Russia.

The jeep in which the political commissar drove around the countryside did not come from America but from Russia. Look! It even had the red star painted on its side! Those British battledresses which the Partisans wore were really Russian uniforms! The rifles were not American but German or Italian, captured by the Partisans in some battle far away to the north!

This "welfare" work functioned under some difficulties during the closing stages of the war because every day found American and British transport planes somewhere over Montenegro dropping supplies to the Partisans who were harrying the retreat of the German armies from Greece, and because, for a time, Montenegrins had an opportunity actually to see Allied troops in the presence of that British artillery force, sent in to blast the German army as it retreated. I began to see a reason for the Partisan pressure on Alexander to withdraw that force. Perhaps the Partisan leaders did not want the people to see the soldiers of any of the Western democracies.

When the artillery force was withdrawn, it left behind certain engineering equipment, including some Bailey bridges, with the specification that they should be used to help in the peacetime reconstruction of shattered communications. With nearly every bridge, dike, and culvert in the country destroyed or damaged, the few bridges left by this force were obviously inadequate, but it was left to the Partisans themselves to decide where they should be used until UNRRA began to function and bring in more equipment. Montenegro asked that at least one bridge be allocated for use in that province. The Partisans decided that they should be used elsewhere. But the Montenegrins were not told that this was a Partisan decision; they were told that the Anglo-American military headquarters had refused to give Montenegro a Bailey bridge, and I had many a discussion on the propriety of these tactics with the key Partisan official in Montenegro, Bozo Ljumovic. Before the war, Ljumovic was the Singer Sewing Machine agent in Podgorica and an underground member of the banned Communist Party. A short, powerful man with flowing black hair, looking rather like Tito himself, Ljumovic had blossomed forth during the war as a leading Partisan official. He was now one of the vice-governors in Montenegro, his function being to supervise the activities of the governor, a non-communist Partisan, who, incidentally, was suddenly removed after Ljumovic flew to Belgrade to report that the governor had unfortunately requested UNRRA to send a medical unit to Montenegro in order to establish an orphanage for Montenegrin children—an action that might have resulted in too close a contact between the Montenegrins and the West. After his removal, the medical unit—which had been sent immediately from Italy to the Dalmatian coast—found itself faced with all kinds of formalities; the weeks drew out into months, and the request was finally withdrawn. Ljumovic was later promoted and sent as Jugoslav ambassador to the Russian puppet government in Poland, which Tito was naturally the first to recognize.

From Montenegro I went into Bosnia and Herzegovina. Surprisingly enough, although further formalities had to be followed in order to obtain the necessary travel permits, there were no warnings about collaborators. Perhaps this was because warnings would have been superfluous. For on several occasions I was stopped by Partisan road patrols who warned us that territory ahead was in the hands of the Chetniks and that we might be ambushed. I was with Alfred Farber, the director of the Displaced Persons Division in the UNRRA mission to Jugoslavia. Both of us were anxious to reach Sarajevo that night and it was for this reason, rather than through any disbelief in the Partisans' words, that we decided to go on. Two Partisan officers, to whom we were giving lifts in our jeep, decided there and then to leave us and to go on as soon as the territory had been cleared. The forests were filled with Partisan patrols and there was no doubting the seriousness of their business.

Officially the war was over. The Belgrade radio denied the existence of any opposition within the country, armed or otherwise. The broadcasts, however, were in English for American and British consumption. In its domestic broadcasts, Belgrade radio was significantly quiet about the opposition, although it talked very shrilly about war-profiteers, collaborators, and traitors. It was some time before we learned that this was the way the opposition was always disguised.

As it happened, we were unable to reach Sarajevo that night

as one of the bridges over a gorge outside Jablonica had not yet been repaired and the raft that had been used in its place to ferry men and vehicles over the torrent had been swept away. As we drove back down the valley, racing the twilight towards Mostar, the strange and beautiful town that is half Balkan, half Oriental, we entered a village and noticed a group of women standing in the street. They waved to us to stop, but we took it as another sign of friendship towards America, of which there had been plenty, and were driving by when they tossed branches of evergreen towards the jeep. They were evidently enthusiastic in their tributes of friendship, for some of the branches looked like young trees as they came hurtling into the road. We pulled up about a hundred yards down the road, and they came running after us. Some of them were weeping. One of them, a young girl in her early twenties, spoke to us in English.

"Please," she said, and there was no mistaking the agitation and urgency of her voice. "I want to leave this country. I am a Greek and I do not belong here, but they will not let me go."

At this call to business, Alfred, who had been struggling with a small pine tree in his lap, gave up the attempt and stuck his head through its branches.

"Madame," he said in his best Cleveland accent, "you have come to the right department." While he explained to the girl the forthcoming procedures for returning to their homelands (he devoutly hoped) all displaced persons within Jugoslavia, I watched the other women in the group. The girl, it was explained, was a Greek who had married a Jugoslav. He had been killed in the war four years previously, and these were his family with whom the girl had lived.

They were ordinary Jugoslav peasants, but it appeared they did not like Tito or the Partisans and what he was doing to Jugoslavia. They loved America and Britain, they said repeatedly, and the frantic way in which they murmured the words, then clasped our hands, then kissed the jeep itself, was evidence that their hearts spoke truly. It was all I needed to convince me that the heart of Jugoslavia was still in the same place and pulsing as strongly as ever.

DEALINGS WITH THE JUGOSLAV UNDERGROUND

These, if you like, were first reactions. As evidence it was too flimsy to offer in proof of the charge that Tito and his Partisans were attempting to foist a dictatorship on Jugoslavia. In those early days, the closing stages of the war—for Jugoslavia was one of the countries where the Germans laid down their arms later than elsewhere—everything could be excused on the grounds that the war came first. The mobilization of all menfolk in a town as soon as the town was liberated, the requisitioning of supplies from the wealthy and middle class, the wholesale arrests of people later accused of collaboration, the introduction of an internal passport system for travel within the country, the restriction of newspapers to those published by the Partisans themselves, the ruthless propaganda drive with its public-speaker systems blaring continuously in every town, the adulation of the Red Army—now in the east of the country—the refusal to allow the king to return until a plebiscite had been held *after* the war, all these and a thousand other evidences of *Tito*talitarianism could be excused by the single Partisan slogan: All for the Front, All for Victory.

The war was offered as the excuse for everything by all those apologists for Tito and his hierarchy. And indeed one had to admit that no one who had not himself experienced it could understand the passions and hatreds let loose by four years of guerrilla warfare. Have patience, it was said, and wait until the war is over. Wait until the Partisans feel settled in the saddle, and you will see how they will relax this tight control.

This is a genuine democratic people's movement. "Why, Tito himself told me," said one of these apologists, an Englishman who had known Jugoslavia for twenty years, and who ought to have known better than to believe it, "there will be a restoration of all democratic rights after the war. He said to me, 'Of all people, we communists know that Jugoslavia can never be ruled by force, and that if rule by force is attempted it will create an opposition which will in time destroy the regime.' "

It seems to me that this first-hand report is testimony not only to Tito's insincerity but to his amazing ability to hoodwink all those who came into contact with him. For, in the last analysis, the consideration that induced America and Britain to throw their whole weight behind Tito's movement, as opposed to Mihailovitch and his Chetniks, was the belief that he was not only killing more Germans than Mihailovitch, but that his movement represented a popular surge towards a fuller and freer democracy than Jugoslavia had ever known.

Enough has already been reported in this book to show that propaganda, in the form in which it is recognized by America and Britain, very often has little to do with the ultimate attitudes of the people to whom it is directed, that frequently democratic propaganda fights a hopeless battle against impressions caused by other events and other agencies over which it has no control and with which it has no concern. Many of the decisions that led to these events in Jugoslavia were defended at the time on the grounds that they were in the interests of military expediency, that they would produce the best immediate results.

In most human affairs, especially in military affairs during the war, there is a strong temptation to take a course of action which will save lives at the time, even though it creates long-term problems which may result in the loss of even more lives. After all, it can be argued, the long-term problems may not arise, and, if they do, they will be for other people to solve.

But there are certain laws of human destiny which ordain that the payment must be made—in full; there is no way of avoiding the reckoning.

For twenty years, British diplomacy in Europe was devoted to the task of warding off an issue with the obscene horror of National Socialism. One compromise after another was made in order to maintain peace in Europe on the old-time basis of "balance of power" politics, with the British holding the balance with one hand while directing their empire with the other. Yet it was already apparent that world shrinkage had rendered the "balance of power" policy out of date; it was equally apparent that the comfortable, prosperous British Empire of the late nineteenth century was not only out of date but represented a challenge to other envious nations who had entered late into the age of empire-building. There was no way of avoiding the issue, and by postponing it the British have paid terribly in lives and financial bankruptcy.

The last war was supposedly fought to make the world safe for democracy. By refusing to work for this aim in the peace that followed, World War II was made inevitable. The sacrifices and loss of privileges that would have been exacted of America and Britain to make the world safe for democracy from 1919 onwards would have been minute compared to those that have been exacted by World War II as a result of their failure to do so.

On this basis alone, it is extremely doubtful whether it is better in any problem to take the easy way out, where that way demands a sacrifice or ignoring of the ultimate ethical goal. For the ethics—the ideals, if you will—of the democracies are their strongest weapon among the peoples of the world. To sacrifice them is not only to weaken democracy but to fight with the other man's weapons in a field with which he is much more familiar.

In no country in the world is this more apparent than in

Jugoslavia today, and in no country have America and Britain paid so swiftly for their past mistakes.

After the swift German conquest of the country in 1941, a four-months' night descended, during which time the capability of the Jugoslavs for resistance appeared to the outside world not merely dormant but dead. The efforts of Britain and Russia (by this time in the war and paying bitterly for her past neutrality) were bent to reviving that spirit of resistance.

Then, in August of that year, the British picked up a radio message from the heart of Jugoslavia. It came from a Colonel Mihailovitch and it notified the world that he had taken to the hills and was rallying around him the surviving remnants of the Jugoslav army.

The policy of both the British and the Russians at this stage was to single out an individual leader or an individual movement in order to create a following within the country, a dangerous surrender to that tendency towards hero worship which is such a weakness in most ordinary people. It was noticeably different from the policy of America after Pearl Harbor in favoring no individual guerrilla organization within a country but in stressing, rather, the idea of general resistance to the occupier. As far as the British were concerned, these tactics were pure "sales campaign" propaganda tactics, preference for any one movement being in direct ratio to the number of Germans its members were killing. Whatever quarrels went on among the British about which movement to select, the choice, when it was made, was based upon military rather than political considerations. How often Churchill defended his actions by reiterating that this was not an ideological war—and how mistaken he was, as he himself admitted in 1944!

As the war developed, it became increasingly plain that in one vital respect American and British propaganda towards all occupied countries, Jugoslavia included, differed from that of Russia. The whole purpose of the underground movements, as America and Britain conceived them, was to organize for the time of the Allied invasion so that they could be of maximum use in destroying German communications, sabotaging German supplies, and otherwise diverting German troops from use on the Allied beachheads. Time and again the American and British governments, and sometimes General Eisenhower, broadcast warnings to the underground against being tempted into premature revolts and so risking annihilation before invasion day. An expensive lesson had been learned in Czechoslovakia early in the war, when German *agents provocateurs* had lured the underground movement of the university students into the open and had destroyed it utterly.

For their part, the Russians believed that underground movements were expendable and should be used at once, a pardonable attitude in view of the rate at which they were expending their own resources. They used intimidatory methods in their broadcasts (and they devoted twice as much time as BBC did in their broadcasts to Jugoslavia) emphasizing that those who did not pass over at once to active resistance should be marked as collaborators when victory came. Hard pressed as they were on the battlefronts, the Russians saw no contradiction between their attitude after the German attack, when they called the Germans beasts and murderers, and their attitude during the years of Soviet neutrality, when, for example, they publicly decorated Herr von Ribbentrop with the Order of the Revolution. Indeed, at one time during the German thrust towards Moscow, the Russian radio desperately appealed to all European movements to rise at once and save the capital of world socialism. It is a testimony to the long memory of the underground, as it was organized in those early days, and to the prestige of America and Britain, that the underground leaders followed the guidance of Washington and London rather than the orders of Moscow. When people glibly say today that only the communists in this or that country fought against the invaders from the start, they forget (or perhaps they never knew of them) the vast numbers of people in every country who, consumed though they were by hatred of the occupier, faithfully repressed their emotions and waited on the word of the Western democracies.

In 1941, Britain had quickly sent liaison officers to Mihailovitch in the mountains of Serbia. Her example was followed by America immediately after America entered the war. Supplies of all kinds were dropped to Mihailovitch and his Chetniks, but always with the caution to reserve them for the ultimate day of action.

Other guerrilla bands made their appearance in Jugoslavia shortly after Mihailovitch and his Chetniks. Although showing no central organization, they called themselves Partisans. They were denounced by the British radio as "bandits and murderers," for the simple reason that this was what they had showed themselves to be. At least one British agent, returning to Jugoslavia to make his way to the resistance forces, had been robbed and murdered by one of these bands. Whatever their suspicions may have been at the time, the British did not know that they were denouncing the underground agency of Russia within Jugoslavia—for the communist press did not announce Tito to the world until the end of July, 1942, doubtless because Russia was not satisfied until that date that the Partisan organization had gained its feet.

Mihailovitch had participated in the popular uprising of March, 1941, more than adequate proof that he was a friend of the Western democracies. By raising the standard of rebellion, he also demonstrated that he was a good patriot. However, he had great weaknesses; he shared the general Serbian resentment against the Croats whom it was generally felt, had aided the defeat of Jugoslavia by their passive attitude towards the German invasion. Much as the Croats had suffered under Serbian rule in the years before the war, the Serbs felt that the war itself should have united all members of the Jugoslav nation in a common struggle against the Germans.

The establishment of Croatia as a separate state after the German conquest seemed to the Serbs to be a reward to the Croats for services rendered to the Nazi cause. They were too overwhelmed by the bitterness of their own defeat to realize that this was a deliberate Nazi device to increase the hatred between Serb and Croat—part of the divide-and-rule technique. The wholesale massacre of Serbian residents of Croatia by Croat quisling troops inflamed the hatred, and one of the war aims of the Chetniks became to obtain their revenge against the Croats. Either voluntarily or in order to gain recruits, Mihailovitch pandered to this Serbian chauvinism.

But, be it remarked, he was not alone in those early days in his distrust of the Croats. Such was the blackout of the German occupation that neither America nor Britain was fully sure of what part the Croats had played in the war and to what extent there had been collaboration with the Germans. Their tendency was to suspect that there had been a certain amount of collaboration, and the suspicions at one time even included the powerful Croat Peasants' Party, headed by Dr. Vladko Matchek. In actual fact, neither Matchek nor his followers had collaborated with the Germans; they refused to take any part in the government of the puppet republic set up by the Germans, and on Matchek's orders they settled down to a policy of passive resistance towards both the Germans and their Croatian quisling organizations. It was some time, however, before America and Britain became fully aware of these facts and by that time Mihailovitch and his Chetniks had been isolated as an organization—but for different reasons.

Mihailovitch was a royalist officer. He had taken the oath of allegiance to the young King Peter. Moreover, he was a cabinet minister in Peter's government, whose predecessors had banned the Jugoslav Communist Party. With the hard lesson of previous Russian neutrality in mind, it was not difficult for Mihailovitch to suspect the Jugoslav communists of ulterior motives when they came out openly for resistance in the shape of the Partisan organization.

As they grew in power, he became more and more convinced that the so-called National Liberation Movement was a front for the communists and that its ultimate aim was to seize control of the country.

But at the same time he fell more out of step with the Americans and British—the British especially. For by this time Russia was in the war as an ally. Britain and Russia had signed a twenty years' pact, a natural corollary of which was that neither partner should seek to offend the other. Russia had now openly sponsored the Partisan organization of Tito as being the only true national movement inside Jugoslavia. Both the Americans and British had attached liaison officers to Tito as well as to Mihailovitch. And Tito had not hesitated to follow the orders from Moscow of proceeding at once to active resistance against the Germans.

TITO AND THE PARTISANS

What follows now is not a criticism or belittlement of the heroism of the rank and file of the Partisan soldiery. As far as they were concerned, as far as the vast majority of its members were concerned, the National Liberation Front in its early stages was all that its name implied.

Unlike Mihailovitch, it appealed to all nationalities within the country, to all religious denominations, and to all classes to join in the common fight against the invader. It promised a new and more democratic Jugoslavia after the war. To the most overpopulated country in Southeastern Europe, with the lowest average level of income, with one half of the population illiterate, the movement appeared to be a break with the intransigeant past. Tito promised that victory would usher in a new period of social and economic reform, on which general principle there was more than general agreement. But Tito and his henchmen carefuly avoided a more specific definition of the scope and degree of such measures, and, when questioned, justified their attitude with the reply that this would involve controversy, and controversy might split the popular front. If the present specimen of totalitarianism is what Tito had in mind for Jugoslavia at the time, his reply was indeed true!

But the rapid growth of the Front was due, not so much to its political programs or its ability to rouse the spirit of the Jugoslavs, as to the ruthlessness with which it followed its revolutionary tactics in order to drive the population onto its side.

Mihailovitch had been deterred from his raids on German positions by the indiscriminate massacre of Serbian hostages which followed every raid. The Serbian population of Croatia had already been wiped out in the early stages of the occupation and the shooting of Serbian hostages in Serbia itself at one time reached a peak of five hundred a day. Rightly or wrongly, Mihailovitch felt he must call a halt to his operations or face the ultimate annihilation of the Serbian people.

He was already supported in this attitude by both America and Britain, whose radios were appealing to all undergrounds to lie low until invasion day. It is hard to reconcile this truly humanitarian attitude with the present one of condemning Mihailovitch because he did not fight the enemy enough. He was only anticipating American procedure.*

* The Naples edition of *Stars and Stripes,* the U.S. Army's daily newspaper, published the following story on June 1, 1945: "Manila, May 31— Filipino guerrillas had to be ordered not to kill Japs in order to save entire villages from reprisals," Lt. Colonel Bernard L. Anderson, a 31-year-old U.S. Air Force officer, said today. Anderson escaped from Bataan by crawling through the Jap lines and organized 60,000 Filipino guerrillas on Luzon. "We finally learned that every time we killed a Jap, they went to the nearest

Tito had no such inhibitions. He knew that if his forces attacked a German or Italian supply column, the next twenty-four hours would see an enemy punitive expedition to the vicinity and that every village in the area, together with its inhabitants, would be wiped out. It was not long before the peasants themselves learned this lesson. Whenever Tito wished to recruit in any neighborhood, therefore, all he had to do was to make a raid on enemy occupation garrisons in that neighborhood, thus confronting the inhabitants with the alternative of fleeing to the towns, where their future would depend upon the good will of enemy garrisons, or fleeing to the hills and forests, where they could only subsist by joining the Partisans.

When the Partisan radio boasted that the movement had a membership totalling some 250,000 people, it omitted to mention the tactics by which it had gained the majority of its following. And it is significant that in spite of its boasted strength, the Partisan army never captured a single town of any size in any part of Jugoslavia. With the exception of Belgrade, which was liberated by the Red Army, the large centers of population remained firmly in German hands until the Germans evacuated them in their own good time. Even at the time of the Italian capitulation, when Italian garrisons in the Jugoslav coastal towns were ordered to surrender to the Partisans, the latter were easily expelled by the Germans, who rushed in to take over the territory occupied by their former allies. From then on, until the Germans began to withdraw from Dalmatia, the Partisans never again descended in force to the coast from the mountains behind it. Several thousand Jugoslavs, in danger of German reprisals, had to be evacuated by the British from Dalmatia to the Middle East as a result of the Partisans' inability to retain control of the territory handed over to it by the Italians, and it was some time before the Allies

village and massacred everybody in retaliation," he said. "By early 1943 I had to forbid anybody killing Japs without specific information."

were able to re-establish direct routes into Jugoslavia other than by air or by nightly sneak-visits to isolated parts of the coast.

In the final German offensive against the Partisans in the late spring of 1944, the situation for the latter became so grave that Tito himself had to be rescued and brought out of Jugoslavia to the safety of Allied occupied territory in Italy, until communication had been regained with his scattered forces. Needless to say, Tito has never allowed the Jugoslav people to learn that on one occasion he was forced to flee the country; and strangely enough neither America nor Britain has embarrassed him by mentioning the incident in broadcasts to Jugoslavia.

BRITISH POLICY

If this was the unhappy situation within Jugoslavia, why was it that Britain, followed by America, gradually withdrew support from Mihailovitch and turned instead to Tito?

There was, of course, the desire not to offend Russia by supporting a movement which was waging a civil war with the Partisans. For the British at least, this was an important consideration.

The British themselves began to change their policy towards the Jugoslav underground. They pressed Mihailovitch more and more to take positive action against the Germans. Mihailovitch refused.

By this time Mihailovitch saw in the Partisans a threat to his own authority and a symptom of the social revolt to which he was by training and temperament opposed. The fight against the Partisans appeared to him to be more urgent than the fight against the Germans—which he could rely on the Allies to wage. He was thus relentlessly driven from the attitude of preparation for the Allied invasion to one of passive resistance against the Germans, from which point the deadly slope led towards actual collaboration with the enemy.

No evidence exists that Mihailovitch personally had contacts with the Germans, but there is abundant evidence to prove beyond doubt that many of his local commanders struck up bargains with the Axis in order to obtain weapons with which to fight the Partisans—a course of action which it was in the German interest to encourage to the maximum. By the time the British endeavored to rouse Mihailovitch to active warfare against the Germans, it was too late; his organization was too deeply committed to actual collaboration with the occupier.

But for the British to call him a quisling, as they later did in their official documents, was the height of ingratitude. They themselves had originally encouraged him to remain inactive. They themselves had been hostile to Soviet Russia in the days when Russia was friendly to Germany. The fact that the courses of Britain and Russia later ran parallel in the war against Germany constituted no reason for Mihailovitch to cease regarding the Partisans as a method for the communists to infiltrate into the seats of power. Time has proved him right.

If Mihailovitch had been a greater man, the tragedy would never have occurred. If he had possessed the gift of comprehending the forward urge of the Jugoslav people and of representing it, instead of representing the rancor of one embittered and frustrated section, there would have been no occasion to fight the Partisans—for the Partisans would never have come into being as a united force. The people would have followed Mihailovitch, and the communist core of the Partisan movement would have been exposed for what it was.

As it was, Mihailovitch was an ordinary career soldier, not a leader of people but a man who regarded his conscience as clear if he followed his orthodox duties towards his king.

But if the position of Mihailovitch was destroyed by the

limitations of his military mind, the position of the British in Jugoslavia was equally destroyed by the limitations of the military minds of their liaison officers in the country. It was on their reports that the Churchill government took decisions of policy.

It was early in 1943 when the Free Jugoslavia Radio broadcast an appeal to the British to send representatives to the Partisans. The Free Jugoslavia Radio was important then in making known to the world the activities of the Partisans. It was even more important later on as a mouthpiece of Partisan policy.

Nobody ever explained to the world that the Free Jugoslavia Radio was neither free nor in Jugoslavia, but was a Russian transmitter located in the Soviet Union.

The British Government knew it at the time—as did the American Government, which was one reason why America was considerably more reserved than the British in her attitude towards the Partisans as an independent organization. Knowing the real nature of the Free Jugoslavia Radio, the British asked the U.S.S.R. in April, 1943 to give information and establish common contact with the Partisans. The U.S.S.R. declined the British request, and British liaison officers went in alone the following month. Contact was established and the British press and radio were immediately encouraged to give increasing prominence to news of the Partisans.

There was no doubting the bravery of the Partisans or their capacity to endure great privations. In that respect, they lived up to the reputation that Jugoslavs have earned. But for some reason the British liaison officers felt it their duty to justify co-operation with the Partisans not only on grounds of their fighting ability but on grounds that they constituted a really democratic movement, that is, on grounds which ought to have been beyond their terms of reference.

For this reason, they chose to ignore the tight control held

.193

by the communists of all key functions within the movement, playing up rather the fact that the movement consisted of several political factions. The function of the political commissars was minimized. The fact that wherever a non-communist occupied a leading position there was always a commissar behind him to see that he toed the line, was ignored. Not content with the evidence on which Mihailovitch stood condemned as an inadequate and confused leader, they adopted tactics towards him which showed a marked tinge of those dishonest dialectics which so mislead the world nowadays.

They proclaimed the fact that Tito was so anxious to insure genuine national resistance that on one occasion he had even offered to serve under Mihailovitch, and that Mihailovitch had refused the offer. They played down and minimized the importance of the conditions Tito had proposed to Mihailovitch, conditions that no army commander could accept from a Fifth Column. These were that there should be a joint headquarters, with the Partisans retaining their own separate identity, their own political commissars, their own propaganda directives and propaganda organization, and so on down through the whole list of subsidiary agencies which Tito had created for the indoctrination of the non-communist Partisans.

It was necessary to hide the revolutionary nature of the Partisan movement which had driven Mihailovitch to oppose it—so Mihailovitch was portrayed as having first attacked the Partisans and having adopted what was officially known as a "stab-in-the-back" policy. In an Allied military survey of Mihailovitch and the Chetniks, it was written:

"The uneasy alliance between Chetniks and Partisans continued with interruptions throughout the summer of 1941. The first meeting between Tito and Mihailovitch had taken place in September, 1941, but was without result. A second parley was held in October, 1941. An agreement was then reached for common action against the Germans.

"Clashes between Chetniks and Partisans, however, soon broke out. Each side has subsequently blamed the other for causing a breach of the truce: the Chetniks appear to have been the aggressors on the Partisan garrison at Uzice on the night of 1–2 November, whereas the Partisans may have been to blame for clashes elsewhere, as at Loznica."

The dishonesty of this report can only be understood by analyzing the implication that the Chetniks were the first to break the truce by their attack at Uzice, and that the Partisan attack at Loznica was a retaliation.

But the reverse was the case! On October 20—a few days after Tito had signed the truce with Mihailovitch—the Partisans appeared at the Serbian town of Loznica and demanded that it be handed over to them and, when this was refused, attacked the Chetnik garrison there on three consecutive days, but failed to take the town. Before the end of the month, they attacked a nearby smelting works at Zajaca which had been captured from the Germans by the Chetniks, overpowered the Chetnik guards, and occupied the place. The onus of having broken the truce therefore falls upon the Partisans. The subsequent Chetnik attack on Uzice was a consequence of, and not a prelude to, the attack at Loznica.

By such tactics as these, Mihailovitch was portrayed as a man whose popular following had disappeared, as a man who was being driven to collaborate more and more with the enemy in order to maintain his authority in the countryside. Tito was portrayed as a man who represented the majority of people in Jugoslavia, as the head of a genuinely democratic movement.

Undoubtedly one of the greatest factors in this self-hypnosis was the ability of Tito to persuade those British officers with whom he came in contact. He convinced them that democracy in Jugoslavia had nothing to fear and everything to gain from his movement. He convinced them that Britain herself had no reason to fear his rise to power. He said that he recognized Britain as the dominant Allied Power in the Mediterranean, and therefore as strategically responsible for the war in the Balkans. The statement was cheap at the time for Russia was still far away and still on the defensive. But when the Russians broke through into the Balkans, Tito modified his attitude. Russia was to be responsible for the Balkan land front, but responsibility for coastal warfare was still left to the British.

Notice how careful Tito was not to offend the susceptibilities of the British as a naval power! And notice how, when the time came, he told the British navy to stay away from his shores! Notice the treatment, for example, of the British cruiser in Split. As late as January, 1946, Allied ships were still being sunk by mines that had drifted away from the Dalmatian coast because British minesweepers were forbidden by Tito to enter Jugoslav coastal waters.

Another facet of Tito's hypnotism over the British was his constant assurance that after the war he intended to work for the widest and strongest Balkan federation as protection against foreign interference. This was a policy with which the British themselves were in agreement; they had realized at last that the Balkans, split up into a number of separate and hostile countries, represented a constant temptation for any strong European power wishing to conquer the whole continent. We shall see later how this intention of Tito's, if ever it really was genuine, was altered at the behest of Russia, and transformed into that policy which the British most feared.

AMERICAN POLICY

American policy during this formative period of the new Jugoslavia took no definite line.

There was not the same urgent compulsion, felt by Britain as a European power, to make compromises with principle in order to reach an understanding with Soviet Russia. There was therefore not the same urgency to recognize the Tito movement.

The American observers in Jugoslavia, having this detached attitude, were able to look at Tito and his movement with a more casual eye. What they saw was evidently by no means so convincing as the picture presented by the British officers, for America continued to maintain her contact with Mihailovitch long after the British mission had been withdrawn.

That they finally withdrew their mission is evidence that they, too, eventually regarded the Chetniks as a lost cause. But they never succumbed to the swooning fits of adulation which the British manifested towards the Partisans.

Consequently it is a tragedy that America never developed a foreign policy towards Jugoslavia. For America, far more than Britain, was fitted by her youth and energy to recognize the emotions and ambitions which prompted so many non-communist Jugoslavs to throw in their lot with the Partisan movement. Only America, admired in pre-war Jugoslavia as the greatest democracy in the world, could have captivated these emotions and ambitions, and turned them into channels leading away from the totalitarian system that Tito imposed as soon as he no longer felt dependent upon the material and moral support of the Western democracies.

But America had formulated no policy towards Jugoslavia. In her propaganda, she had withdrawn from the Anglo-American PWB, preferring to postpone her information services until conditions permitted diplomatic relations to be established between the two countries.

Back in New York, however, the American short-wave radio maintained a markedly cautious note towards Tito. Credit for this analysis of the real basis of Tito's power must go to Reuben Markham, the director of OWI's Southeastern Europe section. During his work in the Balkans before the

197

war, Markham had made a reputation among correspondents as being the foremost authority on the Croats. In those years he was more closely in touch with Dr. Vladko Matchek, the leader of the Croat Peasants' Party, than any other American or British correspondent. His misgivings concerning Tito arose when the Partisans began to criticize Matchek, first as a collaborator, then as an outright quisling. Knowing that Matchek was incapable of collaboration with the Germans, Markham's suspicions were aroused and it was not long before he had convinced himself of the utter unscrupulousness of Tito's tactics.

While Matchek refused to give allegiance to Tito, although refraining from assisting the Germans, many other Croats who had actively assisted the Germans were taken into the Partisan fold, purely because their names gave the movement prestige value among other Croats.

Vladimir Nazor, the best-known of Croatian poets, who wrote fervent odes for the fascist press after the conquest of Jugoslavia, was taken into the movement in 1943 and immediately produced a string of poems as rabidly pro-Tito as his earlier stuff had been pro-Pavelitch (Pavelitch was the quisling head of the Croat republic). For these services he was appointed first president of Tito's National Council of Liberation for Croatia.

A Moslem colonel named Suleiman Filipovitch, who had been a commander of the Ustashi, the Croat puppet army which massacred the Serbian population, went over to the Partisans after the Italian armistice and was appointed Acting Minister of Mines and Forests in Tito's Provisional Government. Antun Augustinchitch, the second-best of Croatian sculptors, who created a bust of Pavelitch, the chief Croatian quisling, was made one of the vice-presidents of the National Committee of Liberation a few months after he joined the Partisans in the summer of 1943.

The best-known of Jugoslav sculptors, Ivan Mestrovitch, never gave his support to the Partisans and has so far refused to return to Jugoslavia from Switzerland, in spite of Partisan pressure upon him to do so.

By 1943 Markham was so thoroughly convinced of Tito's devious tactics that he took issue with the British on their suddenly adopted policy of giving all-out and uncritical support to the Partisan movement.

But the British continued to go their way and there began a noticeable divergency between the content and philosophy of British and American broadcasts. That it went no further, that the American radio never took a positive attitude towards events in Jugoslavia, is attributable to the fact that America had not yet developed a foreign policy towards Jugoslavia.

As it was, the Partisans were furious. They were enraged by the neutral attitude maintained towards them by America, they were enraged by the fact that America continued to maintain a mission with Mihailovitch after the British had withdrawn theirs, they were furious at the activities in America of the Jugoslav Government-in-Exile's ambassador, Mr. Fotic, who continued to denounce the Partisans as a threat to the future independence of his country.

But much as the Partisan press and the Free Jugoslavia Radio denounced America to the people of Jugoslavia, they were careful never to show an outward appearance of hostility. It is an attitude they still maintain. For the Jugoslav colony in America is an extensive one. It has a long nose for chauvinism in its former homeland and, if its active hostility were aroused, it might perhaps be capable of rousing America to take an active interest in suppressing Titotalitarianism.

Russia's policy towards the Partisans during the time that they were establishing their position, was not that of all-out support as might have been expected. Perhaps for the reason that America and Britain would be suspicious of Russian interference in Jugoslavia, the Russians deliberately abstained from a direct active interest. With the exception of the Free Jugoslavia Radio, Russia had no direct connection with the Partisans.

Their attitude was rather one of benevolent support, such as they adopted towards EAM in Greece. For two and a half years no Russian missions were sent to Tito in Jugoslavia. Not until Tito formed his temporary government and received the *de facto* recognition of America and Britain by their continued support, did Russia feel it was time to establish a direct connection; the first Soviet Mission accordingly was sent to Jugoslavia in February-March, 1944.

Materially, the Soviet Union sent no supplies to the Partisans, principally, of course, because there were no direct communications between the two countries until the Soviet offensive in the Balkans in 1944.

From the time of the German attack on the Soviet Union, the Russians built up their propaganda towards Jugoslavia. Moscow devoted twice as much time as New York or the British radio to Serbo-Croat broadcasts, but it is interesting that the Belgrade paper *Novo Vreme*, published during the German occupation, reported that it was British and American broadcasts which were mainly responsible for Serbian resistance. "Moscow is responsible to a lesser degree," added the paper, forsaking for a time the official German policy in the Balkans of attributing all resistance to "Communists and bandits."

Despite the absence of material ties between Jugoslavia

and Russia, there was no doubt that the Soviet Union's moral influence was very great, especially among the Partisan leaders. Russian victories were praised and Russian sacrifices in the war were compared favorably with those of America and Britain. Stalin was celebrated in poems as the teacher of Tito, and the Red Army, with its Partisan detachments, as the larger symbol of the Jugoslav National Army of Liberation, as Tito now called the Partisan soldiers.

Undoubtedly one reason for the Russian abstention from any overt connection with the Partisan movement was that the Jugoslav communists had been trained in a hard school and could be trusted on their own. Tito himself had fought in the Red Army during the Russian Revolution; on his return to Jugoslavia after World War I, he had been arrested as an agitator and had spent some years in jail. Most of the other men around Tito had been jailed as communists at one time or another; they had been accustomed to underground work ever since the Jugoslav Communist Party was banned in 1921; time and suffering had tested both their endurance and their loyalty. When I went to Belgrade in 1945 and had an opportunity to observe the Partisan leaders at the actual task of government, there was no doubt who were the real henchmen of Tito and who were the politicians who had been taken into the government for the sake of giving it an all-party appearance. Tito's men, Russia's men, were men of steel. They were beyond all emotion. They had the power at last; for once, the ends had justified the means they used to obtain it. Jugoslavia lay exhausted, far more so than after the German conquest four years previously.

She was exhausted physically because she had endured a war against the Germans and a multiplicity of civil wars: Chetnik against Partisan, Chetnik against Croat Ustashi, Partisan against Ustashi. In the fighting, some villages had been fought over and had changed hands sixteen times. In one province alone nearly half of all the houses and buildings had been destroyed. The railroad system, except for a portion in the northwest which had been surrendered intact with the German defeat, was gapped and useless. In the savagery of German and Italian reprisals, the population had suffered nearly as badly as the Poles. And in addition to the slaughter by the Germans, there had been the massacres of Serbs by the Croat quislings.

She was exhausted mentally and spiritually by the series of civil wars. In spite of the ostentatious national claims of Tito's movement, the minorities were suspicious and fearful of each other, fearful lest the rise of one be followed by the ruthless subjugation of the others. The people were bewildered and helpless because of the wide vagaries of British policy as manifested over the British radio, and because of the apparent disinterestedness of America. Only the Partisan press and radio, by now the only means of public expression, blared out the slogans that pointed to Russia as the only road towards the future.

Into this charnel house of general destruction, official hostility, and public despair, America and Britain came tiptoeing to find out where they stood.

V. JUGOSLAVIA: PART TWO

JUGOSLAVIA: PART TWO

PERHAPS the greatest lesson of the war, and one not yet thoroughly digested by those most concerned, is that democracy is on trial for its life and that the outcome is by no means certain.

I know that this statement has been made before and that there is a tendency to point complacently to past crises as proof that democracy has a tough fiber which enables it to endure all trials and to emerge triumphant. This very complacency is in itself a menace, for it breeds a feeling of lassitude, a general trend to "Let George do it," whether George be our elected leaders, or some other nation or group of nations, or merely the man next door. It is a menace because the very crisis in which democracy finds itself points the way to the only possible cure —democracy can endure as a system only if every individual person makes it his or her personal business to see that democracy functions properly for all.

Belgrade at the end of World War II presented a perfect specimen, in capsule form, of a democracy whose death agonies were brought on by this abnegation of personal responsibility.

It was a city on which three and a half years of German occupation had left a deep and ineradicable trace. The physical destruction was not great. Compared with the London Blitz, the bombing of Belgrade by the Luftwaffe in April, 1941, had done little damage. Indeed, by far the worst damage had been caused by the U.S. Air Force in its raid of Easter, 1944, when some six thousand people had been killed as a result of inaccurate bombing through overcast. But even after this raid, which had been directed against the bridges over the Danube and the Sava, and not against the city itself, Belgrade looked a great deal tidier than any city on, say, the Italian front.

The real damage to Belgrade was the destruction of the political and economic way of life of its inhabitants.

Commercial life had been reduced to an abject state. Of nearly eleven thousand shops registered before the war, only some six thousand remained in existence on the city's liberation by the Red Army. The rest had been formally wound up during the occupation. Of the three hundred and twenty-seven factories in the Belgrade area before the war, only one hundred and eighty-eight existed after the liberation, due mainly to the repressive economic policy of the Germans. Of the small businesses, the reduction was from sixty-eight hundred to forty-two hundred.

The difficult economic conditions of the German occupation hit chiefly at the smaller man, that is, the small shopkeeper and craftsman. With his business wiped out, the small man was forced into the ranks of the proletariat. The better capitalized businesses were able to ride out the occupation by resorting to black-market operations or to discreet collaboration.

Consequently Belgrade on its liberation had been divided into the two extremes of economic life, the very rich and the very poor, each with its own jealousies and suspicions of the other.

Superimposed on these economic hostilities were political fears and prejudices formed during the occupation. For three and a half years, the people of Belgrade had nursed their hatred, and their ambitions to see Serbia once more the dominant state in Jugoslavia. The Germans had seen to it that their hatred was fed with stories of Tito and the Communist Danger, and even the Partisans had to admit that their organization had never succeeded in penetrating deeply into Belgrade during the occupation.

So when Belgrade was liberated, the greater part of its population looked upon the liberation as the replacement of one kind of occupation by another, and set themselves to the task of enduring it until they were really liberated by the armies of America and Britain. There were even coffee-house rumors at one time that American and British troops were marching on Belgrade from Dalmatia in order to expel the Partisans.

In general the population adopted an attitude of non-cooperation towards the Partisans. The people grumbled continually, gossiped, and exchanged rumors—but did nothing to carry their opposition into the sphere of activity.

The Partisans did little to appease the public hostility. True, their acting Minister for Trade and Industry, Andrej Hebrang, assured Belgrade businessmen that there would be a special sphere in which private enterprise would have full liberty of action within the framework of a general economic plan. But in the very person of Hebrang, active and able as he is, the Partisans had chosen an uncompromising communist, an action that could hardly be expected to reassure private industry and business.

They also made difficulties by removing competent and experienced men from positions they held during the occupation, without detailed investigation of their behavior. And in general these positions were awarded to Partisans as rewards for wartime services rather than on a basis of competence. For example, the despatches of Allied correspondents in Belgrade were held up because the Censor's Department could not find an English-language censor who possessed both a good knowledge of English and a certificate of four years' service in the Partisan organization. And, as another example, one of the men in charge of the rehabilitation of Jugoslavia's mining industry was a Partisan veteran whose only connection with mining was that he had learned during the war how to use explosives in the demolition of roads, railroads, and bridges.

It is significant that even among the Partisans there was much headshaking over this favoritism and much talk about the Jajce Clique as the group which centered round the wartime headquarters of the Partisans at Jajce was known. It was said that members of the Jajce Clique were securing for themselves all the best jobs and obtaining real control of the state. At that early stage of post-war activity, no one could take this dissatisfaction as a sign that the Partisan movement was splitting up. It was a sign, however, that Tito's troubles were still to come. With the tangible support of America and Britain and the moral support of Russia, it had been comparatively easy for him to hold together a national movement in wartime, postponing all political and social issues until after the war. But his great problem would be the demobilization of the Partisan army and the general rehabilitation of the country.

These problems were still ahead. Meanwhile the vast majority of the Partisans remained under military control.

But the citizens of Belgrade were civilians, and the only hope for a democratic way of life lay in the manner in which they accepted inevitable social changes, the extent to which they themselves participated in creating a new way of life by establishing political parties to temper the proposals of the new extremists.

Instead, they damned the whole Partisan movement as being communist; they failed to realize that it was an amorphous group welded together in war by the revolutionary tactics of the communists, but that complete communist control hung in the balance and could be abolished by the rise of a genuine democratic movement.

It could be said, of course, that the communists would have prevented the rise of such a movement, and there is plenty of evidence that truly democratic Jugoslavs were damned as "collaborators" whenever they ventured to take a positive attitude against the extremist control of the Partisan movement. The strict curfew system in Belgrade, preventing the movement of anyone without a pass after 10 P.M., the patrolling of the streets by squads of Partisan guards armed with machine guns, the wholesale arrests of people, and the encouragement of rumors to the effect that all those seen with Americans and British were likely to disappear within twenty-four hours—all these were symptoms of an attempt to isolate and outflank whatever opposition existed, and to prevent it from becoming organized. Any opposition to Tito's totalitarian wing within the Partisan movement—an opposition whose freedom Tito professed to guarantee, but whose rise he was determined to prevent—required heroes and martyrs not only for its leaders but for its whole rank and file. It was a situation which called for a spontaneous and irresistible surge on the part of the people in much the same spirit as they had shown in the rebellion against the quisling government in 1941.

But the spirit was not there. The annihilistic tactics of the German occupation authorities, the terrible physical and spiritual destruction, the inexplicable vagaries of American and British policy as manifested through their attitudes towards Mihailovitch and Tito, had destroyed its resilience. The people lived in memories of the past, but they themselves were not the same as in the past. Their politics were the politics of 1941, but lacked the flaming passion that could carry them into action. They were unsure and unafraid. They gossiped and grumbled, whispering over the coffee-house tables and in the restaurants, hushing their voices even in the security of their own homes. The spark that would have brought them bursting out of their doors into the streets in one mad, impassioned effort to retrieve freedom or die . . . that spark was dead.

They developed an émigré mentality, living in a spirit of nostalgia and discontent, working up a series of imaginary situations in which America and Britain would intervene to restore their former way of life.

By doing nothing, by refusing to collaborate with the Partisans and yet refusing to create an active opposition, the people handed over to the communists the final assurance of complete power.

In May, 1945, the Partisan Provisional Government introduced a new national currency to replace the eight different currencies that were in circulation. By closing their shops rather than accept the new currency, the tradesmen gave the communists the excuse they wanted to go back on their pledge to reserve a sphere for private enterprise. The shops were confiscated and their former owners imprisoned.

Hoarders of food, owners of factories, and wealthy owners of villas in the fashionable suburbs of Belgrade, the peasants who refused to bring their food to market, the former civil servants who refused to adapt themselves to new conditions—all of them were driven backward step by step. Instead of resisting immediately and voicing their opposition, they gave in at the initial stage of the campaign. They knew—far better than those British liaison officers who had written that this was a democratic movement—that this was a movement to create conditions in which a revolution could take place.

Tito and the other Jugoslav communists had obviously studied their history of the Russian revolution. They set out deliberately to abolish all private wealth, all private ownership of means of production. The new currency was a revolutionary device. It set a rate of ten old dinars for one new dinar; no one was allowed to exchange more than a certain amount, the same in all cases; all money over this amount was confiscated by the state, which simply took the money and issued "bonds" in return. After a certain date the old currency was declared illegal, thus wiping out the funds of those who had sought to evade confiscation by hoarding their old currency.

The requisitioning of privately held food supplies was another revolutionary device. So was the requisitioning of housing space from the pre-war upper and middle classes. All of it was carried on under the excuse of emergency conditions— which really existed. But no one believed for a moment that compensation would be made after the emergency was over. Neither Tito nor any of his henchmen even bothered to make any such promises.

SIGNS OF UNREST

The bright spark of resistance to revolution was lacking. It was hard to see how the embers could be revived by the people themselves. True, here and there, some people had taken to the woods, determined to fight to the last rather than surrender, and at times their activities were embarrassing to Tito and his henchmen. And the resisters were not merely Chetniks or the quisling Ustachi troops; among these rebels were bands of former civilians, principally Roman Catholics who refused to accept the suppression of the Church's role in Jugoslavia. They called themselves "The Crusaders."

By the end of 1945, the Jugoslav Government was compelled to abandon temporarily its internal propaganda line that no unrest existed within the country. As usual on such occasions, Tito personally acted as spokesman. Waiting until after the "elections" in November had confirmed his government in office, Tito gave a press conference at which he admitted the existence of resistance movements including the Crusaders. He denied at the time that the latter was any sort of a religious movement, contending that it consisted of those Ustachi who fled into the forests after the end of the war. According to Tito, the Crusaders operated in groups of from five to ten men and singled out high executives of the Partisan movement for their attacks. Evidently they had had some success, for Tito showed considerable annoyance at their activities, calling them common bandits and criminals. "Our military authorities will have to see to it that our countryside is cleared of these bandits in the winter," he said. "In the snow it will be easier to track them down."

Before the end of the year, when the snow lay deep in the hills of Bosnia, some of the Crusaders were tracked down and brought to trial. In strange contrast to Tito's denial that the movement had any religious character, the prisoners were all Roman Catholic priests.

But these anti-Tito guerrilla groups have little chance of success. Those that remain are isolated, having in common only a hatred of Tito and his regime. Unless their movement spreads from the hills and forests into the towns and succeeds in linking up the people in a general feeling that national opposition to Tito really exists, their ultimate annihilation is unavoidable, and draws nearer with every month that enables the Partisan extremists to turn their attention away from the primary task of the consolidation of their power.

The people in the towns were cut off from each other. It is still forbidden to a Jugoslav to travel in his own country. A citizen of Belgrade may not go to Zagreb, or vice versa. There exists, therefore, no way of breaking down the fears and suspicions which were born during the occupation. A native of the Dalmatian town of Split hates Tito just as much as the citizen of Belgrade hates Tito. But the townsman of Split is in all probability a Croat, and as a Croat he has his reservations about taking part in any revolution against Tito which may put the Serbs back into power and thus enable the Serbs to take their revenge on the Croats for the massacre of

Serbs in 1941. The citizen of Belgrade is a Serb, and as a
Serb he has his own fears about linking up with the Croats in
a revolution against Tito.

Among the most Hitleresque of Tito's tactics is the manner in which he uses these fears and hatreds to keep the people divided and to perpetuate his own power.

Just after the end of the war, I spent an evening with some
Croatian friends in their home in Split. There was a certain
wistfulness about the celebration and it was pathetic to notice
how they had brought out their own special rations of food
in an effort to make believe that the war and all its suffering
was really over for all of us—for them, as well as for us. My
host brought out his guitar (and no one need fear that this is
a clue for Tito's secret police, for nearly every middle-class
Dalmatian has his own guitar) and we sang the old Dalmatian
songs, from which the Partisans borrowed so many of their
tunes.

Inevitably, of course, one of those present broke down and
asked the question which had come to be asked of us more
frequently wherever we went. "How long will this go on?
How long shall we be asked to suffer under this regime?"

There was nothing to say, except to repeat that America
could not be expected to intervene, and to forestall any embarrassing questions about American interest in the well-being
of other democracies by emphasizing the truth, common to
the people of all other countries, that the future of democracy
in Jugoslavia lay in the hands of the Jugoslavs themselves.

One of the curious effects of the occupation was that it left
these people with the feeling that relatively nearby towns were
in another world and that no two sets of conditions were the
same. They asked searching questions about conditions elsewhere in the country.

"Look," I said finally on this occasion. "If you feel that no
one else but you is suffering in this way, you surely have no

213

ethical right to be discontented. But if you feel that conditions here are intolerable and that the same conditions apply everywhere, then you must realize that in every district where those conditions exist people are talking as you are talking."

"Ah yes," said somebody. "The Serbs probably feel as we do towards Tito . . . but we know what they would do to us if ever they got power into their own hands."

In Belgrade two months later, I went with some American and British friends to the home of a Serbian family. The fiancé of the daughter was a Partisan and obviously not by any means in sympathy with the extremist faction at the head of affairs, though he appeared ill at ease when the daughter spoke bitterly of some of the lengths to which the extremists had gone in their efforts to wipe out the upper and middle classes.

"We thought they came as liberators," said the girl. "They talked about freedom and democracy, and they kept promising us free elections as soon as the war was over. But they behaved like a conquering army in a conquered state.

"They went into houses and looted worse than the Germans. One night four of them came into this house. They had machine guns and they peered suspiciously into all the rooms and all the cupboards as though we had collaborators hidden away. When they were satisfied that we had no strangers in the house, they said they had decided to stay. They took three rooms and we had to move into the kitchen and one bedroom. They stayed four months. They paid nothing for their keep, and gave us a requisition slip for the rooms. When they left, they took most of our crockery and some of mother's silver ornaments.

"If you go to the Military Commander of Belgrade to make a complaint, you are asking for trouble. First they say that you must be mistaken as the Partisan army never steals. And then if you persist, they act as though you were a collaborator and ask all kinds of questions about your background as though you, and not they, were the thieves."

And then there followed the usual outburst about the people's disillusionment in the Partisan movement and questions about when the totalitarian regime would end.

"You do not know how we Serbs have suffered," said the girl, almost wringing her hands in an attempt to convey to us who had not been there what the war had done to her country. "You do not know how the Germans took their revenge on us for the revolt in 1941 and what it was like to endure their oppression.

"You blame Mihailovitch now for having collaborated, but it was you who told him to wait and not to attack. And Mihailovitch is a Serbian priest. He did not want to see the Serbian nation wiped out. That is why he stopped fighting the Germans—because he knew that for every German he killed the Germans shot a hundred Serbian hostages.

"The Croats did not suffer so much. They were protected because they were made into a separate state and they had Croats to rule them. They were quislings, but they were Croats and they took care of their own. But the Serbs in Croatia suffered terribly, and it will be a long, long time before we Serbs can forget."

The girl frankly proclaimed that she was a royalist.

"Nicki, here," she said, pointing to her fiancé. "He is a royalist too. He does not say so now because he is wearing the Partisan uniform. But he is a Serb and if we could vote freely for our King, Nicki would vote in favor of his return."

One of my colleagues was unable to reconcile this idea of kingship with democracy as he conceived it.

"You do not understand," said the girl. "We know that King Peter has his faults. We know he may be weak in some respects. But he is ours; he is a Serb, and we are strange enough to want a Serb for our ruler. This man Tito is not of us. Who is he? No one knows who he is or where he comes from. They say he is a Croat, but he does not speak Serbo-Croatian either like a Serb or like a Croat. We listen to him on the radio and we ask ourselves, 'What is this man? Where does he come from? He does not speak our language like one of us.' "

WHO IS TITO?

On five different occasions, in different parts of the country, I have heard people raise queries about Tito's antecedents. They were people antagonistic towards the government and could not therefore be judged to be above attempts to slander Tito personally. Nevertheless, it was curious to hear such widespread remarks about Tito's origin, especially since communications inside the country were rigorously controlled by the Partisans.

I know as little about Tito as any other Allied official who has been to Jugoslavia during and since the war. The continual outpouring of praise for Tito, blared forth by the controlled press and radio, give nothing of Tito's background. The attempt is to build him up as a mysterious redeemer who appeared from nowhere to rescue the country in the hour of its need. The techniques of the build-up are identical with the techniques of the Nazi propaganda machine towards Hitler —even to the studied effect of slogans to be shouted by the official claque. At any mass demonstration, the word Tito— shouted in two syllables, "Ti-to! Ti-to! Ti-to!"—has exactly the same rhythm and resonance as "Sieg Heil! Sieg Heil! Sieg Heil!" at the Nazi demonstrations, or "Du-ce! Du-ce! Du-ce!" in Fascist Italy.

A Partisan choral recitation, quoted by Major Temple H. Fielding, who was out on an American military mission to Tito, runs as follows:

"He was born of an angry father and the people.
. . . You ask, who is Tito?
Write, my darling machine gun. Write Tito.
Tito is the army, earth, and river."

This mystical balderdash is typical of the Partisan attempts to put across a man who is obviously not yet accepted by the people as being completely one of themselves.

To attempt an appraisal of the man at this stage of his career is an impossibility. Too little is known about him. Nevertheless, the fact remains that Tito is the undisputed head of Jugoslavia. As dictator of his country, he must assume responsibility for the policy of his government in its attempts to isolate Jugoslavia from all spiritual or physical contact with America and Britain and to incorporate it, against its wishes, in the strategic, political, and economic sphere of Russia.

Tito's real name is Givenas Josip Broz. The British account, which is the most complete, says he was born of Croat peasant stock on May 25, 1892, in a village in the Croatian Zagorje, the hill district north of Zagreb, capital of Croatia. In the Zagorje the nickname of Tito is not uncommon. He was conscripted into the Austro-Hungarian Army during World War I, but went over to the Russians in the Galician campaign of 1915. After the Revolution he joined the Red Army, and fought through the Russian Civil War where he acquired his first experience of guerrilla warfare.

In 1923, the British account goes on, Tito returned to Croatia and began to earn his living as a metal worker in different parts of the country. He became a leader of the metal-workers' trade union and engaged actively in political work. This led to his imprisonment for some years in the Mitrovica jail, notorious as the place of incarceration for Jugoslav communists. He used the time to study and continue his education. On his release, Tito resumed his political activities and became leader of the underground communist movement.

Between 1929 and 1939 he paid a number of secret visits to Soviet Russia and met a number of Soviet leaders, who came to regard him as an able and far-sighted man. (The British account does not explain how he was enabled to visit Soviet Russia, whose regime the Jugoslav government did not recognize until 1939. Nor does it point out that if he did go to Russia he must have travelled via the Russian underground in prewar Europe. Nor does it state which Russian leaders Tito visited.)

Tito took no part in the fighting during the Spanish Civil War, contrary to a popular rumor about him, but did organize the secret channels by which volunteers from the Balkans reached Spain.

At the time of the German invasion of Jugoslavia, according to the British information, Tito was living in the Croatian capitol of Zagreb under the assumed name of Josip Tomanek, claiming to be a Czech engineer. (How he could speak Czech in such a way as to deceive the Jugoslav authorities is not explained, but it is a sign that Tito's Serbo-Croatian, supposedly his native language, was not as perfect as might have been expected.) He succeeded in escaping from Croatia after its occupation and in making his way to Serbia. His wife, however, was arrested and interned in the Ustashi concentration camp of Jasenovac, but was later released without her identity being discovered.

On arriving in Serbia, Tito set about organizing the armed uprising, and from that time he personally directed the Partisan movement and became its recognized leader. According to the British, he speaks fluent Russian and good German, and also reads English and French.

Major Temple Fielding, who has written by far the best American account of Tito to date, is more outspoken than the

British.* According to Major Fielding, Tito is not merely a Jugoslav Communist; he is also a Russian agent, who was trained at a super-secret school in Moscow. He married a Russian girl and his son was born in Russia. Major Fielding concurs with the British that Tito was born in the Zagorje, but states his father was a Slovene blacksmith and his mother a Croat peasant, both of whom were illiterate.

According to Major Fielding, Tito possesses a devastating personal charm which never fails to bewitch the man he seeks to convince. This fact, in itself, more than explains the fervency with which the British officers who met Tito advocated his cause to the British Government. He led them into a personal conviction that he was a democrat.

While in Belgrade shortly after the war ended, I discussed Tito with Marcel Fodor, then correspondent for the *Chicago Sun*. Fodor, one of the most experienced of foreign correspondents in the Balkans, noses after facts about its personalities as a bear goes after honey. Fodor told me he had been informed by Tito personally that he had been born not in Croatia but at the watering spa of Rogarska Slatina, in Slovenia, the most northerly province of Jugoslavia.

Fodor spoke in German to Tito and was surprised at the fact that Tito spoke it perfectly with an Austrian accent. "His Viennese dialect was perfect," said Fodor. "Tito explained it by saying that he had studied for years at the University of Vienna."

Another British account places Tito's birthplace in the village of Klanjec in the Zagorje, but gives his birth date as May 25, 1893. His wife, it said, is not a Russian but a Slovene member of the Communist Party whom he met in Moscow. Although he returned to Jugoslavia as an underground worker

* See "Tito: A Portrait from Life," by Major Temple H. Fielding, *Harper's Magazine*, October, 1945.

for Russia in 1923, he did not join the Communist Party of Jugoslavia until 1927.

So far therefore, we have three different birthplaces for Tito—one as reported by American and British officers who worked with him in the war, one given by Tito himself, and a third British story.

The Russians, however, who are probably the best-informed on Tito's antecedents, give yet another. On November 23, 1945, Moscow radio in a broadcast to Latin America gave a glowing account of the Jugoslav elections and said:

"At night the report arrived from Zagreb that the entire population of the Croatian village of Kumirovac—Marshal Tito's birthplace—came to the polls and the entire electorate voted for the People's Front candidates."

Of course, it is unimportant where Tito was born, unless he was born outside Jugoslavia, which would explain the official reluctance to discuss his background. (Even so, he would not be the only dictator to have been born outside the country he controls. Hitler was an Austrian. Stalin, properly speaking, is not a Russian but a Georgian. Kemal Ataturk was not a Turk but an Albanian.)

But it *is* important that there are large gaps in Tito's life about which official accounts are silent and which can only be explained by the fact that Tito was an active agent for Russia—not merely a communist working in behalf of an internal communist system (for he is not on the records of the Communist International in the Balkans) but the paid agent of a foreign power.

As ruler of Jugoslavia, he now lives extremely well. His home is the former royal palace in the suburb of Dedinje overlooking Belgrade. His banquets compare favorably with state banquets in any other country, and, considering the parlous state in which Jugoslavia finds itself today, are disgusting in their magnificence. His ardent followers explain this fact by saying that the Jugoslavs are a primitive people and require their rulers to be ostentatious—thus demonstrating the cynicism with which they exercised power and flouting their public statements that Tito is one with the people. Statements that are also expressively contradicted by the fact that whenever Tito leaves the palace grounds to attend a celebration, Partisan guards armed with machine guns are posted every twenty yards on each side of his route; and whenever the celebration is held in the open air the streets on every side are blocked off for twenty yards.

Captivating though he may be in private conversation, he is not a good public speaker. He lacks the power of a Hitler to induce his native listeners into a state of hypnotism. He tends to strut, but he has not the power of Mussolini to compel the crowd's admiration for his flamboyance. He lacks the witticisms of a Goebbels. The psychological build-up to a Tito speech might have been copied word for word from the textbooks of Nazi or Fascist propagandists, but the voice of the Leader adopts none of the tricks of oratory; it is almost dry and matter-of-fact. His followers say this is a virtue, claiming it as a sign that Tito rejects the tricks of a demagogue. Their acts, however, belie their words, as do Tito's.

OWI: DIRECTIVES AND DIFFICULTIES

Just how far the democracies were out of touch with the trend of events and of attitudes in Jugoslavia can be seen by the methods and channels adopted by American propaganda at the crucial time when Tito was consolidating his power not only as war leader but also as post-war leader of Jugoslavia. British propaganda differed from American only in the fact that the British had earlier capitulated to the Tito movement and had actually beguiled themselves for a time into believing that Tito might be good for Jugoslavia—and good for the general scheme of things in the new post-war world of power politics.

American policy directives for propaganda to Jugoslavia by OWI were purposely vague and restrained. They fell into four main headings:

First, America should be presented as primarily interested in winning the war and, in devoting all efforts to that end, postponing other issues until after the war was won.

Second, America should be presented as intending to obtain the best possible peace settlement for all.

Third, America should be presented as interested in preserving and promoting lasting peace.

Fourth, America should be presented to the best advantage for accomplishing the first three objectives.

Now there was confused thinking in these four points alone. For, surely, point four was not an end but the means—not the why but the how. But to have accepted this interpretation would have committed OWI to an impossible task; on every issue of international affairs it would have committed OWI, on behalf of America, to explaining how each issue could be solved. And this OWI could not do because it had no authority to do so. The State Department could not sanction such a course because it, in turn, had no authority from Congress to commit America to any course of intervention. Congress, representing the American people, had a phobia against any course of action leading to the Frankenstein of overseas commitments.

Next, the directives were based on two incompatible assumptions. The first was that there would be a return to normalcy after the war—at home and abroad. The second was that the policy directives could not be too dogmatic since it was necessary to wait and see how the break with the old regime in Jugoslavia took shape—in other words, there might not be a return to normalcy after all. In actual fact, the Jugoslav directives of OWI were based on the directives for work towards Poland, which were kept short for reasons of state. Thus, the ultimate control of Jugoslavia by Russia was recognized as being as inevitable as the ultimate Russian control of Poland.

No criticism can be made against OWI for this apparent self-emasculation of its policy. OWI was an agency of the administration and represented a state of mind. A state of mind which recognized that the time had not yet arrived when the American people was willing to accept foreign "entanglements" and which had accordingly abandoned ethics in favor of power politics.

It is not even a criticism of America as opposed to Russia or Britain. The Russians had never abandoned power politics, and the British were not slow in joining the game.

It was a game that quickly stripped the Atlantic Charter of all its values, a fact which the British Government realized more than twelve months before the war ended in ordering its propaganda agency to make no further reference to the Charter and to concentrate on the Four Freedoms as a slogan.

In view of the American withdrawal from the Anglo-American PWB in so far as it affected work towards the Balkans, OWI was prevented from any close-range work within Jugoslavia before the American diplomatic mission to that country had been established. Still, this gave no advantage to the British; the entrance of all liaison officers into Jugoslavia was closely supervised by the Partisan high command and was only allowed on strict conditions—that the officer must confine himself to liaison work with the Partisan officers, must not travel more than three miles from his local headquarters, and must have no contact with the civilian population!

After Pearl Harbor, The Voice of America program of the OWI was broadcast to Jugoslavia in Serbo-Croatian by seven transmitters in the United States. As these broadcasts went out by short wave, the program was also relayed in the long-wave band by the British radio and by the captured transmitters in Bari. In addition, the Bari office of the OWI originated its own radio programs to Jugoslavia. With the end of the war, the British radio ceased to relay OWI broadcasts to Jugoslavia.

American leaflets dropped over Jugoslavia during the war were mainly addressed to German troops and were designed to induce the Germans to surrender rather than to inculcate an understanding of Americans among the Jugoslavs.

America, soon after beginning to cooperate with Tito's forces, became more cautious in her air operations over Jugoslavia when it became known that in his directions on bombing targets Tito was including areas in which Chetnik troops of Mihailovitch were operating. Despite the fact that America had abandoned Mihailovitch in favor of Tito, there was no wish to involve the AAF in the civil war now raging in Jugoslavia.

Yet America had several advantages in her propaganda to Jugoslavia. First, there was the large Jugoslav colony in the United States; although the majority of them had been living in America for many years and were out of touch with current trends of thought in their native land, their influence in Jugoslavia was strong.

Then there was the fact that five out of ten people in Jugoslavia either had relatives in the United States or had worked in the United States at some period of their lives. In Montenegro, for example, it is impossible to go into the smallest village without having some grizzled peasant walk up to you and start talking knowingly about copper mining in Montana or silver mining in Arizona.

For a generation before the war, thousands of Jugoslavs annually came to work in America, most of them in mining of one kind or another, and returned to their native land, after making a few thousand dollars, to live in retirement.

All this was in sharp contrast to British or French commercial relations with Jugoslavia. Private financiers in both these countries possessed large mining concessions in Jugoslavia and, whatever their working conditions may have been, both Britain and France possessed a reputation for exploiting Jugoslavia for what it was worth.

There was more than ample evidence that American popularity was great in Jugoslavia. The revolt of March, 1941, had demonstrated America's ability to swing Jugoslavia on to the side of the British. And when America entered the war scores of American airmen shot down over Jugoslavia were hidden by both Partisans and Chetniks until they could be smuggled out to Italy.

As in Greece, the people demonstrated not merely with their lips but by risking their lives that they were devotees of America. Pro-American (and pro-British) feeling ran highest among the Serbs, who constituted nearly fifty per cent of the population, and who remembered that after World War I neither America nor Britain had forgotten their debt to Serbia, sending in extensive relief units to aid the shattered country. They had every reason to expect that the peace following World War II would bring the same practical assistance.

Nay, even more! Both America and Britain preached unceasingly that the world had shrunk, that there must be a greater communion between nations and a greater willingness to share international burdens. To a people accustomed to a primitive way of life, driven by economic poverty in their own land to seek a better way of life elsewhere, the Four Freedoms were a tangible promise that after World War II they would not only have a greater supply of the goods of life in their own countries but would be free to roam wherever they desired to seek their living. For a Jugoslav, the Freedom to Travel meant not only freedom to leave his own country without the restrictions of exit permits, but also the freedom to enter the country to which he wishes to travel.

But specific elaboration of this freedom was omitted from Allied propaganda. The American Way of Life was portrayed in all its detail as the best way of life in the world, and among the Jugoslavs there were few who would disagree with the contention. But it was portrayed as something to be admired from afar, a tantalizing vision of loveliness denied to the spectator. There was no indication that America wished to share her bounty with the world—quite the reverse, in fact.

The different techniques by which American propaganda sought to implement the policy directives laid down for OWI in most cases avoided any indication that there was to be One World after the war.

When OWI established its Jugoslav headquarters in Belgrade after the liberation of the city, it set itself five main lines of operations. They are listed here:

To explain America's sincere interest and willingness to share our obligations in a peaceful world.

To convince others that America is not pursuing imperialistic aims and is *disinterested in the purely domestic affairs of other nations.*

To develop appreciation and good will for America and Americans.

To facilitate contacts and cultural exchanges between Americans and the Jugoslavs.

To make available knowledge about our scientific, technical, professional, and cultural achievements since the beginning of the war.

The last point had naturally been developed before the discovery of the atom bomb was made known, and therefore before Anglo-American-Canadian reluctance to share it with other nations, without tangible evidence of good will, un-covered the nakedness of post-war power politics. What is amazing is that the stage should already have been set for power politics at Tehran, and then that America and Britain should proceed with their propaganda as though power politics could never exist again.

For on the fourth point, of facilitating contacts between Americans and Jugoslavs, OWI quickly found itself in an unexpected situation. Tito did not want the Jugoslavs to mingle with either Americans or British.

POLICE TACTICS IN JUGOSLAVIA

If it were not for the fact that Tito's terrorism is being constantly denied it would not be necessary to amplify this fact. There is not one American (or Briton) who entered Jugoslavia who did not have personal experience of the campaign to isolate the Jugoslav people from the Western democracies.

I have already mentioned the little-known fact that the liaison officers who entered the country did so on condition that they never travel more than three miles outside their area. What is even less known is that after they had been stationed in one district long enough to become acquainted with it, they were regarded with suspicion by the Partisan commissars who were responsible for insuring the requisite indoctrination of their neighborhoods, and attempts were made to have them replaced.

Ordinarily, a simple request from the Partisans to the Allied headquarters in Italy would have been sufficient. But it was not enough merely to secure their removal; for they might carry with them stories which the Partisans did not wish to have believed just then in America or Britain. It was therefore necessary to discredit their stories in advance. In requesting the removal of any American or British officer who had become embarrassingly familiar with Tito's tactics, the Partisans consequently rigged up a series of charges against him in order to make his subsequent complaints appear malevolent and biased. This officer was accused of black-market operations; that one of conspiring against the Partisans with Roman Catholic reactionary leaders; another of having made advances to girls in the Partisan movement.* In yet another case, presumably in lack of any other excuse at the time, a liaison officer who voluntarily requested his own withdrawal was accused of having been unable to withstand the constant strain of guerilla warfare and so having suffered a nervous breakdown.

Occasionally the commissars blundered, and sufficient evidence was accumulated to warrant the Allied headquarters in Italy making complaints against them and, in some cases, insisting on their removal. They were removed—but only from that particular district, invariably turning up somewhere else subsequently, even more anti-Allied in their activities.

Americans of Jugoslav origin were not welcomed because they could more easily familiarize themselves with the countryside and its inhabitants, and unless they showed themselves to be blindly pro-Tito, they were quickly frozen out. At least five Jugoslav-Americans of my own acquaintance reported that their Jugoslav friends had been warned by Tito's secret police to keep clear of them. In all five cases, the men are now back in the United States.

In Belgrade, the largest concentration of anti-Partisan senti-

* After the end of the war, the Jugoslav secret police organized sex as a means of obtaining information for its dossiers, especially where Americans or British were concerned. Dance halls and "night clubs" (in quotes because of the early curfew hours) were closed for two weeks. When they reopened, all their former dancing partners had disappeared and had been replaced by girls whose inquisitiveness and persistence left no doubts as to who their real employers were. Of course, the use of women agents by secret police societies is neither new nor specifically Jugoslavian, although the Jugoslav secret police may have been naive enough to believe so.

ment and of pro-American and pro-British sentiment, the campaign to isolate the population assumed such proportions that it could not be disguised.

The OZNA secret police system (the initials are from its Jugoslav name, Odeljenje za Zastitu Naroda, literally Department for the Protection of the People) was patterned after the notorious Russian NKVD and OGPU. It had its own jails, separate from those of the ordinary criminal police. There were five OZNA jails in Belgrade, and a large barracks on the outskirts of the town, formerly used by the Gestapo, was used for training the enormous numbers of recruits it enlisted.

The jails were kept filled and every morning, walking past one of them from my hotel to my office, I passed long queues of relatives of the incarcerated, waiting with food parcels to be taken in to the prisoners. No communication was allowed between a prisoner and his or her relatives, and frequently the relatives had to go from one OZNA jail to another before they found where their missing sons and daughters were imprisoned.

In most cases, the prisoners were of the younger generation, and of the upper and middle classes. Sometimes they were released with a caution after a few days of salutary imprisonment; sometimes they disappeared permanently.

Frequently OZNA officials, sometimes in ordinary army uniform, sometimes in civilian clothes, would stop an American or British soldier seen walking in the street with a Jugoslav girl and ask for identification papers. The soldier's papers were naturally returned to him without comment. The girl's papers were retained by the police agent with the request that she call for them next day at the OZNA headquarters. When she called to collect them, she was simply taken away to a cell.

In one case OZNA made the mistake of arresting the Jugoslav fiancée of an American G.I. Locating the jail without too much trouble—for the grapevine of anti-Partisan Belgrade is highly developed—he turned up there with his automatic and threatened to shoot his way in unless the girl were released. The jailers promptly produced her and merely asked the G.I. to sign a paper certifying her release. They were so flustered at the time that they did not attempt to prefer any charge against her.

One evening in the summer following the end of the war, two American girls in Belgrade took out the two daughters of the house where they were staying. They dined at a public restaurant and went on to the opera without any suspicion that they were being shadowed. In the middle of the night OZNA agents called at the house and collected the two Jugoslav girls. They were kept in jail for two weeks. At the time of their release, no charge had been preferred against them; their imprisonment was sufficient hint that they should not mix with Americans.

In the early stages of this campaign, both the American and British Embassies intervened whenever there was sufficient evidence to prove that these were cases of intimidation. The attitude of Jugoslav officials was invariably to express shocked surprise, to promise to investigate, and then, after some weeks had elapsed, to reply briefly that the victim had been arrested for "collaboration" with the Germans during the occupation.

As the campaign developed in the late summer after the war, American and British intervention ceased to be of any value. OZNA let it be known to the victims and their relatives that if they sought foreign intervention their sentences would be twice as severe. And time and again the relatives of arrested persons besought the American or British authorities not to make complaints in their behalf.

There was no right of habeas corpus, no public trial, nor even—so far as anyone could determine—any charge. In the eyes of the commissars, the very fact that the prisoners had been seen mixing with Americans and British was in itself the crime and the evidence. For the training of the political commissars in Jugoslavia—both during and after the war—was that no matter how parallel the courses of the Western democracies, on the one hand, and of Tito, on the other, might run for the time being, the two systems were incompatible and that America and Britain were the ultimate enemies.

This is the basic fact which has to be accepted before Tito's policy can be understood. As conditions warranted, he changed his public attitude towards the West, but the party line within the inner councils of the Partisan movement never varied an inch. At a time when he urgently needed Allied supplies, Tito talked loudly of the unshakable alliance between his movement and America and Britain. When he no longer needed their help, he began to differentiate between the American and British peoples and their governments, a tactic necessary in order to insinuate the idea that those governments were not democratic. I have witnessed only one comparable change of attitude in such a short space of time. This was in Germany in the first six months before the attack on Poland when the Germans, convinced that they had obtained by deceit all that they needed in order to wage and win a European war, threw off their wheedling attitude towards the West and began openly to heckle and shout.

So, within the Partisan movement, there was no deviation of policy. Public attitudes were a means to the end, and did not disguise the fact in their cold analytical minds that America and Britain were the real enemies.

The efforts to isolate the population from contacts with Western democracy were not confined to the arrests of those seen in Anglo-American circles. No opportunity, however great or small, was passed up by OZNA.

For a time I had had plans to move out of my hotel in Belgrade and to find rooms in one of the villas in the suburbs. I quickly discovered that some circumspection was required. The Partisan billeting officers were by no means forthcoming in suggestions where to live. Housing space was terribly short, they said—which was true in view of the wholesale requisitioning of villas by the Red Army and Partisan High Command. However, Jugoslav friends were more helpful and before long I was shown many villas with vacant rooms. But the owners were anxious not to let it be known publicly that they had space, fearing that the Partisans would requisition the whole house. I was warned that if OZNA learned I was negotiating for a certain room it would certainly be requisitioned under my nose.

The trick, I learned, was to move into a room before the Partisans found out, and then if necessary to dare them to remove me. The owners were only too keen to have American residents in their homes as it gave them a certain amount of protection from visitations by OZNA.

I was not alone in my experience. Alfred Farber spent so much time in vainly trying to find accommodation other than his hotel that he confessed to feeling almost like a displaced person himself.

Two American officers, having found rooms in a suburban villa, told the woman who owned the villa that they would return in the afternoon with their clothes. When they arrived, she told them that she had to withdraw her offer as her sick son had suddenly returned. They questioned her and she eventually invited them inside. Once off the street, she told them that shortly after they had left she had been called upon by two OZNA officials who interrogated her about their visit. When she confessed to the police agents that she had rented rooms to the two officers, they ordered her to withdraw her offer and threatened her with imprisonment unless she obeyed.

She begged the two Americans to keep her secret. "Don't

worry," said one of them. "You're the sixteenth person in the last two days who has offered us rooms and then backed out of the deal."

If private attempts to find residences were discouraged, travel outside one's area was even more strictly controlled. American or British officials were forbidden general travel permits, except in special cases where their work absolutely required them. Foreign correspondents were allowed to travel only by certain routes to certain places and ran the risk of expulsion if they strayed off the path.

In such a situation, OWI discovered that its plans to foster contacts and cultural exchanges with the Jugoslav people were next to impossible to carry out. Its showroom in the center of Belgrade was crowded and its printed material, mostly produced in Italy on directives from the Belgrade headquarters, was superb. The people needed no convincing about America, however. What they wanted was advice on how to get rid of their regime. And that advice America was not prepared to give because America was "disinterested in the purely domestic affairs of other nations."

An OWI executive reported a conversation he had had with one of Jugoslavia's leading writers. "Do not send us political articles," the writer told him. "That would make trouble. But I hope that you will send us many articles about the laws and arts in America. Today we Serbs are very uncertain and you must not expect too much of us. We know that our culture is not a high one, that we are backward in many respects, but we are intelligent and we are observant, and we are anxious to learn."

In other words, the writer understood that Jugoslavia could expect no active help from America, and that without active help any American encouragement to the people might result in an abortive revolt. For Tito had by this time demonstrated that he intended to retain power even if he had to use machine guns to do so—Allied machine guns shipped to the Partisans by the thousands during the war. The Partisan guards on the street corners, the marching squads of soldiers parading the streets every day in every principal city were silent threats to the people.

But the Jugoslavs had not given up the idea of ultimate liberty. In spite of the fact that every attempt was being made to turn their faces toward Russia, at the University of Belgrade one hundred and seventy students had set themselves to learning English, forty to learning French, thirty to learning Russian.

RUSSIAN POLICY

The Russians did little direct propaganda in Jugoslavia, preferring to leave that work to Tito, who could be expected to be energetic in the Soviet cause. Certainly Moscow could find no fault in the display put on by the Partisan propagandists in favor of Russia.

The greatest concentration of propaganda in Jugoslavia is in the radio. In every town, public-speaker systems are set up in the main squares and the programs of Belgrade radio are relayed continuously, with the speakers blaring so loudly that one has to develop a deaf spot in order to ignore the noise.

The Belgrade radio station is operated by Russian engineers. Needless to say, its output is carefully controlled. OWI, which hastily shipped out recordings of the Voice of America programs, has succeeded in having only a small number accepted for broadcasting purposes.

In the movies, America found herself squeezed out; the Partisans realized fully the propaganda value of the movies. In 1938 America had sold 582 movies to Jugoslavia; Nazi Germany had sold 207, France eighty, Hungary fifteen, Britain fourteen, Czechoslovakia thirteen, Italy five, Switzerland four, Sweden three, Russia one.

234

On establishing their provisional government in Belgrade, the Partisans organized a State Film Corporation, which was a complete monopoly. Private enterprise in the movie industry was forbidden. The corporation quickly made a deal with Russia for a total of seventy-three films in its first post-war year. Much as they disliked to deal with a monopoly, the British shrugged their shoulders and realistically sent in delegates to arrange a similar deal, accepting a smaller quota than the Russians. America refused to deal with the corporation, but eventually accepted a compromise arrangement permitting the importation of American films into Jugoslavia, with the arrangements subject to cancellation on short notice.

In books, the Russians are naturally given the same advantage as in all other propaganda media. The largest bookstore in Belgrade was taken out of the hands of its owners and turned over completely to the exhibition of Russian books. Not only Russian books, however, but Russian translations of American and British books, suitably chosen for their content. The Russians were not hampered by any such international restrictions as copyright. Nor were they hampered by the Jugoslav censorship which went over every word of every sentence in every American or British book brought in by the OWI or the British Ministry of Information.

Nor were the Russians hampered in their cultural contacts with the Jugoslavs. They had plenty of money (the new Jugoslav currency was printed in Russia, a fact which constituted one of the reasons for popular prejudice against it), plenty of showrooms, and a whole string of Russian artists, writers, and musicians with whom to beguile the public at teas, soirees, and official receptions.

The press, of course, is controlled as thoroughly as in any other totalitarian country. Only two daily papers are published in Belgrade: *Borba*, the organ of the Communist Party, and *Politika*, once one of the best newspapers in the Balkans but now rendered unrecognizable by its subservience. *Selo,* organ of the Agrarian Party, was nominally supposed to be a daily newspaper; one of the conditions which the Agrarian Party posed and obtained before it entered the National Liberation Front was that sufficient newsprint would be issued to *Selo* to enable it to publish daily. But *Selo* proceeded to criticize some of the extremes to which Tito was proceeding in his revolution of the political and economic systems; its newsprint was accordingly cut down by way of reprisal until *Selo* barely manages to appear weekly.

The editor of *Borba* was Lt. Col. Vlada Dedier, son of a well-known Belgrade family. Dedier spoke fluent English, having spent many years in America during his childhood. He fought and was wounded in the Partisan army, but his most useful service to Tito was his clever public-relations work in the Middle East at a time when the question of Mihailovitch versus Tito was still undecided in Allied minds. Dedier cleverly laughed off the idea that there could ever be such a thing as a communist menace in Jugoslavia and soothed Allied worries about Tito's ultimate aims. "You people are too scared about communism," was his line towards Allied officials and correspondents. "It is just a bogey and only exists in your own minds." It was identical with the line Tito himself adopted towards American and British officers, and it worked.

Perhaps because the fear is cropping up once more, this time among the powerful Jugoslav-American groups in the United States, Dedier was detached from *Borba* and sent to San Francisco at the time of the conference. When the conference ended, he was attached to the Jugoslav Embassy in Washington.

The Russian-Jugoslav efforts to deal with the hostility of the Jugoslav-Americans are interesting as an exhibition of totalitarian teamwork. No totalitarian regime can afford to admit that it is unpopular with its people—even though its people have become citizens of another country and are living three thousand miles away. Especially if those emigrants constitute an important colony with great influence in their former homeland. On the problem of the Jugoslav colony in the United States, the Russo-Tito teamplay is therefore for Tito to tell his people that he has the full support of all Jugoslavs in America, and to leave to Russia the problem of a frontal attack on the colony.

Thus, Belgrade radio on the eve of the so-called free elections in Jugoslavia:

"Jugoslavs residing in the U.S.A. sent a message to Marshal Tito, expressing fraternal greetings to the peoples of Jugoslavia. The message says, 'You led the peoples of Jugoslavia through all hardships and trials of the war of liberation, and you will just as brilliantly be able to lead Jugoslavia to economic prosperity. The Jugoslavs residing in America helped their brothers in their struggle for liberation and will help them in their economic rehabilitation which will bring Jugoslavia to glory.'"

Moscow radio, a few days earlier in its overseas service: "Recently it has been possible to observe in the United States a certain effervescence among Serb reactionary organizations opposed to democratic renascence in Jugoslavia. They are endeavoring to mislead American public opinion. In this respect particular activity is shown by Fotich, former Jugoslav Ambassador in the U.S. (for ex-King Peter's Government) and by the leader of the Jugoslav renegade organizations such as the Serb National Federation and Serb National Defence.

"The increased activity of these organizations coincides with the electoral campaign in Jugoslavia. The Serb reactionary organizations abroad are giving a helping hand to the Jugoslav opposition so that it may achieve its main aim; namely, to provoke intervention of foreign forces in matters of Jugoslav home policy."

Or Moscow home radio:

"The secretary of the American Slav Congress, Pirinsky, has stated to press representatives that the U.S. State Department must cease interfering in the internal affairs of Bulgaria and Jugoslavia. Pirinsky also stated that the great majority of the Bulgarian and Jugoslav populations have given their support during the elections to the anti-fascist candidates and have dissociated themselves from the opposition. Pirinsky said that the Balkan peoples are not impressed by the sample of Churchill-Bevin democracy in Greece, or the sample of Byrnes democracy in South Carolina, where the greatest majority of the citizens cannot take part in the elections because of voting taxes."

An interesting point in the latter broadcast is the linking of Bevin's name with Churchill's; it is an indication that the Soviet Government's propaganda campaign to portray the British Government as fascist, a campaign that was halted by the British Socialists' victory at the elections, had been resumed.

RUSSIA AND A "BALKAN FEDERATION"

The most important aspect of Russo-Jugoslav relations is in the use of Jugoslavia as a spearhead for advancing Russian interests in Southeast Europe.

It was clear as the war drew towards its close that its end would bring a severe reaction on the part of the American public, a rush to recapture the peaceful way of life that had existed in America before the war. There would be an enormous disinclination to become involved in any European situation which would entangle American troops. The British Government could be expected to have its eyes and ears open, but would be considerably hampered by the war-weariness of the British public. The American Government, no matter how much it might take an interest in European affairs, could be depended upon to turn the major part of its attention to American interests in the Far East. The first few months after the war presented to Russia and her friends the most suitable opportunity for consolidating and expanding their positions in Europe.

Jugoslavia was in the best strategical position to be used by Russia to exploit these ambitions. At three places along her frontier, there exist areas whose possession is important to any power wishing to extend its sphere of interest into the heart of Europe.

In the south there is Greece, foreign control of which would deny the eastern Mediterranean to the British. In the north-west, there is the Italian port of Trieste and its surrounding countryside. Trieste is the largest port in the Adriatic, whose eastern coastline is Jugoslav territory. Jugoslav possession of this port would convert the Adriatic into a Jugoslav lake.

In the north there is the Austrian province of Carinthia. Jugoslav possession of Carinthia would not only emasculate post-war Austria but would render impotent Anglo-American attempts to reconstruct Austria as an independent state after seven years of Nazi rule. And when the Western Allies withdrew their occupation forces from Austria, the rump state would be ready to be snapped up by the Red Army, lurking like a hungry trout in the eastern section of the country.

There appeared no reason to prevent Jugoslavia from gaining virtual control of all three areas, providing Tito used the right mixture of nerve-war tactics, the sudden seizure at the appropriate moment followed immediately by the requisite assurances of good intentions.

At one time, Greece seemed to be "in the bag." The latter stages of the war had seen American and British support for EAM, British support amounting almost to complete abandonment of other Greek movements. EAM was closely in touch with Tito's National Liberation Movement. It had sent delegates to his conferences. Its hierarchy, like his, was composed of experienced and disciplined communists, who knew the techniques of power.

It was true that at Tehran, Stalin had promised Roosevelt and Churchill that Greece should be in the British sphere of interest, and that as a result there could be no open seizure of the country. But what better method for snatching Greece from under the noses of the British than by appropriating the American and British idea of a post-war Balkan federation? If the communists could control the so-called all-party fronts in each country, they could certainly control a combination of fronts in one Balkan group.

Tito must have smiled at their naïveté as he watched the British liaison officers swallowing his bait. Down in Macedonia, the southernmost province of Jugoslavia on the Greek border, he had one of his most trusted henchmen, a man whose activities were so secret that he was known only by the nickname of Tempo. Tempo, it was discovered in 1944, was a young Montenegrin communist named Svetozar Vukmanovitch. Born in Cetinje in 1912, he had joined the underground Jugoslav communist movement before the outbreak of war and, after the German occupation, had been sent to organize the Partisan resistance in Bosnia.

He did so well that in November, 1942, he was sent as Tito's personal representative to Macedonia, that ancient land which now exists only as a province of Jugoslavia but whose territory, according to Macedonians, takes in chunks of Albania, Bulgaria, and northern Greece, including the port of Salonika.

In February, 1943, Tempo crossed from Jugoslavia into Greece with two Macedonian battalions and marched almost to Salonika. With General Sarafis, the head of the Greek

ELAS forces, he attended a conference of EAM at Trikkala in Greece, and the same year found him conferring with leaders of the young Albanian Partisan organization, a duplicate in every way of EAM and Tito's National Liberation Front.

The Bulgarian capitulation to Russia in 1944 opened fresh territory to Tempo. Part of the Russian conditions were that the Bulgars should hand over the Greek territory they had occupied to the ELAS forces, and that their occupation forces in southern Jugoslavia should place themselves under Tempo. The outbreak of the Greek civil war thus found the whole of ancient Macedonia—comprising southern Jugoslavia, western Bulgaria, northern Greece, and part of Albania—occupied by "National Front Liberation" troops of one nationality or another, all under the direct control of Tempo, who by this time had been made a Lieutenant General by Tito, and decorated with the Order of Kutuzov First Class by Stalin.

The collapse of ELAS in the Greek civil war and the consequent disintegration of EAM as an "all-party" Greek front, robbed Tempo of the Greek portion of his territory. It also took the Balkan federation platform from under Tito's feet. For this tool of Russian imperialism wanted only a particular kind of Balkan federation. He wanted a federation of all-communist governments, not a federation in which one government was communist, another non-communist.

In the winter of 1945–46 a group of British Members of Parliament visited Jugoslavia and asked Tito about the possibility of forming a Balkan federation. "The question is premature at present," replied Tito, "Because, for the creation of a Balkan federation, certain prerequisites are indispensable. In the first place, it is necessary to remove what separated the Balkan peoples in the past, create friendly relations and realize economic and cultural cooperation. These are the main prerequisites because a federation created without these con-

241

ditions would be weak. I think that this question cannot be considered now." *

Having failed to gain a toehold in Greece by Trojan Horse methods, Tito tried other ways. The Macedonians in southern Jugoslavia raised an agitation to be united with their non-existent Macedonian brothers over the Greek border. They demanded that Greece cede her northern provinces to them and that an autonomous Macedonia be set up within the framework of Jugoslavia. By a strange coincidence the Jugoslav press was filled with stories of atrocities by "Greek chauvinists" against the "terrorized" inhabitants of northern Greece—which was carefully called Aegean Macedonia, not Greek Macedonia.

Tempo came out openly under his real identity and made a speech at the National Assembly in Belgrade, declaring that the whole Macedonian people wished to achieve complete unity, and advocating the union of the people of "Aegean" and Bulgarian Macedonia with the Jugoslav Macedonian federal unit.

MACEDONIA

The Macedonian agitation was the first use of minority problems by the totalitarian Left-wing. Its techniques were followed closely by Jugoslavia in her later agitations for Trieste and Carinthia. They were also followed closely by Soviet Russia in the "spontaneous" revolt in northern Iran and the equally spontaneous demands of Soviet Armenia and Soviet Georgia for eastern Turkey. The techniques were not new by any means. As a matter of fact, they were exact imitations of the various campaigns used by Hitler in Czechoslovakia and other countries whose territory Nazi Germany wished to acquire.

* Reported by Belgrade radio.

In the case of Czechoslovakia, it will be recalled that the German technique was to work up a furious press and radio campaign accusing the Czechs of terrorizing the Sudeten Germans who wished only to be united with the Germans of the Reich and to live peacefully ever after. The German press, especially the *Völkischer Beobachter*, the now defunct organ of the now defunct Nazi Party, invented a series of specific incidents in which Germans had been beaten or murdered by Czech gendarmes. I was in the Sudetenland at the time and spent considerable time and energy in dashing from one Czech village to another to investigate these "atrocities," only to find that in most cases, far from Germans having been murdered by Czechs, the reverse was the case.

Anyone who remembers the German methods of eight years ago will recognize a familiar ring about this extract from *Borba*, organ of the Jugoslav Communist Party. It was published on June 19, 1945, when the agitation for Greek Macedonia reached a peak:

"News from Salonika describes the terror of the Greek chauvinists, who are being aided by troops of the Greek regular army. It describes the unbearable situation for the Macedonian people. Groups of armed monarcho-fascists, assisted by the monarchist Greek nazi-police, the army of the Greek Government, are attacking villages, terrorizing, maltreating and murdering the democratic citizens.

"These bands are raiding the villages, stealing everything they can find. In the Drama area especially there exists an unbearable situation. Lawlessness exists and the bands of the traitor Andor Chaush, now collaborating with the regular Greek army, are preparing orgies of extreme fury. Chaush's bandits arrest, beat, murder, and plunder wherever they will. In one day alone, there were nine cases of murder in Drama. The victims are always the poor peasants of Macedonia.

"The villages of Philnia, Europos, Mesna, Agnos, Petros,

and others are being blockaded and the villagers beaten en masse. The attacks surpass those of the Germans in their barbarity. The aggressors have attacked and destroyed houses, beaten peasants, and plundered their property. In the village of Acrini, the Greek police dishonored a young girl. In the village of Pollilaco, Greek Gestapo men arrested the national liberation fighter Marco Kokra, who was so terribly beaten that he is in danger of his life.

"In the village of Maritza, the soldiers of the regular army killed seven people and wounded seventy-five others."

And so on. Slightly more primitive in its style, but in the true *Völkischer Beobachter* tradition.

Another extract from the same paper showed how closely the Jugoslav and Greek communists were working together:

"The unbearable situation in Aegean (*sic*) Macedonia is described by *Agraticos Aponos*, the voice of the Greek Agrarians. It reports that thousands of peasants and workmen are escaping to Salonika as the drive of the wild fascist terror spreads in the towns and countryside. They believe they will find protection in Salonika in spite of the fact that the Greek regular forces are taking part in the terror. Blockading of villages, arrests, torture, murder, plunder, and all other well-known fascist methods are rampant in the country districts, much the same as during the German occupation. All this makes it impossible for the working people to start with their work."

The meaning of the last sentence is obscure. The Greek Agrarians referred to by *Borba*, however, were not the old Greek Agrarian Party, but the Agrarian Party founded during the war by the Greek communists; by such tactics it was possible to create an impression of veracity about the reports. What might be discounted if it came from openly communist sources became more credible if its authors appeared to belong to such moderate groups as the "Agrarians."

Naturally, propaganda was not used alone. Selected men

244

from the well-indoctrinated section of the Jugoslav Partisan army were posted along the border with orders to create "frontier incidents," and several detachments of the Jugoslav Army were moved quietly into Yugoslav Macedonia, including the Twenty-first, Twenty-fifth, Fifth, and Lika "Shock" Divisions, ready to move as soon as the time was judged opportune.

A Jugoslav airman, who escaped to Allied territory in October, 1945, and who refused to return to Jugoslavia, revealed to Mr. C. L. Sulzberger of the *New York Times* that some three hundred Soviet planes given to Marshal Tito during the summer had been moved to southern airfields near the Greek border.[*]

Tito was compelled to order his propagandists to place special emphasis on "terror" rather than on the ethnical aspects of the problem, because ethnically no case existed. The population of Greek Macedonia had been predominantly Greek since before the Christian era and, after World War I, the influx of some 600,000 Greek refugees from Turkey had accentuated its Greek character. Furthermore, Greek Macedonia is not only nearly ninety per cent Greek in population, but is an area where millions of American dollars and British pounds were expended in relief work after the last war, and where several American organizations and American individuals worked for years, after the influx of the Greek refugees, in order to help to settle one of the oldest of Balkan minority problems.

Of course, what Tito wanted was not so much the hinterland of Greek Macedonia but its great seaport of Salonika, the outlet for the Morava-Vardar Valley. Possession of Salonika by Jugoslavia would enable Russia to outflank the Dardanelles and to put an extra squeeze on Turkey for their complete possession. It was not a new ambition on Jugoslavia's part. In

[*] *New York Times,* October 19, 1945.

1929 she had acquired a small free zone in the port, an arrangement which did not prove completely satisfactory. Possession of Salonika was one of the rewards promised the quisling Jugoslav Government by Hitler for signing the Tripartite Pact in March, 1941. On that occasion, however, the Jugoslav people had refused the temptation in order to be on the side of the Western democracies.

Tito's maneuvers did not succeed because he overplayed his hand. One crisis at a time should be the recipe for all totalitarian states. Tito was trying to handle three simultaneously; for while the Macedonian crisis was in full swing he was also trying to snatch Trieste and Carinthia, and the British, who might have given way on one of the three if it had occurred alone, dug in their heels and made it plain they would fight if need be. And much as the press of Jugoslavia blustered about its rights, the last thing Tito wanted was an open clash between his regime and the Western democracies. It might have provided that spark for which the Jugoslav people were waiting in order to overthrow him.

TRIESTE

The Trieste crisis occurred in the last few weeks of the war and was obscured by the gigantic developments taking place between the main Allied and German armies.

On the eve of the final Allied onslaught that brought about the disintegration of German resistance, the Partisan armies in Jugoslavia were still unable to do anything more than harass the German occupation forces in their country. The whole northern sector of the country was still securely in German hands, including Zagreb, capital of Croatia. The Partisans held a strip of the Dalmatian coast and had only just succeeded with the capture of Sarajevo, in establishing communications between their forces there and their main forces in the east of the country.

Both America and Britain were aware of Tito's ambitions to seize Trieste and the Istrian peninsula of Italy and were equally determined that its future status should be decided only at the peace conference and not by a *fait accompli*. With this in mind, General Alexander, at that time the Supreme Allied Commander in the Mediterranean Theatre, had flown to Belgrade and had agreed with Tito on the coordination of Allied and Partisan offensives. The Allies were to take on the main task of smashing the German armies, driving up through northern Italy and round the Adriatic, capturing Trieste and meeting the Partisan armies on the old Jugoslav frontier.

Tito's task would be to launch a drive for the liberation of Zagreb, second capital of the country. By attacking the Germans on a broad front, the main German armies would be squeezed between the Partisans and the Allies, who would see to it that they were held relentlessly in Jugoslav territory until they surrendered to Tito.

Having signed this agreement, Tito promptly proceeded to break it. The fleet of little boats that constituted the Partisan navy—most of which should have been engaged in shuttling relief supplies from Italy across the Adriatic for the civilian population of Dalmatia—was moved quietly up the coast to points where it could supply the Partisan land forces in their dash to reach Trieste before the Allies. The main Partisan army was shifted from the Zagreb front to strategic points for this offensive.

As soon as General Mark Clark announced that he had broken German resistance in Italy, the Partisan offensive on Trieste was opened. Zagreb was by-passed and actually remained in German hands until after the Partisans had taken Trieste; it was, in fact, the last important city in Europe to be liberated. Zagreb could wait; in Tito's opinion it was more important to seize Trieste before the Allies arrived there.

Having succeeded in this, the next objective was to present Trieste to the world as a truly Jugoslavian city. With this in mind, some four thousand leading Italian residents were deported from their homes and vanished into the interior of Jugoslavia.

The usual "spontaneous" demonstrations were organized. To create the impression that the Italian citizens themselves wished to belong to Jugoslavia, an Italian language paper was founded. Its title, at least, was Italian—*Il Lavoratore*. The same could not be said for its founding-editor whose name was Georg Jakcetich. Jakcetich was an officer in the Jugoslav Partisan army, and was later removed from *Il Lavoratore* to serve a term of imprisonment to which he was condemned by the Allied Military Tribunal in Trieste as a result of his participation in the Partisan terror. On his release, he became organizing secretary of the local Communist Party.

Alexander was furious at the attempt to seize Trieste. He sent a telegram to Tito, the terms of which he made public, accusing Tito of having broken his word of honor as a soldier and of using the tactics of Hitler and Mussolini. Tito replied publicly expressing his outrage at such an insult. He also sent a private telegram to Alexander, the contents of which were not made public in Jugoslavia. In it, Tito said in effect, "When I signed my agreement with you, I was commander-in-chief of the Jugoslav army. Now I am also prime minister."

As commander-in-chief, he was bound by his word. As a politician, he could break it. There is no finer exposition of the ends-justify-the-means principle of totalitarian foreign diplomacy.

On this occasion, however, cocksureness upset the apple cart. Alexander moved the British Eighth Army towards Trieste and made it plain to Tito that he would fight his way into the city if necessary—and Tito realized too late that in his overconfidence he had omitted to tell his generals to blow the bridges between their lines and the advancing Allies.

America hastily jumped into a neutral position. American troops who had participated in the liberation of the Istrian peninsula, on which Trieste is situated, were moved to positions where they could not be involved in fighting, should it start. OWI employees who had gone along with the Allies as part of PWB, on the supposition that Trieste was to be part of the Italian occupation zone and in no way involved with the Balkans, were withdrawn—at least temporarily. The Trieste situation developed into a naked showdown of strength between the British and Tito, backed by the Russians, whose frontier positions in Austria were in the vicinity.

The awkward aspect of the Trieste crisis for Tito was that he had gone out on a limb, not only with the Allies but also with his own people. He could, if necessary, crawl back as far as the Allies were concerned, but he knew that no dictator could afford to suffer loss of face among his own people. In Belgrade we had fed for weeks on headlines about "Trst" as the Jugoslavs call Trieste. We had been told how the residents had jubilantly welcomed the Partisan liberators, how they had paraded in praise of Tito, how even the Italian residents had clamored to belong to Jugoslavia, and how the population was predominantly Jugoslav anyway! How the Partisan army had distributed relief supplies to the people of the city— though without mentioning that these were supplies borrowed from UNRRA on the Dalmatian coast. True, the liquidation of the Italian opposition in the city had not yet been carried to the point where American correspondents in Belgrade could be taken to Trieste on a sightseeing tour. William King of the Associated Press and Panos Morphopoulos of *Newsweek* had been pressing the Jugoslav Propaganda Ministry for permission to go to Trieste, but were fobbed off with the excuse that no transport was available. Nevertheless, in order to help them gain a picture of the true state of affairs, little Sava Kosanovitch, the Jugoslav Minister of Information, flew to "Trst" with a group of Partisan journalists and sent back a stream of exuberant reports from which they could take their information, if they wished. Needless to say, they declined with no thanks.

Also needless to say, Tito did not fight. He allowed the British and New Zealand troops to enter Trieste and after moving his troops from one position to another in one threatening gesture or another, he finally accepted a compromise which compelled him to leave Trieste to the Allied Military Government, but gave him occupation of just enough territory on the Istrian peninsula to enable him to save face with his own people.

To say that this was the end of the incident would be deceptive. It was merely the end of an attempt. Withdrawing his forces, Tito set to work to build up a propaganda campaign for Trieste. The Russians sent one of their top writers, Ilya Ehrenburg, to Jugoslavia to assist the more amateurish Partisans. Ehrenburg went to Istria and wrote a series of articles, in which he claimed that the population earnestly desired to become part of Jugoslavia. He also whitewashed some of the tactics of the Jugoslav occupation authorities, notably their attempt to create economic hardship by pumping millions of worthless paper lire, printed in Jugoslavia, into the district.

On the future of Trieste, Tito changed his tactics. Its status should be left until the peace conference, he said, stating as a demand a fact to which he had been compelled to agree. But its status should be decided only by the Big Three, he added, and not by the United Nations as a whole. In other words, Tito believed his prospects were brighter if the future of Trieste were left to power-politics haggling, between the

Big Three, rather than to an open assembly of all the United Nations.

CARINTHIA

Carinthia lies over the Austrian border from the northern Jugoslav province of Slovenia. Its population, though predominantly Austrian, contains a minority of Slovenes, a natural consequence of the days when both provinces were part of the Austrian Empire with no frontier between them. On these flimsy ethnical grounds and on the grounds that the Austrians, as part of the German Reich, were enemies deserving of no consideration, Tito demanded that Carinthia should be incorporated into post-war Jugoslavia.

As in the case of Trieste, he was told that the future of all territories should be decided at the peace conference; as in the case of Trieste, he attempted to forestall any dispute by racing to seize the province before the Allies arrived.

He had less fortune than in Trieste. The Allies arrived before him at Klagenfurt, capital of Slovenia, and although the Partisans had succeeded in crossing the border, they were promptly turned back over it with little ceremony.

The usual howls arose in the Jugoslav press. The British, who were responsible for occupation of this section of Austria, were accused of having arrested numerous Slovenes known for their "anti-fascist convictions." AMG, in conjunction with the local police, was accused of arresting members of the former Slovene National Liberation Committee in Carinthia, an organization which was formed by the Partisans during their brief sojourn over the border and which was subsequently closed by the Allied military authorities because of its subversive activities. It was alleged that the provisional Carinthian Provincial Government contained former Nazis and was pursuing an anti-Slovene policy, unimpeded by the British; that the police force was recruited from former members of the

Gestapo and the SS and was carrying out a reign of terror, and so on.

By the time this press campaign had developed in Belgrade in the summer of 1945, I had become interested in the idea that Tito had adopted what might be termed Hitler's Rule of The Big Lie—the bigger the lie, the wider will be its acceptance. I therefore made a point of following up the specific allegations of the Partisans and ascertaining what the true facts were.

Up to June 7, 1945, I found, 732 arrests were made by the Allied Military in Carinthia on security grounds. Of these 696 were officials under the Nazi regime. The remaining thirty-six were all arrested on various grounds of security within the existing directives issued to the Allied Military authorities on the spot. Of the total of 732, only six were Jugoslavs, all of whom had been employed by the Germans. Almost half the arrests had been for offenses against the military government, such as contravention of the curfew and movement regulations. Far from arresting anti-fascists, as Tito alleged, the reverse was the case.

The action against members of the Slovene National Liberation Committee was purely military, in accordance with the agreement whereby Tito agreed to withdraw his troops, commissars, and other officials over the border. The civilians whom the Jugoslav press had alleged were arrested and carried away to "an unknown destination" were Jugoslav citizens who had been escorted to the Jugoslav border after confessing their nationality.

No local Slovenes had been deported from Carinthia. The only cases of deportation were those of Jugoslav Slovenes, falsely claiming to be local.

When Allied troops entered Klagenfurt on May 8, the Provincial Government, established three days previously, offered its services to AMG but ceased to exercise any authority. On

May 28 it was dissolved and during the following weeks a consultative Committee was established which included well-known local anti-Nazis. All its members were first checked and approved by AMG authorities. One of the twelve members on this committee represented the Slovene minority. Moreover, the local Slovene leader was given a special pass to travel from his home to Klagenfurt at any time and invited to make any complaints to AMG on behalf of the Slovenes. Up to June 5, he had made no complaints.

The local police force had been de-Nazified, and all special Nazi police formations had been dissolved.

Now the only point to be served, in dealing in such detail with Tito's agitation over Carinthia and his similar campaigns for Italian and Greek territory, is to illustrate that we have entered on another period of nerve-wars during which immense pressure will be exerted from abroad on the American public. The crises have started at a time when the American public is least prepared mentally to withstand them. Our war agencies are dissolved—not merely branches of the War and Navy Departments, but those agencies which made it their special business to analyze the intricate web of stories spread by foreign radios, by newspapers set up under faked auspices, by stooge organizations and political parties with grandiose and misleading titles, by the much-travelled "foreign observers" in neutral capitals, and by all the other devices of a ruthless and well-oiled propaganda machine, still in active service.

During the war, the restrictions imposed on the American press for reasons of military security were compensated to a certain extent by the enormous amount of background information disseminated by these agencies in order to help the press assess the news with which it was being bombarded from a thousand different directions.

Today, with these American agencies gone, the American correspondent entering a country is in a position similar to that of Commander Perry when he forced Japan to open up to the outside world. Conditions are not what they used to be (a platitude) and never will be again. Even if a man has worked in a particular country before the war, he possesses an advantage only in his "Know-how," in the fact that he can more quickly assess its background than the correspondent who has never been there before. But the old faces are gone, new conditions apply, there are new ways of doing things and seeing that they are done. The devious ways of power politics are still there, if anything more rotten than before, but the cynicism and disillusion have percolated from the top to the people below. The war has destroyed not only the bodies of the dead but the morale and morals of the survivors.

DEMOCRACY IN JUGOSLAVIA

If this is true as a general rule for the whole of Europe, it is pointedly so in the specific case of Jugoslavia. In no other country in Europe is the prestige of America so high—among the people. If Britain is almost as popular, it is only because the British, though second choice, are three thousand miles nearer and therefore in the minds of the Jugoslav people at least, more apt to take an interest in what is going on inside Jugoslavia. In actual fact, of course, this is not so; the British Government was prompt to follow the example of America in affirming its determination not to interfere in the Soviet sphere of influence.

So far as power is concerned, the Russian position in Jugoslavia is unshakable. The Red Army is no longer needed for Tito to maintain his position. The active opposition to Tito has been broken up into scattered bands, eking out a bare survival in the hills. As Ilya Ehrenburg put it during his tour of the country, "The Chetniks control areas of Jugoslavia only on paper." The vast mass of the people hostile to Tito are

254

dispirited and disunited. Even the moderate politicians, who quit ex-King Peter's government-in-exile in order to find a common platform with Tito and who have since resigned from Tito's government, lack the spirit of leadership.

The Partisan movement itself is still a tightly knit organization. So far Tito has stalled off his reconstruction problems by mobilizing the men in every town he liberated and shipping them off to other parts of the country—an old Balkan technique. Today Jugoslavia has the largest standing army in the world for its size. With the call-up of the seventeen-year-old class during the Macedonian agitation, the army was estimated to number nearly three quarters of a million—an enormous number considering the numbers of Jugoslav prisoners of war from the former royal army who had either not yet been returned home or who, on return to Jugoslavia, had been clapped into internment camps pending decision on their political suitability.

The consolidation of power by the communists within the Partisan movement has done a great deal to undermine that unity, however. Some indication of this was given in the fall of 1945 when Tito suddenly dismissed General Arso Jovanovitch, who had been his chief of staff since the beginning of the Partisan movement. Jovanovitch is not a communist; his successor, Lieutenant General Kocha Popovitch, is. Popovitch is the son of a rich and well-known Belgrade lawyer. Only thirty-six years old, he fought in the Spanish Civil War, at the end of which he succeeded in returning to Jugoslavia, where he was imprisoned for some time. In June, 1941, he raised the Posavski Partisan odred (or guerrilla detachment) and later became commander of the First Brigade, then of the First Division, and finally of the First Corps.

The meteoric rise of this young communist did little to soothe the feelings of the non-communist Partisans; nor did the chauvinism with which loyal members of the party were rewarded with the choicest positions in the post-war civil administration.

For a time, the morale of the overswollen army was maintained by pep talks about "our suffering brethren" in Greece, Austria, and Italy, but such wordy campaigns cannot go on forever. There comes a time when the men must either be given action or sent home.

It will be after demobilization that Tito's real troubles will start and the real totalitarian ruthlessness of his regime will be exposed. When the soldiers become peasants again, they will demand their land—and it is significant that so far Tito has proceeded most cautiously with his plans to create a collective farm system.

For the time being, he contents himself with creating a dictatorship which will enable him to retain power in spite of all discontent. Each increase of power encourages his ambitions; his appetite came with the eating, as the French proverb puts it.

Tito is canny enough to admit there is discontent, but he is sufficiently powerful at this stage to issue threats. When the Roman Catholic leaders in Jugoslavia issued a pastoral letter protesting against the persecution of the church, Tito went to the radio and said, "It is my duty to give warning that there exist laws which forbid the spreading of chauvinism and dissension as well as the endangering of achievements of our great liberation struggle."

He proclaims that his system is a democracy—as indeed it is *on paper*. Article 27 of the new constitution states that freedom of press, freedom of speech, and freedom of association—including holding of conferences, public meetings, and demonstrations—are guaranteed to citizens. This freedom exists on paper only, and there are thousands of cases of people arrested for attempting to exercise those rights. The press is controlled to an extent equalled only by Russia, and its contents, where matters of policy are concerned, are identical even to the commas and headlines.

Article 28 says that the right of habeas corpus is guaranteed. What does this mean when any pedestrian in Belgrade can look up at the windows of the OZNA jails and see, pressed against them, the faces of people whisked away without any legal charge and condemned without any legal trial?

Not even Tito—when taxed with these and other facts by foreign visitors to the country who cannot be fobbed off with the meaningless platitudes of the Partisan radio—claims this to be true democracy.

When a group of British members of Parliament visited Belgrade and asked Tito what type of democracy existed in Jugoslavia, he replied (according to Belgrade radio), "We have created that kind of democracy which best corresponds both to the mentality of our country and to our economic conditions, because Western democracy does not fully correspond to us. Naturally we cannot agree to a type of democracy such as exists in other countries."

On another occasion, explaining the meaning of the new constitution, Tito said over the radio, "The relationship between the people and authority in New Jugoslavia has changed so that there is no longer a conflict between them, but a political and organizational unity."

In view of the manner in which the people are prevented from entering into any conflict with the State, this statement, stripped of its hypocritical verbiage, means simply that the people have been submerged in the new State. "*L'état c'est moi!*" says Tito.

THE GOVERNMENT OF THE PEOPLE?

Which is more important—to possess prestige and influence among the people of a country, or to possess power to influence the government of that country against the people's wishes?

The very essence of power politics demands that a nation engaged in it must choose the latter, whatever its sentimental attachments may be, and every large power in the world has plenty of such examples in its history. But to presume that because this has always been so, it must always be so in the future is to speak with a voice of despair. For there is a difference between the power politics of the past and those of the future.

America takes a vital interest in the affairs of Mexico, but this vital interest does not demand that the people of Mexico shall be cut off from all contact with other peoples, especially with the peoples of other large powers. It does not demand that the press, radio, movies, civil administration, police, and armed forces of Mexico shall not only be free from all influence by other powers but shall be hostile to them.

Yet this is what is happening in Jugoslavia, despite whatever denials the propagandists of Tito may make for the sake of obtaining some concession or another.

When Field Marshal Alexander visited Belgrade in order to make joint plans with Tito for the final offensive in Jugoslavia, the people of Belgrade attempted to show their warm feeling towards the Anglo-American armies. They were not allowed to do so lest they also show their hostility towards Tito. The spontaneous demonstration was kept back from the square where Alexander's hotel was situated. There was a crowd outside Alexander's hotel, but it was an organized claque. I have spoken to people who attempted to join in the demonstration. One of them, a woman, said she managed to break through as far as the Partisan guard. He told her to go away. From his accent, she recognized him as a Serb and asked, "Why must I go away? You are a Serb and you know that we must welcome the guests to our country." He scratched his head and replied, "I don't know, but my orders are to send you away."

A few days later, Anthony Eden, who was then the British Foreign Minister, reported to the House of Commons that from the evidence he had obtained the demonstration given to Alexander was a spontaneous expression of good will and showed the democratic nature of Tito's regime.

Now who was it who so grossly misinformed Mr. Eden? And what do the British Conservatives expect if they so wilfully pass on misinformation to their people? In so ignoring the true state of affairs, they have shackled themselves.

On May 1, 1945, the May Day Celebrations took place in Belgrade. For days beforehand—in spite of their complaints to the Allied Military headquarters that they were desperately short of transport—the Partisans had been shunting people into Belgrade from all parts of the country. This was to be a really grandiose "spontaneous" demonstration. It was in the true style of Mussolini's "spontaneous" affairs, even to the postcards sent to all civil servants requiring them to present themselves at mustering points some hours beforehand.

The night before the demonstration took place, I was shown by an American Embassy official a list of thirty-two slogans which were to be distributed to the marchers to be shouted "spontaneously" as they passed the stand where Tito was to take the salute.

After the march-past had taken place, a crowd of people, mainly young Belgrade boys and girls, gathered outside the offices of OWI and shouted, "Long Live Roosevelt! Long Live Truman!" and other pro-American slogans. It was a spontaneous demonstration not anticipated by the Partisans. A group of these youths was taken into custody by OZNA agents. Some of us knew some of the parents, but they begged us not to have any intervention made by the American authorities, and in view of their reluctance it was impossible to collect

259

any evidence warranting a protest—although protests were made on other similar occasions.

There are other ways of isolating a people in addition to the crude tactics of direct intimidation. Tito's new currency was such a method, for in addition to using it in his program of destroying the upper and middle classes, he used it to destroy commerce between Jugoslavia and the West. The method was simple. The Jugoslav Government merely fixed the new *dinar* at the exorbitant rate of fifty to the dollar, thereby raising the prices of goods to the foreign purchaser to five times what they used to be before the war. The American living in Belgrade when the new currency was introduced in the summer of 1945 found his cost of living raised from two dollars a day, approximately what it had been before the war, to ten dollars a day.

It is still premature to write about the ultimate effect of this measure since it is being disputed vigorously by both America and Britain. So far, however, Tito has remained adamant, and it is safe to say that if the rate of exchange remains in force, trade between Jugoslavia and the Western democracies will cease to exist, and, lacking her former customers, Jugoslavia will be forced into the economic orbit of the Soviet Union. In fact, trade and barter agreements have already been signed with Russia and with Czechoslovakia, also an unwilling member of the Russian zone.

At present, the only Americans or Britons inside Jugoslavia, apart from the members of both diplomatic missions and the foreign correspondents, are the workers of UNRRA. It is impossible to overemphasize the importance of their work and the effects it is having on Jugoslav public opinion. These Americans and Britons represent the sole democratic contacts remaining to the Jugoslavs. Though they happen to be operating under a Russian chief, they have demonstrated that whatever their private opinions of Tito and his regime may be, they are in the country on an errand of mercy. They are seeing to it that relief reaches the people of the country who are in need of it. The only criticism that could be levelled against them to date is that so far they have been unable to investigate the conditions under which the political prisoners are incarcerated and to ensure that they are being adequately fed, as the UNRRA mission in Greece has done.

If the policy of Tito continues, these will be the last unofficial members of the Western democracies to enter Jugoslavia en masse. Wherever they went, they were welcomed by the people and found that the name of UNRRA had gone before them.

Therefore, when the members of Congress talked angrily of cutting off supplies to those countries under totalitarian rule, they were cutting off their noses to spite their faces. Had there been attached to them conditions requiring him to change his system, Tito would have refused the supplies and let his people suffer. If the communist mind can excuse and condone the massacre of two million Russian peasants in order to create a collective farm system, it is easy to see Tito willingly accepting the death of a quarter of his population by disease and starvation rather than relax his power to the point where he may be overthrown.

By working on the principle that it is concerned with peoples and not with governments, UNRRA has laid the foundations for immeasurable post-war good will towards America. Much as he dislikes the broad contact involved in UNRRA work inside his country, Tito has been forced to give in. Strangely enough, he has never attempted to pick an issue with UNRRA since it sent its mission to Jugoslavia. He has even been forced, in spite of protests made in private, to accept the principle of relief to all, without discrimination as to race, creed, or political belief. The reason is comparatively simple for those who care to see it. In Jugoslavia, UNRRA has a stronger influence than either the American or British diplomatic missions, because UNRRA is concerned with practical ideals rather than so-called practical politics. In the latter game, the Partisan leaders are old hands. They know all the tricks of protocol, of throwing discussion of ticklish subjects from open session to the privacy of special committees. But with UNRRA they are comparatively helpless, because UNRRA is concerned primarily with one thing only—the principle of helping people. And in attempting to fix limitations on UNRRA's work in Jugoslavia, Tito would be exposing the emptiness of his own doctrine.

When, therefore, Congress approved the allocation of funds permitting UNRRA to carry on with its operations, and when they withdrew the various conditions they had posed in permitting their use, Congress was being infinitely wiser than perhaps it realized. No conditions need be attached to the use of UNRRA funds, discriminating between one country and another because of the nature of their regimes. In Jugoslavia the people realize fully whence their help is coming, and any attempt by Tito to belittle UNRRA only besmirches him still further in the minds of the Jugoslavs.

It will be many years, and there will be much bloodshed, before Tito can destroy the prestige of America and of Britain among the Jugoslavs. The democracies still possess a large credit balance to draw upon, but . . .

If they forget the people in their anxiety to deal solely with the government they will be destroying their own position.

VI. ITALY

"There was a bit of a storm in the intellectual spheres of Albania, which explains why twenty or so persons will immediately be sent to concentration camps. There must not be the least sign of weakness; justice and force must be the characteristics of the new regime."
—Diary of Count Ciano, May 12, 1939

ITALY

ITALY AFTER THE WAR

THE plane rocked violently 16,000 feet above the earth. Below were the jagged snow-streaked peaks of the mountains that lie behind the Dalmatian coast. As the plane flung itself into one cloud after another, it was hurled up and down sideways. The clattering of the hail on its body drowned out the noise of the motors. Then, suddenly, as though reluctant to release us, the cloud gave us one final toss into the air and we burst out into the blue. There was sunshine all around. The tiny towns of Dalmatia lay far below us, licked by the green fringe of the Adriatic. Far ahead, the heat haze darkened to the low flat coast of Italy.

Southern Italy, with its olive groves, its plodding peasants' carts with the dogs trotting patiently between their six-foot wheels, its dirty little sun-bathed villages; Italy, with its confusion, its struggle to rise from disillusion and defeat, its temporary reversion to pre-fascist chaos and dishonesty and inefficiency—its air of freedom.

Our pilot, a young American lieutenant, took his hands off the controls, threw his arms in the air, and shouted, "Whoopee!"

Those who do not realize that the air of freedom has a physical reality, actually exists, should go to Belgrade for some months and then make that flight to Italy. They will never realize the transition that occurs in them while in Jugoslavia, for the pressure of the atmosphere only gradually restricts their personalities. But as their plane wheels over the olive groves to make its landing at Bari, they will feel their chests expand. And suddenly they will realize that they are taking their first deep breath for months, not only a deep breath but a breath of clean air. And they will realize, perhaps for the first time in their lives, how immeasurably fortunate they are to belong to a country where men are still comparatively free. They will get a deep satisfaction like a smoker enjoying his first cigarette for months, and become aware of the deep joys and privileges of a democracy. The moment may be brief, for in a few weeks they may be submerged in the general stream, once more preoccupied with the troubles and problems of democracy, and, like the majority of others around us, they will perhaps lose that awareness of democracy's values.

To lose that awareness is, sooner or later, to lose democracy itself; and the re-creation of democracy, if ever the opportunity occurs, is a long and laborious process, as the example of Italy shows.

The formulation of Italian attitudes towards the three large Allies to the point where they exist today, falls into three main stages. There was first the period when Italy was at war against us. Next, came the period of Italian surrender, when the southern half of the country lay under the joint occupation of America and Britain, and the northern half lay under the occupation of the Germans. The final period has seen the liberation of the whole country, the surrender of control by the Allied authorities, and the present attempts of America and Britain to resuscitate the country's shattered economy and restore democracy to a people whose younger generation has never known the meaning of the word.

The first period can be dealt with briefly, for the very speed of the Italian collapse demonstrated that the hearts of the people were not in the war. Indeed, in the years before the war, there were plenty of indications, to those of us who lived and worked in fascist Italy, that their hearts were not even completely in agreement with fascism as it manifested itself in later years. Their Latin temperament inclined them to regard the more flamboyant aspects of their system with a mixture of cynicism and amusement, as evinced by my Rome office boy when he came to me one evening in the summer of 1939, asking to have the next day off and saying with a grin that he had to attend a spontaneous demonstration outside the Palazzo Venezia. He showed me the postcard he had received, with its instructions. In those days Fascist Italy did not even trouble to go to the extra expense of an envelope. A penny postcard would do!

Ostensibly, Italy at war was even more bitter towards the Allies than Germany. Both the British Eighth Army and the Americans who landed in North Africa had had experience of the cruelty with which they were treated by Italians when taken prisoner. Because of that treatment and because of the readiness with which Italian troops surrendered, American and British troops developed a contempt and loathing for Italy which were by no means justified. In a fight, the Latin is by nature cruel and vindictive, but his blood cools as quickly as it grows hot. And those who believe that the Italians are by nature cowards received a shock to their preconceptions when they learned how ferociously the Italian Partisans behind German lines fought to free their fields and villages.

By the time they surrendered to the Allies, the Italians were weary of the war. Those dreams of empire, for which they had been persuaded to suffer through years of deprivations, were shattered. Hundreds of thousands of their men were prisoners in America, in Britain, in India, in Russia, and in the Middle East. In its disintegration, fascism had dragged down the whole nation to share its degradation, and there was nothing to which the people could look for rescue.

They had, it is true, developed an almost morbid anxiety to listen to the American and British radios. The very small proportion of radio sets in Italy before the war was nearly doubled in the two years after the invasion of Poland, and almost three-quarters of these sets were equipped to receive programs over the short-wave bands. Nevertheless, this could be ascribed to Gallic apostasy, a refusal to accept docilely the inanities of the Axis radio, rather than to a tangible admiration of the democracies.

In the early stages of the war neither America nor Britain promised anything to the Italians in return for unconditional surrender. Soviet Russia also had no "line" differing from the one adopted towards Germany of dividing the people into those who were in favor of the regime and those who were against it. It was not until the American and British armies stood opposite the Italian mainland on the coast of Africa that Anglo-American propaganda to the Italians took on the positive trend of attempting to build up an Italian resistance movement, and promising ultimate membership in the United Nations as a reward. Adolf A. Berle, Assistant Secretary of State, promised to all those true patriots of a free, friendly Italian nation who rose against the fascists, that they would not lack in assistance. "The armies of America and Britain are behind you," he said.

But when the Allied armies crossed to the mainland, entering upon that second phase of the conditioning of the Italian minds, they found a nation seemingly beyond all hope of recovery . . . physically, socially, or spiritually. It was a land of ruin and despair.

Frank Gervasi of *Collier's* told me in Cairo at the end of 1944 that Italy was finished. Frank had worked in Italy for many years before the war. It was the European country which he knew best and of which he was fitted to speak with authority. His sojourn in Italy as a war correspondent had done nothing to lighten his depression. "The Italians have taken a terrible beating," he said to me. "It will be generations before they recover and they will never be even a second-class power again."

It was some months before I could go to Italy and spend some time there, but I was then able to see what had caused Frank to form this opinion. The war had proceeded up the length of the country in a series of spasmodic jerks as the Germans retreated from one series of prepared defenses to another. Where the Allies had been compelled to fight for ground the devastation was enormous. The weapons of modern warfare had accomplished in a few days what had taken years of guerrilla warfare to accomplish in Jugoslavia—and, unlike Jugoslavia, the inhabitants of the shattered towns and villages had had no time in which to find refuge for themselves or to find places of safety for their most cherished possessions.

One day a town had existed under as nearly normal conditions as are possible in a country where a modern war is being fought. The German army had lived a life quite distinct from that of the local inhabitants. The enormous streams of supplies flowing through to the front lines had hardly impeded the normal customs of the peasants tilling the tiny fields as though no Moloch were stalking the land a few miles away. Then, suddenly, the traffic began to flow in the opposite direction as the Germans withdrew their forces northward, and, within a few hours, war struck at the town with the speed and force of a whirlwind, leaving it shattered beyond recognition, its inhabitants dazed and homeless, its tillable land sown with mines and unapproachable. Following the Germans came the Allies, who cleared the verges of the roads of mines, but left the fields still sown with sudden death—there was no time to do more.

If the town were fortunate, the Germans had pulled back sufficiently far to leave it well behind the Allied lines and therefore in a position where the townspeople could set about the laborious work of clearing up the wreckage. But if the front line were not far away, the town was once more subjected to attack, this time by the Germans.

The effect of modern war on southern Italy was catastrophic. Even in peacetime, this part of Italy had never been far above the level of feudalism. It is poor agricultural country, but nearly half the population of the country lives there. Yet before the war its earning capacity was so poor that it paid only about one-fifth of the country's taxes. The tough land is carved up into tiny holdings and the waste of manpower is prodigious. The land is literally dug up by hand, every square yard of it, and the sparse harvest is also cut by hand. Modern methods of agriculture are unknown.

In Naples, capital of southern Italy and the chief Allied supply port for most of the Italian campaign, squalor reigned and crime abounded. It seemed on the surface that with the sudden removal of fascism the Italians had reverted to the chaos, inefficiency, and dishonesty of the eighteenth century. For twenty years the fascists had been allowed to tie up, ever more intimately, their own fate with that of the whole nation. So in their sudden downfall they had dragged the nation into the abyss with them.

Far more serious than the physical destruction was the spiritual degradation. For the most awful aspect of totalitarian rule, an aspect which is at once its greatest menace and its most attractive feature to the bewildered and disillusioned masses of people, is that in offering a panacea for all economic evils it insists that the people should renounce all attempts to face problems individually, and should allow the regime to do all the necessary thinking.

With the collapse of fascism, the Italian people appeared to have forgotten how to think for themselves. Their press had been accustomed to automatic praise of every governmental gesture, and with the disappearance of the regime and its replacement by an Allied occupation, it knew nothing better than to give the same slavish praise to the Allies that it had once given to Mussolini, and the same outpouring of invective to Mussolini that it had once devoted to the Allies.

The Anglo-American PWB laboriously endeavored to remove this psychosis—for it was nothing less. The weight of fascist authority had left its imprint on the Italian mind just as deeply as air raids had affected those soldiers of World War I who dived under the nearest table whenever an automobile backfired. To give the Italians fine-sounding definitions of democracy would have had about as much effect as telling a shell-shocked soldier that the war was over. These people had to be taught to think for themselves.

There were many fine people in AMG and not least among them were those American and British journalists, foreign correspondents of before the war, who had enlisted for the painstaking, mole-like task of grubbing up the roots of fascism.

Their successors in the profession, those war correspondents who wrote with a flourish that General Eisenhower was perpetuating fascism in Italy by maintaining the original Italian police force, seemed to think that an evil disease could be removed merely by waving a magic wand. There did exist many weaknesses in AMG but the decision to proceed step by step with the re-education of the Italian people was not one of them.

The basic weakness was that America and Britain decided to go into Italy and rule the conquered country without the participation of Soviet Russia. This decision, in its turn, was based upon the fact that by the time the Italian campaign arose, both Roosevelt and Churchill had sufficient evidence to convince them that Russia was pursuing the war for her own ends. True, for foreign consumption, Russia gave lip service to the Allied cause, but as both America and Britain knew through their diplomatic missions in Moscow, the Russian propaganda campaign for domestic consumption was quite different. To the Russian people the war was portrayed as an event which had temporarily caused the courses of their country and the Western democracies to run parallel—but only temporarily. There was no attempt by Russia to "sell" the democracies to the Russian people as intensively as the democracies "sold" Russia to *their* own peoples. And the manner in which the Russians were behaving in Iran indicated in the strongest possible fashion that Russia intended to pursue a unilateral course of action after the war.

The only way in which America and Britain, still closely tied together by the intimate cooperation of Roosevelt and Churchill, knew how to reply to these tactics was to institute a unilateral system of military government in Italy. Its folly ought to have been apparent at the time, for Russia made no protest. Indeed, it was probably welcomed by Stalin for it established a precedent to which he could point later when the Red Army liberated the Balkans and proceeded to set up unilateral systems of military government in those countries.

And, furthermore, he could count on it as a certain fact that the military government of Italy would commit mistakes —as which military government does not? Shrewd tactics by the Italian communists could capitalize these mistakes and swing a certain amount of public opinion to the idea that perhaps the Russian system of doing things would be better.

Later, both America and Britain saw the trap into which they had fallen and established an Allied Commission on which all countries with which Italy had been at war were invited to serve—Soviet Russia, Greece, Jugoslavia, and France, as well as America and Britain. But by that time the mistakes had been made.

The Anglo-American blunders in the early days of occupation were of two categories. On the British part, they were mistakes of commission. On the American part, they were mistakes of omission.

This statement is a generalization, of course, and one which is liable to be challenged. Nevertheless, it is true as a generalization that America failed to provide a sufficient number of officials of all categories qualified to take a proportionate share of responsibility for the government of Italy. On the other hand, the British had an abundance of men whose previous connections with Italy qualified them as experts. The inevitable result was that the AMG machine became heavily weighted in favor of the British, not by British maneuvering, but by American default.

And as if this were not bad enough, the two countries approached the Italian problem from diametrically opposed angles. American connections with Italy were with its common people, thousands of whom had emigrated to America in search of a better life. Their annual remittances to their relatives formed a considerable part of Italy's pre-war revenue. It was from the ranks of the huge Italian colony in America that the majority of American recruits for AMG was drawn.

British experts on Italy were from an entirely different category. They had become experts by virtue of having lived and worked in the country before the war. The Italy they had known was the Italy of landlords, officials, bankers, and industrialists. An Italy whose navy not only had close ties with the British Navy but was very much the "senior" Service and, like the British Navy, intensely royalist.

Having themselves reconciled the idea of a monarchy with their own ideas of democracy, the British saw nothing unusual in the perpetuation of the monarchy in Italy. They realized that Victor Emmanuel was too deeply entangled with Mussolini to remain as king, but they saw no reason why his abdication in favor of his son should not succeed in saving the monarchy. They did not realize that the monarchy was too deeply associated with fascism to retain its power among the defeated and disillusioned Italians. It is possible, as a speculation, that if the throne had been abdicated in favor of the third generation, in favor of Victor Emmanuel's grandson, thus permitting the establishment of a temporary regency, the idea of monarchy might have ultimately endured as a unifying force among the different political parties.

But Churchill would not hear of it. He refused to recognize that the war had an ideological character and said as much. When Count Sforza returned to Italy from his exile in America and attempted to convince the Allies that the monarchy was a dead force, it was Churchill who insisted on Sforza's removal from political power—as though it were possible to remove a popular prejudice by removing the man who reported it.

The decision to retain the monarchy was taken largely by virtue of the British preponderance in AMG and by virtue of the fact that in the trend towards post-war power politics it was recognized that Italy was in the British sphere. American reaction to the decision was a mixture of contradictions. In Italy itself, American officials accepted the decision as one that had been taken by "higher quarters" and was therefore unchallengeable. But there were some in the New York office of OWI who refused to accept the decision, in spite of directives from Washington. With more skill than caution, these people set out to ignore or circumvent the directives from Washington and there followed a succession of broadcasts to Italy from New York which devoted themselves to the task of undermining the monarchy.

Their efforts culminated in a broadcast which referred to Victor Emmanuel as the "moronic little king." It was a good epithet but by no means true, for however small Victor Emmanuel may be he is not by any means moronic, as demonstrated by his shrewd political maneuvering during his reign. When its contents became known, the broadcast raised a storm of public comment and resulted in Mr. Elmer Davis, then director of OWI, making inquiries which led to disciplinary action. Unaware of the irresponsibility which led to the broadcasts, however, the Italian listeners could conclude only that American policy in Italy had not yet been formulated.

The American and British officials of PWB were not really concerned with the question of whether Italy would remain a monarchy or not. They were devoting themselves to the task of helping the Italians to restore freedom of expression in all its phases. Every newspaper in the Allied-occupied zone was operated by PWB. The official news service, Stefani, was abolished as being a fascist agency and a news service by PWB was instituted. In addition, PWB controlled nearly all the transmitters in the Allied zone. Stocks of movie films and equipment were impounded, and all films were examined before being released for distribution. All distribution, releases, and film showings were controlled by PWB.

It was slow work and mistakes were made. It would perhaps have been more immediately efficient if PWB had not taken Italians into its organization. In such an event, the Italian press, edited solely by American and British journalists, could have vaulted overnight into a position of presenting a sober and well-balanced picture of daily events. But PWB was looking ahead to the time when the Italians would once more be masters in their own land and it was not enough merely to do a good job of presenting the news during the occupation; the Italian fourth estate itself had to be taught to do the job after the occupation was over.

In this and in other problems of the occupation, AMG authorities were continually in competition with the other

Allied military leaders who were concerned solely with the task of expelling the Germans. Ships were needed desperately to carry supplies for the rehabilitation of the liberated portion of Italy, but shipping could not be obtained because it was commandeered by AFHQ. One of the armistice conditions was that not only the Italian Navy, but the whole Italian merchant marine, must be handed over to the Allies. The condition was a wise one, but the Allies would have been still wiser if, having obtained possession of Italian shipping, they had devoted a portion of it to the reconstruction of the shattered country they occupied.

The Italians were desperately in need of footwear, of meat, and of coal, to name only three of the items which were almost completely lacking. The Italian island of Sardinia had a surplus of all three and the Sardinians were seething with discontent, to the point of autonomy, because they were unable to export their surplus to the mainland. On three separate occasions attempts were made to secure the release of a few small coastal ships in order to bring meat, hides, and coal from Sardinia to the mainland; and on each occasion the attempt came to nothing because the relevant papers wound up on the desk of an Allied official who chose the bureaucratic safety of abiding by a literal interpretation of the armistice conditions rather than take the initiative of releasing the required ships. The result was that Italians lived on short rations, watched the price of shoes soar to sixty dollars and eighty dollars a pair, and remained unemployed while the factories stayed idle for want of fuel.

It was not surprising that the idea slowly grew and spread that the Russians, whatever their extremes might be, would have done things differently. A casual observer visiting Italy in the first six months of 1944 would have decided that Italy was ripe for communism.

In 1944, behind the German lines in northern Italy, the industrial workers of the towns were preparing for action. They had their own Partisan organization which was closely in touch with the Jugoslav Partisans. Like Tito's National Liberation Committee, they presented the face of an organization in which all Left-wing and liberal parties united in a common endeavor to fight the Germans. Like the Jugoslav Partisans, they were in touch with AFHQ in Italy. They also had their communications with Allied officers stationed in Switzerland.

Unfortunately for the course of events in Italy during the last six months of the campaign, the very word Partisans had come to have an unpleasant connotation in the minds of the American and British commanders. The Greek civil war had already demonstrated the ambitions and abilities of the Greek communists within the Greek Partisan movement. And it was at last beginning to dawn upon the Western Allies that Tito also was not what he had pretended to be.

Since the game of power politics was already well under way, both America and Britain would have been well advised to realize that Russia was now approaching that point where it was impossible to satisfy everybody.

There was the question of Trieste and the Istrian peninsula. The territory had been Italian. Tito wanted it. Perhaps the Italian Communist Party, on instructions from Moscow, would not have opposed its cession. In which case, the Italian Communist Party would have committed political suicide in Italy.

It would have been shrewd politics if the Allies had allowed the Italian Partisans to participate in negotiations with Tito over the Trieste question, thus facing the Italian communists with the embarrassing necessity of choosing between their patriotism and their ideology.

Shortly before the question of Trieste arose, however, Allied policy in Italy underwent a drastic change.

Mr. Churchill paid a visit to Italy in the early fall of 1944, not long after he had declared that the struggle was becoming less and less an "ideological war." The situation he found in Italy gave him a swift and sobering shock. Perhaps for the first time since he became Prime Minister of Britain, he realized that the war was becoming rather more than less ideological, and from Rome in September, 1944, he proclaimed to the Italians and the whole world the "ideology" for which, in his opinion, the Allies were fighting.

Mr. Churchill said that the Allies were fighting to restore freedom to the oppressed peoples, including those who, like the Italians, had fought against us: and these, said Mr. Churchill, were the tests of freedom:

1. Is there the right to free expression of opinion and of opposition and criticism of the government of the day?

2. Have the people the right to turn out a government of which they disapprove, and are constitutional means provided by which they can make their will apparent?

3. Are their courts of justice free from violence by the executive and free of all threats of mob violence and all association with any particular political parties?

4. Will these courts administer open and well-established laws which are associated in the human mind with the broad principles of decency and justice?

5. Will there be fair play for poor as well as rich, for private persons as well as government officials?

6. Will the rights of the individual, subject to his duties to the state, be maintained and asserted and exalted?

7. Is the ordinary peasant or workman, earning a living by daily toil and striving to bring up a family, free from the fear that some grim police organization under the control of a single party (like the Gestapo, started by the Nazi and

Fascist Parties) will tap him on the shoulder and pack him off without fair or open trial to bondage or ill-treatment?

Now it was obvious at the time that, in this speech, Mr. Churchill was seeking to justify in advance the intervention which he by then saw was inevitable in Greece if the country were to be saved from the communist-controlled dictatorship of EAM. He may also have had in mind the inevitable oligarchies in Rumania, Bulgaria, and Jugoslavia. Whatever the cause, the vital importance of the speech was that Mr. Churchill had at long last realized that the seven points went to the very root of Europe's terrible experiences, and that the time was overdue when the political dreams of the people had to be considered in order to secure the victory and insure a lasting peace.

The temptation to regard Allied supremacy in arms as alone sufficient to insure both victory and peace had been overpowering for years—and indeed there was no doubt that the large battalions would be needed to cauterize the poison of Fascism and National Socialism. But the condition which permitted the lawlessness of totalitarian rule had also to be ended, and force alone could not end that condition.

It had been a long time coming, but Mr. Churchill had finally realized the importance of full political warfare. It was too late by now to apply it to the countries of Eastern and Southeastern Europe, but it was not too late to apply it to Italy.

Six years previously, the British Minister in Belgrade, the late Neville Henderson, had drawn a line north of the country to which he was accredited and had estimated that this was the line where Nazi expansion could be halted. He had been tragically wrong, as events swiftly demonstrated.

Now, in the fall of 1944, America and Britain drew a line extending northward from the eastern frontier of Italy and noted it as the line where they might hope to halt the westward expansion of Russia. It remained to be seen whether they were right.

A NEW ITALY TODAY

Let us jump ahead and look at Italy today. First of all, it is the most promising country in Europe. Its will to live has not only been revived but is spontaneously stronger than that of any other European nation. Its political animation is infectious and an ever-growing spate of newspapers increases the long-frustrated love of the southern Latin for polemics and diatribe.

Economically, standards are extremely low and would be regarded with abhorrence by Americans if they existed in the United States, but the excitement of rebuilding their own country has permeated throughout all classes of the country, and the new shoots of life are already thrusting their way through the debris of the war.

What are the reasons for this sudden transformation of a country which at one time seemed utterly beyond recovery?

First, there was the realization by America and Britain that their only hope in preserving a free Italy lay in supporting the formation of self-government at the earliest possible opportunity.

Second, there was the decision to throw in the utmost economic help in order to bolster the sagging economy of the country.

Third, there was the sound common sense of the Italian people, bursting to give expression to itself.

By the end of 1944, the decision had already been taken to turn over to the Italians more and more responsibility for running their own affairs, and this decision began to be put into effect early in 1945. A few railroad services were placed at the disposal of the civilian population. The Italian newspapers were allowed to take their news from whatever sources they wished and permission was given for Italian news services to be established. The armistice terms still remained in force but were modified and sometimes annulled in practice, much to the annoyance of Moscow.

The liberation of northern Italy took place so rapidly that its hydroelectric generators and industrial factories were recovered almost intact, thus placing manufacturing possibilities at the disposal of the whole country once it was possible to acquire raw materials. And the people of northern Italy brought with them a vigorous ability and willingness to share the general burden of reconstruction. The Allied Commission, ostensibly the governing body of the country, devoted itself to the task of repatriating the enormous numbers of refugees found in the north of Italy and, this well-nigh accomplished, hastily turned the territory over to the Italian Government, contenting itself with guarding Italian interests in the Trieste zone.

America and Britain began to ship back as quickly as possible the hundreds of thousands of Italian war prisoners scattered round various parts of the world, and with their arrival new reserves of manpower were at the disposal of the government.

The task of reconstruction was prodigious, so prodigious that it was difficult to know where to begin. The normal coal requirements of Italian industry had been a million tons monthly, all of it imported from British, French, and German coalfields.

The steel factories required a minimum of sixty-five thousand tons of scrap iron monthly, and although some of this could be made up from the debris of war scattered around nearly every field and hillside, it would not be by any means sufficient.

There was not enough food to feed the people, and what

there was could not be properly distributed, so shattered were the road and rail communications. In the south alone, more than a million people had lost their homes, and there were about a hundred and fifty thousand refugees. The average ration provided only two thousand calories a day, even when relief supplies from the military were included, and over a long period two thousand calories is not sufficient to prevent people from deteriorating physically.

For the crops there were almost no fertilizers, and the amount shipped in during 1945 was less than ten per cent of normal Italian fertilizer imports.

Transportation of existing supplies was next to impossible. Of the one hundred thousand trucks possessed by Italy in 1940, most had been requisitioned and later wrecked by the Germans. The remaining civilian transport had to be devoted to moving minimum food supplies from the countryside into the principal cities. The main railroad lines were still in the hands of the Allied military authorities, who had not yet had time to repair the secondary lines. Nearly every rail and road bridge had been destroyed by the Germans as they retreated.

Homes and offices were without windows. In Naples alone, nearly one half of the city was without glass. But glass could not be manufactured because the glass factories could not obtain electric power. And power could not be provided because there was no coal.

Public health had steadily deteriorated because of shortages of food, clothing, medical services, and shelter. In the winter of 1943–44 Italy had been threatened with a major typhus epidemic whose conquest was one of the most important medical victories of the war—but for each conquered epidemic a dozen others were threatening.

The flooding of the Pontine Marshes, a little south of Rome, by the Germans, had destroyed twenty years of land reclamation in that area and had made it once more the breeding ground for malarial mosquitoes. In retreating over the marshes, the Germans had not only destroyed the power stations which kept the land drained. They had also destroyed the dikes that kept the water in channels. They destroyed even the wire screens with which every house was fitted. There were no supplies of Paris Green with which to prevent the mosquitoe larvae from breeding in the swamps. The elaborate system of inspection was wrecked because there were no tires for the bicycles of the marsh inspectors. And already there were one and a half million cases of malaria among the Italians.

The annual tuberculosis mortality had risen to at least three times the pre-war figure of sixty thousand. At least two and a half million children and nursing and expectant mothers were in need of supplies that could only come from abroad.

There were other facts, plenty of them, all equally depressing, and it was when the problem was most acute that UNRRA decided to send a mission to Italy.

The mission was headed by an American who had had much previous experience of relief work in various parts of the world, Mr. Spurgeon M. Keeny. He took with him a staff of Americans and Britons and set up his headquarters in Rome at the end of 1944.

It is yet too soon to do full justice to the work of UNRRA in Italy—that work will still be appreciated many years after UNRRA has passed out of existence; but there is no doubt that it gave the Italians the wherewithal with which to set about the rebuilding of their country.

Mr. Keeny's tactics were, from the outset, unorthodox. On the one hand, he had the problem of the Allied Military Commission, the cautiousness with which they proceeded from one task to another in a situation whose urgency demanded speed, and their reluctance to grant full autonomy to a new civilian agency. On the other hand, he had the apparent apathy and lethargy of the Italians themselves. It was not enough for

UNRRA to do the job; the Italians had to be cajoled and pushed into action.

Relief work in a country so shattered as Italy (or any other country ravaged by this war, for that matter) is not a job for the dreamy idealist. Although Mr. Keeny may be an idealist, he could not by any stretch of the imagination be called dreamy. His effect on the Italians was that of a seltzer powder dropped into a glass of water.

For his first year of operation in 1945, he had the comparatively tiny budget of fifty million dollars, or about one-eighth of that allocated to Jugoslavia. In less than six months he had galvanized the Italian officials into activity. Refugee camps previously operated by the military had been taken over, a system of rationing established, and the control of threatening epidemics put on an organized basis.

To give all the credit to either UNRRA or Mr. Keeny would be invidious. It would be nearer the truth to say that UNRRA operations began in the right way at the critical moment and found an immediate response in that inward urge of the Italians to do something for themselves.

RUSSIAN OPPOSITION

The speed with which America and Britain turned over northern Italy to the Italians, the energy with which UNRRA operated in Italy, the alacrity with which the Italians jumped to the work of rebuilding their country, were all signs to arouse Russia to a sense that a halt was at last being called to the spread of her influence.

Physically, the halt had already been called in the firm Allied stand at Trieste, but this was something different. This was the rejuvenation of a country, both economically and spiritually. To the politically minded Russians, accustomed somewhat like the Germans to regard modern society from a fixed and precise point of view, there was a disquieting tendency on the part of the Italians to regard political polemics more as a safety valve, than as the shaft which drove the engine.

In my travels during the previous two years I had met and become friendly with a Russian official whose name for obvious reasons must remain a secret. On one occasion I remember discussing with him Stalin's decision to dissolve the Comintern. I commented on it as a wise decision to allay the fears of Russophobes among the Americans and British, and said that, if genuine, the decision represented a reversal of all previous revolutionary doctrine.

"On the contrary," said my Russian friend, "if you look at the world today you will see there is no future need for a Comintern. After the war, every liberated country in Europe will be shattered beyond the point when it can return to your kind of an economic and political system. You, of course, will wish it to return. You will therefore be compelled to pour your wealth and supplies into a bottomless hole, for, if you stop doing so, the country will turn towards us. But it is a process that will impoverish you without contributing anything to the return to capitalism of any other country.

"At one time, perhaps, we believed that it would be necessary to give the branch a shake in order to collect the fruit. In that respect you can say we have changed. Today it is obvious that the fruit will grow ripe of its own accord and drop into our laps without any effort on our part."

Of course, this was the doctrine of Marxism carried a stage further than its pre-war conception. No true communist, I think, would have found fault with it in the closing stages of the war.

He would find fault with it today because Russia learned in Italy that it was too optimistic a conception of the shape of things to come. For, indeed, far from not opposing financial and economic aid to Italy, Russia was sufficiently alarmed by

285

the trend of events in Italy to oppose this aid with all the devices in her power.

In the early fall of 1945 the UNRRA Council met in London, and considered among other things an American proposal to increase the extent of UNRRA aid to Italy. The American delegate, Mr. William L. Clayton, Assistant Under-Secretary of State, proposed that the UNRRA budget for Italy in 1946 should be for full-scale operations as in other countries, such as Jugoslavia and Greece. This meant increasing allocations for Italy from the 1945 figure of fifty million dollars to about four hundred and fifty million dollars. There was some opposition to this proposal from the delegates from the Russian sphere—Jugoslavia, Poland, and Soviet Russia—but Mr. Clayton made it clear that America was determined to do her utmost to restore the economy of Italy.

Less than three months later Soviet Russia demanded that Italy be required to pay a total reparations bill of three hundred million dollars of which one-third would be given to the Soviet Union and the rest would go to Jugoslavia, Greece, and Albania, while Britain and the United States should waive any share.

Simultaneously Russia refused to accept an Anglo-American recommendation that the armistice terms be abrogated for Italy and replaced by a less onerous interim arrangement.

The Russian demand for reparations was conveniently attached to a Russian news agency interview with an Italian communist leader, Luigi Longo, who was quoted as saying that neither Britain nor America could reasonably expect reparations from Italy since they had already had about two billion dollars worth of valuables and property turned over to them by Italy. The latter statement was not tempered by any recognition of the fact that America had undertaken to back with dollars the occupation currency issued to American troops in Italy, thus opening dollar revenue to the country.

The effect of the Russian reparations demand, if acceded to by America and Britain, would have been that the dollars UNRRA poured into Italy would have been taken out in reparations, thus nullifying two-thirds of the proposed UNRRA program. Of the four hundred and fifty million dollars proposed for Italy, approximately three hundred million would have been contributed by America, the rest being made up by Great Britain and the other contributing nations of UNRRA. In fixing their demand for reparations, the Russians thus gauged to a nicety the amount of free exchange which it was proposed to spend in Italy.

Needless to say, America quickly put her foot down on the proposal, having no intention of allowing her Italian policy to be so neatly disembowelled. Meantime, however, Russia was having some success in another direction.

Next to food, the commodity most desperately needed by Italy is coal. Coal was needed immediately to get the idle factories working, to supply the power plants, to rehabilitate the railroads, and to keep down a dangerous pool of unemployed. Emergency supplies could be obtained from stockpiles built up in the Middle East during the last year of the war by America and Britain for just some situation such as this; but these supplies were only a third of Italy's requirements. British coal mines could supply only a proportion of the need. America had stocks of coal, but it would obviously be impractical from a long-term point of view to make Italy reliant on supplies three thousand miles away, when other supplies lay closer to hand in the Ruhr.

During the fall of 1945, a desperate effort was made by UNRRA to get Italian factories into production by bringing in coal from South Africa and the United States, but, as Mr. Keeny pointed out in a press conference in Washington at the time, this was a bad situation because of the cost. "One of the first things that must be done," he said, "is to get European coal—to make European coal available, including coal from the Ruhr." The coal situation, he added, was at the heart of the recovery program, not merely of Italy but also of a number of other European countries.

Shortly after the end of the war, a tour of inspection of the rich coal mines in Western Germany was made by a delegation of the Combined Production and Resources Board, whose headquarters were in Washington and which had been responsible throughout the war for the allocation of vital supplies to the places where they were most needed. Their report urged the rehabilitation of these mines as soon as possible, but was first submitted to the Allied governments for consideration on the highest official level—for any suggestion to rehabilitate a German industry involved questions of high policy.

Fully aware of the implications of this proposal, Russia opposed it, and proceeded to a radio and press campaign alleging that America and Britain were attempting to reconstruct German heavy industry. It was an argument calculated to appeal to the popular mind, and deliberately ignored altogether the fact that whatever country possesses the Ruhr in the future, the coal that lies in its ground is of vital importance to the economy of the continent.

RUSSIA'S ECONOMIC WARFARE AGAINST ITALY

In adopting these almost open tactics to devitalize Italian reconstruction, it was clear that Russia had abandoned, at least temporarily, any hope of winning Italian popular sympathy and admiration. The change of Russian policy began to become more evident, however, with the refusal of America and Britain to give way tamely to Tito in Trieste.

The compromise permitted Jugoslav troops to occupy a portion of the Istrian peninsula until the future of the whole area had been decided. The area occupied by the Jugoslavs was called Zone B; the rest of the peninsula, occupied by American and British forces, was Zone A.

Some of Tito's tactics in Zone B, such as his kidnapping of the Italian residents, his creation of fake "Italian" newspapers demanding incorporation of Istria into Jugoslavia and so forth, have already been described.

But Tito also used Zone B as a method of undermining Italy's economic system. This zone, although occupied by Jugoslav troops, is still officially Italian territory until its future status is decided. This means, among other things, that Italian currency is still the only legal means of tender. Towards the end of 1945 the Partisans began to manufacture quantities of Italian lire notes and to pump them into Zone B, whence they found their way into the rest of Italy, thus depreciating the value of the currency.

Perhaps the best way to describe this maneuver is to give the account broadcast by the Italian radio, Venezia Giulia:

"The Bank of Istria, Fiume, and the Slovene Littoral has issued notes to the value of five, twenty, fifty, one hundred, five hundred, and one thousand lire. This procedure recalls that of Chicago gangsters. The Jugoslav administration should know that before issuing notes it is necessary to cover their amount. Moreover, only military authorities may issue notes. In fact, the Allies, who are well aware of international law, did just this, and did not give the bank set up by them any order to issue the new notes.

"The Bank of Istria, Fiume, and the Slovene Littoral is not a State bank, for the territory where it carries on its business is at present a disputed territory, militarily occupied by Jugoslav troops, just as the territory to the west is militarily occupied by the Allies. It is, then, a private bank whose existence is governed by the international statutes of the area. From an international point of view it is, therefore, not dependent on any state, and not connected with the military occupation. This currency is not only illegal but false."

It was two weeks before Tito could think out a suitable reply for domestic use. (He has not yet issued a reply for consumption outside Jugoslavia.) The reply, distributed in Serbo-Croat Morse by the official Jugoslav agency Tanjug, was as follows:

"Newspapermen from Ljubljana, Zagreb, and Fiume visited the deputy commander of the Jugoslav Army administration for the Slovene Littoral, Colonel Holjevac, who replied to a number of topical questions.

"Question: What are the reasons for the military administration of the Jugoslav Army having put into circulation more lire?

"Answer: This was necessitated by economic and financial difficulties with which broad popular masses of this territory are faced. Lately there has been danger that we would be unable to undertake essential reconstruction work, issue regular payments to employed workers, or meet the needs of industry for raw materials and products because of lack of currency. It is common knowledge that many banks, previous to and during the liberation of this territory by the Jugoslav Army, withdrew a greater part of their monetary assets into Italy or blocked monies in their branches through central offices.

"The same applies to more important enterprises which transferred their capital to Italy or Zone A, and left behind workers and employees and demolished installations, without means for their reconstruction. The Jugoslav Government is giving this territory enormous material assistance, and has placed at the disposal of the Jugoslav Army Administration the entire stock of lire she had. These lire, however, had gradually been disappearing from the territory.

"For the lire which had been put into circulation minor and

insufficient articles of use were imported from Zone A, and these were not goods which were most needed by the broad masses of people. Thus this territory remained without sufficient quantities of currency in circulation. This would seem to dispose of the reasons why we put more lire into circulation.

"Question: Is improvement in financial and economic conditions, resulting from more currency being put into circulation, already being felt?

"Answer: It is now exactly one month since we issued the first batch of the new lire. This fact certainly aided us in the execution of vital operations and insured regular payments being made to workers and employees. Special credits which we granted to some of our institutions and enterprises helped to restore the life of the community and in particular that of individual and other damaged enterprises. At the same time I assisted in the struggle against black marketeers and speculators and to them, it seems, this is the greatest thorn in their flesh.

"Question: What is the established rate of lire in relation to the dinar and is the population of this zone in a position to buy both in Jugoslavia and Zone A?

"Answer: In agreement with the Central Ministry of Finance, measures have been taken enabling the population of Zone B to buy in, and to exchange goods with, Jugoslavia. The entire import and export of goods is carried out on the strength of permits issued by the economic section of the military administration. All payments for imports from, and exports to, Jugoslavia are carried out exclusively through a clearing account in lire which has been opened in Fiume.

"The export of goods from Jugoslavia into Zone B is against dinars. The rate of exchange for all payments through the clearing account provided is for thirty dinars to one hundred lire. It is strictly prohibited to use dinars as tender on the territory of this Military Administration.

"As regards commercial relations with Zone A, we are at this moment in consultation with the Allied Military Administration on this matter and we believe the problem will be solved in such a way that business men here will be able to purchase necessary articles in Zone A."

Now this statement exposes certain facts. First, there is the admission that Tito was pumping fake currency into the area. Fake, because it was not backed by anything. The inhabitants of Zone B could not even use it to buy necessities of life from Jugoslavia. For this purpose Jugoslav dinars had to be used. But the inhabitants of Zone B were not allowed to use dinars. In consequence a debt in dinars was being piled up. If the territory were incorporated into Jugoslavia, this debt could be wiped out or adjusted. If not incorporated into Jugoslavia, Italy would have to redeem this debt.

The use of dinars was prohibited because some of these would inevitably have found their way into Italy proper and would later have to be redeemed by Jugoslavia.

But the lire were not only forged currency; they were also issued at an exorbitant rate of exchange—thirty Jugoslav dinars for one hundred so-called lire. The American dollar in Italy is worth one hundred lire and in Jugoslavia is worth fifty dinar, even at the unreal rate of exchange officially established by Tito. The dinar-lire rate should therefore be fifty dinar to one hundred lire and not thirty to one hundred.

There were, of course, protests from the population of Zone B, and on occasion there were demonstrations which were put down by force by the Jugoslav Partisans. In one demonstration, in which two Italians were killed and business premises were damaged, the Partisans admitted there had been excesses, but passed off the incident as one which had been organized by pro-fascist elements.

292

The Trieste problem united the Italians nearly as strongly as the problems of reconstruction. Whatever the problems of intermingled minorities in the hinterland of the port, there is no doubting the preponderantly Italian character of the town itself; and the Italians, as they read of Partisan tactics, became increasingly incensed. By their silence, doubtless enforced on them by instructions from Moscow, the Italian communists isolated themselves from popular feeling on this issue.

Ferruci Parri, the veteran Italian Partisan leader and at that time Premier of Italy, voiced the public feeling in a broadcast:

"The government has serious duties of which it is aware. It is impossible to ignore the appeals of the lands which we regard as ours, and of our Italian brothers. It is impossible to ignore them because these mass deportations, this system of depriving families of all news, and of trying to eradicate that indelible Italian character which marks our towns and cities —these things cannot be permitted.

"Fascism does not enter into this matter," added Signor Parri, anticipating Tito's propaganda methods. "What we protest against are the evident and intentional signs of eliminating everything which might be an island of Italian resistance. It is an intentional plan, systematically carried out, that we must denounce, as indeed we have denounced, with determination.

"I belong to those groups who, after the last war, were called defeatists and renouncers because they believed that a policy of wisdom was that of respecting the rights of others, and of other peoples, convinced that there can be no justice unless it is other peoples', convinced that there can be no justice unless it is mutual. All our cards are therefore in order and we have the greatest right to defend openly the rights of our people—just because we have shown that we know how to respect other peoples' rights—and the right to ask that justice should be accorded to us, just as we invoked it in those days for the Jugoslav people."

An interesting swift sequence to this broadcast was that the Italian news agency which issued the text, later sent a message cancelling its report. Evidently Signor Parri had used words which were considered too strong for Italo-Jugoslav relations at that time.

The same day, however, demonstrations in favor of Italy took place in Trieste. Thanks to the work and tact of the Allied and civilian police, there were no clashes at the time; but when a number of workers who had attended the demonstrations returned to their work in the shipyards, they were suspended by the Works Committee of the United Adriatic Shipyards and were expelled by force from their places of work.

The AMG Labor Office investigated the incident, learned that the Works Committee was dominated by communists, and ordered the shipyard management to reinstate the dismissed workers.

On his return from touring the district, Premier Parri held his usual press conference for foreign correspondents in Rome. "In Udine, Venice, Padua, and other towns, I received a moving welcome from refugees and from a number of delegations from Venezia Giulia," he said. Venezia Giulia is the Italian name for the whole Istrian area whose future status was under dispute.

"I had to face such a sorrowful and pressing appeal for protection and help that no Government worthy of its name could ignore it," Signor Parri continued. "The number of those who have been deported from those regions to the interior of Jugoslavia is not three thousand but many more—no less than seven thousand or eight thousand. Not only did some of them not come back, but their families cannot get any news of them. These deportations were designed to remove those who might take part in the Italian Resistance Movement and were also designed to alter the ethnical aspect of the region.

"I repeat that before we can arrive at an entente and at

direct negotiations with the Jugoslav Government, the necessary conditions are that all persecutions should cease—that is, the present regime of persecutions, not against fascists, but against Italians; and that there should be justice for the Italian population in that region."

The turning point had been reached at last. The Left-Wing leader of an apparently weak country was finally refusing to negotiate with the most important protégé of the Soviet Union —and, furthermore, doing something that the statesmen of America and Britain had not yet done, exposing the imperialism of the totalitarian Left.

MOSCOW AND ALLIED VIEWS OF ITALY'S DOMESTIC POLITICS

Neither Moscow nor Belgrade was slow in retorting. Ilya Ehrenburg quickly paid a visit to Zone B, writing articles in praise of Jugoslav occupation methods.

Moscow radio criticized the Allied administration of Zone A, and began to adopt the same attitude towards the rest of Italy as it had done towards Greece—namely that the people of Italy were being oppressed by foreign reactionaries.

The cudgels were first taken up by Belgrade radio in a manner of which the following broadcast is a specimen:

"Belgrade—Today's *Borba* publishes an editorial, entitled 'Neo-Fascist Tendencies in the Internal and Foreign Policy of Italy,' saying that the situation in Italy has recently drawn the attention of all quarters in the world, which believed a consistent democratization of Italy was a condition of preserving peace in Italy. In Italy not only are the principles of the Moscow Declaration of the Foreign Ministers not being realized, but there are serious signs that fascist remnants in Italy are reorganizing and that they are increasingly influencing the political life and the present official Italian foreign policy.

"This neo-fascist trend in Italian foreign policy is especially shown in the attitude towards Jugoslavia. Even Parri attempted to influence international public opinion to place the defeated aggressor Italy in the position of prosecutor against an attacked and wounded Jugoslavia, while the leader of the Christian Democrats, De Gasperi, with his proposal at the London Conference of 'separate status for Zara and Fiume' attempted to dispute the right of our peoples even to these towns of ours.

"*Borba* concludes that the neo-fascist tendencies in Italian foreign policy strengthen Jugoslav public opinion in the conviction that Italian imperialism is not reconciled to defeat. Therefore, Italian imperialists are a serious threat to peace. The Jugoslav people know very well how to differentiate between the Italian people and Italian imperialists. But, always prepared for friendship with the Italian people and with a truly democratic Italy, Jugoslavia firmly requests that which is here."

At the same time a Moscow radio commentator named Grishanin broadcast that fascism "is still very strong in Italy," and that although Italy was occupied by Allied forces, no energetic measures for the elimination of fascism had been taken, so that the power "is still in the hands of the reactionaries."

A few days later, towards the end of November, 1945, the Parri Government fell and its fall brought forth this comment from Moscow:

"No one who has followed the situation in Italy closely could have been taken by surprise when the government crisis arose. The government headed by Parri was a coalition government of six parties of the National Liberation Movement. In the teeth of immense difficulties, both economic and political, the Parri Government carried through measures to promote democracy, root out fascism, rehabilitate the country's economic life, and also to bring Italy into the orbit of international cooperation.

"For the policy it pursued, the Parri government was attacked by the reactionaries, who deliberately set out to bring on a crisis. The instigators of the campaign were the surviving fascists, neo-fascists, monarchists, and clericals backed by the Vatican. Their pressure made itself felt inside the government coalition, too. As their spokesmen, they have the Right-wing of the Liberal Party, supported by the Christian Democrats.

"About two months ago, the Liberal leaders and press launched a drive to have the Liberation Committee dissolved, and the government coalition broken up. Just about this time there were numerous reports of a monarchist conspiracy and increased reactionary activities, and the public indignation they aroused made the Liberals and Christian Democrats postpone action. They did not give up the plan, and a week ago all the Liberal cabinet ministers handed in their resignations. Seconded by the Christian Democrats, the Liberals demanded that the government should resign, and a new government be formed by a well-known political leader outside the coalition. The government crisis thus became a fact.

"Both in Italy and abroad, the papers note that foreign policy factors as well as domestic ones operated in bringing on the crisis. They point out that the Italian reactionaries rely on outside support, that the Anglo-U.S. authorities in Italy often adopt an attitude of neutrality which actually serves the end of these Italian reactionaries, and that in some cases these authorities bring direct pressure to bear on the democratic forces.

"In an article printed in *Avanti* a correspondent of the American Overseas News (*sic*) registers an emphatic protest against Allied, particularly U.S., pressure which is exerted through delivering or withholding supplies, and which is intended to impose on Italy a reactionary government that the people do not want. The people of Italy have shown quite plainly what they think of the machinations of the reactionaries. In all the big towns there have been meetings, demonstrations, even short strikes of protest against these intrigues. What the people demand is a democratic government of national unity."

I have given the text of this broadcast so completely because it goes to the very heart of post-war Europe and illustrates aptly the trap into which both America and Britain fell in the early stages of post-war politics.

The question is simply this: Are the different National Liberation Committees that sprang up in so many countries during the German occupation entitled and fitted to constitute the government of each respective country after its liberation?

The immediate emotional reaction is to answer in the affirmative. After all, one can argue, these were the people who actually fought. These were the resisters. These were the men and women who suffered, who went into the hills determined to kill the enemy rather than surrender and live the tame life of the occupied towns.

But, it can be argued, the people who joined the resistance movements (excepting those who were forced to join by revolutionary tactics, such as those used by Tito in Jugoslavia), those who voluntarily left their homes in order to take up the fight fell into one general type—those who had nothing to lose but their lives. They were the unemployed who could look forward to nothing better during the occupation than prolonged unemployment at home or slave labor in the Reich; the teen-aged school youth of both sexes, whose schools were closed by the Germans; the peasants whose homes had been burned by the invader. These were the people who joined the underground movements at whose core were the communist and other related Leftist parties, whose members were experienced organizers, bred to techniques of agitation.

This is not to underestimate the heroism of the resistance movements nor to belie the undying enmity of their leaders towards fascism. When the Nazis were driven out of northern Italy, and when Mussolini was discovered in a German vehicle heading towards the safety of Switzerland, it was a communist who pulled off his blanket in order to verify his identity. And it was a communist who executed him less than twenty-four hours later.

But when the war ended, far too many young men and young women were left with machine guns and hand grenades whose use they knew better than their alphabet. Far too many of them had spent the years which, under other conditions, they would have spent in school or in work, as outlaws accustomed to licensed murder and brigandage. They had helped to win the war, but had their experiences equipped them to function as statesmen or civil servants in the peace?

For the victory they had helped to secure brought with it political freedom, not for them alone, but for the whole mass of their people. Could this mass of people be excluded from civic rights by the glib and false generalization that they were collaborators, because they had not taken to the hills and forests?

This mass of people had been excluded from participation in public affairs throughout the whole of the German occupation and, in some cases, for many years beforehand. This was true in Greece and it was even more true in Italy.

But liberation would bring with it—after a period of delay while the process of awakening took place—a realization of political responsibility, a desire to create representation through other parties than those represented in the various National Liberation Committees. It would be a test of the genuine democratic intentions of each of these committees if it recognized this tendency and gave way to it.

The Russian formula, however, was unequivocal. In Russian

eyes, the National Liberation Committee was the only body fit to rule in any country and it was the Russian refusal to recognize any other means of public representation which led to the transformation of the Jugoslav committee into a dictatorship in that country. It was the EAM attempt to impose a similar form of dictatorship in Greece which led to the civil war.

But in Italy, thanks to the combination of circumstances, the people had had time to awaken to their realization of political aspirations. Countless thousands of Italians who belonged to no party began to tire of government by an admitted minority composed of party leaders in the Italian National Committee of Liberation. As Mr. Milton Bracker of the *New York Times* put it in an admirable dispatch from Rome, "Only seven to ten per cent of the population belonged to recognized political organizations." The rest remained passive.

So long as they remained passive, the Anglo-American authorities in Italy had no choice but to accept the authority of the National Committee of Liberation, which, though representing a minority, was at least the largest organized minority in the country.

Mr. Bracker continues, "But once signs developed that the vast unrepresented were showing signs of political life themselves, it was obviously the strategy of self-preservation"— for the pre-Allied elements within the national committee— "to kick over the traces and try to join forces with those stirring outside the party fold."

There were many other reasons for the party revolt which precipitated the fall of Signor Parri. Undoubtedly the main reason was the fact that government of Italy by the National Committee of Liberation, without an opposition, was breaking down—as it had already broken down in Greece and Jugoslavia, with tragic results.

To accept Moscow's point of view for the moment, the big question is: whether such a development means a return of fascism; whether the (as yet) undeveloped political sophistication of the Italian people will leave them helpless victims to the machinations of the "neo-fascists," as Moscow likes to call them.

The new Italian Government, headed by Signor De Gasperi, showed its determination to prevent a retrogression towards fascism by proceeding to a series of raids in which men accused of being fascists were arrested. The new Italian Government was a Rightist government, that is to say, it was more Right in its politics than the former government of Signor Parri—although it would be Leftist according to American standards.

What it would ultimately be would depend upon the votes of the Italian people at their elections. But at least they would get their free elections—which is more than they got in Jugoslavia!

ITALIAN VIEWS ON COMMUNISM

In the face of this popular demonstration of political rebirth, the communists could put up only a helpless stammering. While Moscow radio talked about incipient "fascism" in Italy, the Italian communists hurriedly redressed themselves to cater to patriotic sentiment. Their new program, broadcast by Rome radio in the Italian Home Service, was as follows:

"The Communist Party deplores the creation of the government crisis at this moment and sums up in three points the task of a government which wants to interpret the country's interests at the present time. It outlines a foreign policy whose primary object is the restoration of all national territory to Italian administration, and the maximum possible national independence, the maintenance of social peace, and the strengthening of unity between workers and all anti-fascist democratic forces.

"After declaring that these objectives, on which Italy's rebirth depends, cannot be achieved by a government which does not enjoy the unconditional support of the democratic parties, the statement concludes by asserting that any attempt to break this unity must be energetically repelled by all who have the people's interests at heart."

In other words, the Italian Communist Party attempted to appeal to popular interest by coming out in favor of Trieste remaining an Italian city, but maintained that the government of Italy must be maintained by parties which (to refer once more to Mr. Bracker) represented, at most, only one-tenth of the Italian people.

Their reasons were transparently clear. By pressing for the maintenance of a government by the National Liberation Committee, most of whose constituent parties were admittedly democratic, the communists hoped to be able to maneuver in such a way as to control the actions of the committee and therefore of the government as a whole.

It was a barren policy, not merely because it presented the farcical picture of the Italian Communist Party quarrelling with the Jugoslav communists—by this time a hoary tactical maneuver—but because the Italian people themselves realized that it was time for the basis of their government to be widened. The Motherland of Communism, whence all these tactical moves were dictated, was fully aware that for the time being the Italian communists had shot their bolt.

Italian domestic press service, November 24, 1945:

"Pavia.—An unknown aircraft dropped by parachute a number of radio transmitting and receiving sets in the neighborhood of Certosa di Pavia. They were picked up by peasants. More radio sets were found near Sizano, sixteen kilometers from Milan."

There was no subsequent explanation of this story, either from the Italian Government or from AMG officials.

But from which country did the airplane come to drop those radio transmitters and receivers? Perhaps America and Britain were trying to launch some secret organization in Italy? If so, why should they send an airplane over territory which they were occupying? How much easier it would be to load a truck with these radio sets and drop them off at precise spots, rather than adopt the haphazard method of dropping them from a plane. If Nazi Germany and Fascist Italy were still extant, one might regard the incident as an attempt to establish or supply a Fifth Column. Since the surviving leaders of Fascism and National Socialism were in no position to take an airplane trip, one can dismiss this supposition.

Perhaps the incident did not take place? If this were the case, one could have expected either a retraction of the story or a subsequent denial from Italian or Anglo-American officials. No denial was issued.

Perhaps the incident did not take place, perhaps the whole story was a fake, planted by Italian or Anglo-American officials as a warning against some power which owned airplanes and which was suspected of trying to establish a fifth-column organization in a country with which it had no direct communications!

Now if the transmitters were dropped to the Italian communists, it is possible to make some deductions. Realizing that an immediate seizure of power in Italy along the same lines as in Jugoslavia, and along the same lines that had been attempted in Greece, was no longer possible, perhaps Moscow had ordered the Italian communists to revert to the tactics of communist parties in other democratic countries before the war —namely, to adopt the old policy of an extreme oppositional party in public politics, while creating an elite underground organization for subsequent use, as tactics dictated.

The following broadcast from Berne, Switzerland, where the Swiss had been closely watching the trend of events among their southern neighbors, gives a clear picture of the situation as it existed at the end of 1945:

"It seems that the present Italian Government crisis forms the basis for a new Allied policy toward Italy. Various statements reveal that, more than ever, the armistice conditions of September, 1943, are being adapted to the special position which Italy has gained by her cooperation in the final phase of the war against Nazi Germany.

"The Allies are now considerably more liberal in their policy with regard to Italy than they were six months ago. At that time, the Russians had made an unmistakable attempt to gain a decisive influence in the formation of the Italian future by means of the newly reborn Italian Communist Party and by playing the Jugoslav card in the Trieste question. It must not be forgotten that the respective spheres of influence of the Allies and Russia had not been fixed as clearly then as they are today. Since then Great Britain, the U.S., and France have made practically all the concessions which, with regard to the Eastern European policy of Soviet Russia, could be reasonably asked and expected by the Kremlin. The Russian influence in Poland and Czechoslovakia, not to speak of Hungary and the Balkan countries, is not only recognized today but respected.

"As a counterpart, at least for the time being, Soviet Russia seems to have given up an activization of her policy of interference in the Mediterranean sphere of the Western Allies. This she can do all the more calmly as the unopposed, though unenthusiastic, acceptance of the abolition of the monarchy in Jugoslavia has supplied the Kremlin with another trump card without any special concessions on her part.

"Italy seems to be left by the Russians to the influence of the West. At any rate, there are no signs indicating that the com-

304

munist movement in Italy, which some months ago was still powerful but which is rapidly losing ground, is particularly backed up by the Soviets. In many respects the contrary seems to be the case.

"Moscow offers no opposition to the trend in Italy for the middle and Rightist parties to regain more and more of their influence on public affairs, an influence which corresponds much more to the conservatism of the majority of Italians than the extreme radicalism which set the tone in the days of the liberation of Northern Italy.

"Furthermore, the state in which twenty thousand Italian soldiers (the last of the 200,000 Italian soldiers taken prisoner in Russia) are returning to Italy at the moment is not exactly a great help to the communist cause in the country.

"The Allied theory which had been proclaimed during the war—and also, for a certain length of time, after the end of the war—to let Italy stew in her own juice, has made way for a revision of the fundamental lines of Allied policy."

Berne's figures on returning prisoners of war were not correct, but there is no doubt that the treatment of Italian prisoners by Russia (and by Jugoslavia) was responsible for most of the loss of prestige suffered by the extreme Left in Italy. For the returning prisoners were tangible evidence of the state of affairs in the Promised Land of Economic Socialist Security.

The treatment of prisoners by Jugoslav Partisans was medieval. During the war, Tito's men took few prisoners, and in this they were justified by the fact that both the Germans and Italians summarily executed all Partisans whom they captured. It was also right that the invaders should be made to repair the havoc they had created during their occupation. It was cold justice that both German and Italian prisoners should be made to dig up the land mines they had planted, to clear the rubble from the wrecked towns and villages, and, if need be, to act as coolie labor in the ports and on the roads.

All this was part of the terrible retribution brought upon Germany and Italy by the ruthless ambition of their totalitarian regimes. But to realize this fact and to accept as inevitable its prolongation are two different affairs. It is right that the soldiers of fascism and National Socialism, tools though they may have been, should repair the damage they have created. But to regard them as slaves to be worked to death is against every idea of humanitarianism, which alone can repair the shattered ethics of war-ravaged Europe.

The Italian prisoners whom I saw in Jugoslavia had almost no hope of ever reaching their homeland again. Nor did this state of affairs apply only to Italians captured by the Partisans. There were other Italians, who had voluntarily deserted to the Partisans while fascist Italy was still in the role of an enemy. They, too, regarded themselves as prisoners for life.

In the little Montenegrin capital of Cetinje, tucked away in the mountains behind the Dalmatian coast, I came upon two Italian ex-sergeants who had deserted from the fascist army, taking with them the essential parts of an army transmitter. They had made their way to the Partisans, and their transmitter later became the official radio station at Cetinje. It had been invaluable during the war as a means of maintaining communications, and it was equally invaluable after peace came to Montenegro as a means of bringing news to the people. Now the war was over, the two Italians wanted to return home; but they were not allowed to leave. Their prisoner status was brought home to them when they were told that they could not even leave the outskirts of the town, less than ten minutes' walk in any direction.

In Belgrade I talked with the Jugoslav wife of an Italian army doctor who had likewise deserted to the Partisans during the war and had served in Partisan hospitals. He, too, was not allowed to leave the country, and had been threatened with such dire penalties if he endeavored to do so that he had not even dared to come to see me himself, but sent his wife as inter-mediary.

At first there was a disinclination to draw any political con-clusions from these cases, and a tendency to excuse the Jugo-slav Partisans on the grounds that they had not yet succeeded in establishing an efficient system; but subsequently the cases became so numerous that it was only possible to conclude that this was either a cold-blooded totalitarian system or a system whose inefficiency was so widespread that it had no justifica-tion for existence.

The Italian Government was naturally aware of the condi-tions under which its nationals were suffering in both Russia and Jugoslavia, and there was therefore some official indigna-tion when the pro-Russian newspapers in Italy began tactlessly to print stories about the facilities which Russia was placing at the disposal of Italian prisoners returning from Russia. Thus:

"Italian Domestic Press Service, October 17, 1945: With reference to reports published by some dailies, the Ministry for Post-War Assistance states that information that some former Italian prisoners in Russia have returned is without foundation. The prisoners so far repatriated come from that part of Germany which is occupied by the Red Army, and not from Soviet territory."

"Italian Domestic Press Service, November 1, 1945: The Ministry for Post-war Assistance again confirms that no de-tachment of former Italian war prisoners in Soviet territory belonging to the Italian Expeditionary Corps in Russia appears to have been repatriated so far. If isolated elements have reached Germany and have returned to Italy, they are single cases of escaped or dispersed soldiers who have evaded all official con-trols."

Later, however, Italian prisoners did begin to arrive from the Soviet Union, and trouble started when they began talking with those returning from the United States. The result of the comparison was heavily in favor of the United States, and there followed a series of clashes with the Leftists.

The Leftists naturally charged that all these outbreaks were engineered by fascists. In actual fact, they themselves had behaved so tactlessly as to greet the trains returning from Russia, carrying red flags and pro-Russian signs—gestures which often caused the repatriates to storm out of the trains, tear down the flags, and beat up their greeters.

No doubt there were reactionaries who welcomed these clashes, but the Italian communists ought to have taken a glance at the healthy and well-clothed Italians returning from prison camps in the United States and the gaunt, ragged skeletons returning from the Soviet sphere, and to have realized that the situation called for a discreet silence.

AMERICA'S STAND

Since Churchill had elaborated his Seven Points of Freedom in Rome in the fall of 1944, thus cancelling the policy he had formulated twelve months before, the onus of developing the new Allied policy towards Italy fell upon America. For if Italy were to survive, she could do so only provided that sufficient economic help were forthcoming to enable the Italian defenders of democracy to stave off the forces of decay until the Italian people themselves came back to life.

Britain was financially bankrupt. The defeat of Churchill in the elections the following year placed in power a new British Government whose conception of its duties was the reverse of that preferred by Churchill. The new government believed its first duties should be to put Britain's own financial house in order rather than to throw good money abroad for political reasons. The Big Stick policy was gone, at least as far as Western Europe was concerned. The new Foreign Secretary, Mr. Ernest Bevin, clearly believes that if the British position in Western Europe is to be maintained, it must be done on a basis of intangibles, rather than by the hard realities of financial wire-pulling.

But even here, Mr. Bevin devotes himself more to his immediate neighbors than to Italy. It is more important for Britain to maintain a foothold in France and the Low Countries, than a toehold in Italy. Even Greece is more important than Italy to the new British Government, for in Greece the British are committed, as a result of the civil war, to insuring that the country shall eventually become free. But, even in Greece, there is a trend on the part of the British to persuade America and France to share the burden, and thus to strengthen Anglo-American post-war cooperation, and to lay the basis for a community of interest with France.

Of all the countries in Europe, Italy has become the special protégé of America. It was America who proposed that full UNRRA aid be given to Italy. It was America who speeded up the repatriation of Italian prisoners from the United States in order that the level of manpower in Italy could be increased. It was America who advanced money out of Lend-Lease funds to supplement the emergency relief program for the last three months of 1945 until the larger UNRRA program could be started. It was America who took the initiative in proposing a revision of the Italian armistice terms after the failure of the Foreign Ministers' Conference in London.

In mid-November, 1945, nine representatives of the New York Chamber of Commerce paid a visit to Italy in order to investigate the possibilities of a resumption of normal trade between Italy and America. It was made known at the time that by the end of the year all Italian ports, except Trieste and a small section of Naples, would be returned to Italian control. In most of the ports, sections had already been turned over to the Italians. It was also announced that the U.S. Government would concede thirty ships to Italy as part of the plan to aid the country during 1946; that commercial blacklisting would soon be abolished, and that steps had been taken to stabilize the lira exchange rate as soon as the peace treaty was signed.

Shortly afterwards, the U.S. Embassy in Rome announced that seventy firms owned or controlled by Italians had been removed from the U.S. black list and could start commercial connections with U.S. subjects. If the system of private enterprise in Europe were threatened, America was determined to see that in Italy it had a fighting chance to survive.

This was indeed a drastic change from the days when Italy was regarded with cynicism and contempt, when G.I. black marketing reached such heights (or depths) that the War Department refused to reveal its disbursals for pay and allowances, lest the extent to which dollars were being converted into lire at exorbitant rates be also revealed.

The Italians responded to the change with enthusiasm. They had never fully accepted the role of empire which Mussolini had devised for them and tried to make attractive by every device of propaganda. They had never seen any sense in fighting for a piece of desert when the sunny vineyards of home lay so much closer to hand. Not that the peasant life in Italy had ever been a pleasant one, by Western European standards. But the new Italy believed it could be made better without having to seize the territory of another state.

A new and encouraging spirit was born. No one could say where it would eventually lead the country. But some things were already plain.

The Italians had renounced as contemptible the panaceas of totalitarianism, whether of the old regime or of the new Byzantine empire to the East. They had had more than enough of its stifling atmosphere.

The recovery from the septicemia of fascism had been

gradual. For a time there had been signs of a relapse into the disorder of pre-fascist days, but that danger was now past.

Given a chance to emerge into the peace without having her growth stifled by the peace treaty, there was no doubt that the new Italy would be among the leaders in the companionship of nations—if there was to be a companionship.

Two great Italian leaders summed up the future in terms which succinctly expressed the crisis of Italy, of Europe, and, indeed, of the world.

When America met with Russian opposition against relaxing the Italian armistice terms, Benedetto Croce, the most clear-sighted of Italian Liberals, wrote this letter to the Florence Liberal paper, *La Patria*:

"Our moral conscience rebels against the victorious powers' policy towards Italy when we compare it with their attitude before the war and with their declarations and promises during the war. And yet this comparison, however spontaneous and violent a reaction it provokes, is really naïve and devoid of any foundation, because what is happening now is not a fact which can be assessed and condemned in moral or legal terms. It is a political fact, an ever-recurring fact of war with all its ruses and mendaciousness, and with the ensuing *vae victis* revealing itself in the victors' unfettered, bestial craving no longer meeting any obstacles to check the boundless covetousness of nationalistic or imperialistic selfishness.

"Accursed fascism has flung open the gates to this ferocious eruption. And the matter is the more serious because even the intelligent and far-seeing among the victors are being hopelessly swamped by the overpowering crowd which they call public opinion, to whose pressure they yield. And so, although formally the victors, they too are defeated and enslaved.

"By protecting, as our duty compels us to do, our political and economic interests with all the means at our disposal, we can, and must, protect and defend and enhance that tolerance

311

and humaneness which is our virtue, the spirit of freedom which inspires it, and the intelligence which enlightens it.

"No one will ever be able to rob us of this possession. Perhaps it may even happen that on this spiritual plane we may help, or even act as teachers and be leaders for our victors, who, though wealthy in political and economic power, are poor in that sphere—at any rate, poorer than we are. Sorrow ennobles, whereas good luck makes a man vulgar and stupid, and there are still people in the world who, being at the crossroads, choose the way leading to nobility."

Here was no five-year plan for economic security, but an inspiring call to Italians to set an example as the stronghold of individual freedom, to show the world that man could live without a full belly, but not without ethics.

The next Italian leader to sound a warning against materialism was Carlo Sforza, he whom Churchill had had dismissed for his previous warnings against the monarchy. Writing on the atom bomb, in the *Corriere d'Informazione,* he commented that the bomb rightly increased the suspicions of those who did not share its terrible secret. It was clear, he went on, that the bomb would also shortly be manufactured in Russia.

"I hope," he added, "that the atom bomb will become a factor of world peace, for it will make governments realize it is folly to face a new world with the formulas of an unhappy past. The only alternative to new wars is a general, loyal agreement and collaboration between nations. Should Europe be divided into two zones of influence, war will soon become inevitable. In case of war, Italy, placed as she is between two contended seas, will be the testing ground of the atomic bomb."

We have reached the stage where it is possible to sum up the history of power politics as they have affected the positions of the three large powers in Italy.

There was the first period, during which both America and Britain, believing they had reached an agreement with Russia on spheres of influence in the Balkans, paid little attention to the future of Italy, contenting themselves with acting as its military guardians until the peace.

There followed the period of awakening when both America and Britain realized that Russia intended to extend her influence and authority beyond her sphere and was, in fact, already doing so. The nature of previous American and British concessions to Russia made it impossible to halt this expansion short of the Italian frontier. Italy became the front line of resistance in the game of power politics.

Previous British policy in Italy, however, nullified in advance any *volte face*. Moreover, the British were financially bankrupt and, at the time when British policy needed its realignment, Churchill was defeated in the elections. As the senior partner, America took over the burden of shaping the new policy of building up Italy as a bulwark of democracy.

Having succeeded in penetrating as far as Trieste, Russia found it impossible to proceed farther without offending the susceptibilities of her intended victims, not to speak of her two Allies. She had reached the point of discovering it is impossible to please all the victims all the time. Attempting to reconcile the irreconcilables of Russian foreign policy, the Italian Communist Party, which emerged from the war as a virile and strong organization, suffered a grievous loss of influence and prestige. Italian prisoners returning from Russia were able to confirm that whatever staying powers the Soviet regime may possess through its authoritarian system, it had not yet succeeded in even remotely approaching the standard of living assured in the West—a deduction arrived at in reverse, incidentally, by Red Army soldiers, who, as they returned to the motherland, became an increasing cause of concern for the master minds of the Kremlin.

Receiving this sudden buffet, the Russian tendency was to withdraw abruptly from Italian affairs and to render the task of Italian reconstruction by America more difficult, on the theory that economic chaos would accomplish what infiltration tactics had failed to achieve.

There was another buffet in store for the Russians, however, when the Italian people, awakening from a generation of political lethargy, demanded a broader basis for their government than the six-party coalition, which represented only a fraction of the future electorate. Preferring to maneuver within a small enclave—just as they have fought for the principle of international negotiations among the Big Three, instead of at a full and open assembly of all United Nations—the Russians opposed this tendency, and thereby caused the Italian Communist Party to suffer a further loss of prestige.

They were even more dismayed when it became apparent that latent stores of energy in the Italian people had been roused to life by the increasing help which came from America. They therefore cast off whatever propaganda role they formerly adopted towards Italy and forthrightly opposed increased American aid, whether by direct economic help or by a relaxation of the Armistice terms. This completed the rout of the Italian Communist Party as a popular political machine.

For their part, the Italian people were engaged in the gigantic task of repairing the almost incredible ravages of war. They had little time for orthodox party politics. If it had to be a choice between the East and the West, they were definitely for the West; but their political leaders were more and more aware that the war, with its varying effects on world affairs, had left only two powers in Europe whose respective strengths remotely approached each other—Soviet Russia and Great Britain. And that if power politics were allowed to continue, Europe would be divided into two zones of influence with rigid and explosive frontiers.

They therefore believe that a continuation of power politics would be disastrous, and as Italy regains her feet, the more she can be expected to press for a real unity of nations with all the conditions that this implies.

For Italy it is all or nothing. When the Jugoslav frontier is finally sealed—as it assuredly will be, once economic help from the West is no longer necessary and once it is clear that power politics with their zones of influence are to be the prescription for the future—Italy will be to Russia what Poland was before the war, a dangerous source of infection from which may seep ideas whose attractiveness may undermine the stability of all regimes founded on a basis of totalitarianism.

It is not possible to say more. The rest is up to America.

VII. CONCLUSION

"*The brotherhood of nations and of men*
Comes on apace. New dreams of youth bestir
The ancient heart of the earth—fair dreams
of love
And equal freedom for all folk and races.
The day is past for idle talk of Empire;
And who would glory in dominating others—
Be it man or nation—he already has writ
His condemnation clear in all men's hearts.
'Tis better he should die."
                    —*Edward Carpenter, Towards Democracy*

CONCLUSION

It is high time we began to find out where we stand. To say we are mixed up in a game of power politics is not enough. We must know what power politics mean and along what road they lead. We must know with whom we are playing this game, who has the blue chips, and who is winning.

Power politics mean simply this: the maneuvering for position by a group of states, generally large and powerful states, who believe that peace and stability can be secured by the juggling of different strategic areas without regard to the wishes of the people who inhabit them. As a method of international adjustment, it is not by any means new and it used to be fairly successful in the days when kings and emperors could make decisions without consulting their various subjects. When the Napoleonic Empire fell apart, the victors did a neat job of carving up Europe and succeeded in keeping the peace for more than a generation—a fact which seems to have hypnotized statesmen ever since. The Czech cession of the Sudetenland to Germany in 1938 was a piece of power politics between Germany and Britain at a time when the British did not realize they had vital interests in Czechoslovakia. And since World War II, power politics have come back into fashion with a vengeance. Anybody can find plenty of examples merely by looking at a map and intelligently analyzing contemporary events. Soviet Russia's seizure (in effect)

319

of north Iran, the Anglo-American recognition of Tito in Jugoslavia, the British intervention in Greece, the extensive American aid to post-war Italy, are all pieces of power politics.

In the last two cases, of course, it can be pointed out that Anglo-American aid has been welcomed by the people concerned; however, since the aid was extended not for the sake of the people (else how explain the earlier Anglo-American indifference to the hungry and ill-clothed Italians?) but as a means of bolstering up the so-called "free enterprise" system in face of advancing communism, I maintain that they are genuine examples of power politics.

Now it is comparatively simple for a totalitarian state to engage in power politics. An emperor has merely been replaced by an all-powerful ruler. And if his subjects are more intelligent than they were a century ago, he has ample means at his disposal to see that they keep in line. The complete control of all means of expression, both internally and externally, through the press and radio, the consequent ease with which it is possible to play up any incident and to blow first hot then cold on any issue as necessity dictates, give the rulers of states such as Nazi Germany, Fascist Italy, and Socialist-Nationalist Russia a great degree of flexibility. Furthermore, constant purges and liquidations and the rise of a new oligarchy have rendered the masses apathetic and the younger generation eagerly agreeable to apparently contradictory changes in attitudes and foreign policy.

No such state of affairs is possible in a democracy, where people are accustomed to voice their opinions and to have them heeded by their government. As a result, in order to maintain a continuity of American policy in power politics, the American administration is being driven to more and more secrecy in its negotiations, especially its negotiations with Soviet Russia. As in domestic affairs, it would seem that the trend in

America is towards, and not away from, centralization of power and ultimate government by an elite bureaucracy.

But the matter does not stop there. There might be a case for power politics if the people could delegate their responsibilities to a bureaucracy without any worries for the future, as they seem to want to do. But once these responsibilities have been renounced by the people, a slippery incline is opened up in world affairs. For it then becomes the responsibility of the large states to maintain peace and order; smaller states are allowed no opinion.

The whole case of Soviet Russia is that there should be consolidation of world power in fewer and fewer hands. Stalin's argument is very plausible. He claims that the large powers, who have maintained the burden of the war, should maintain the responsibility for the peace. If they can agree, there will be no war. If they quarrel, war is inevitable. In Stalin's opinion there is, therefore, no point in allowing the smaller states an influential voice in world affairs. The process of consolidation is continued. First the Big Four. Then the Big Three. And now Russia is trying to convince America that between the two of them all world issues can be solved and that there is no reason to bring in the British.

When this stage is reached, our rule by bureaucracy is well under way. There arise a host of officials, minor and senior, who claim to be able to handle specific problems. The downward grade of democracy is littered with them—the Neville Hendersons who thought the British Government could safely entrust them with the handling of Goering (and lived to write books on the failures of their mission), Chamberlain who thought he could handle Hitler behind closed doors, Churchill who thought he could handle Tito through his liaison officers and who became short-tempered whenever the British Parliament asked him for awkward details. If ever there arises an American statesman who thinks that the democratic world can trust him to "wow" Stalin—that will be the time to start choosing a bomb shelter.

No world war has yet been started by the great powers. They have everything mapped out—or think they have. World Wars start with the obstinate refusal of some small states to be kicked around. In some cases, the small states may be sacrificed, but ultimately there comes a case when the large powers take opposite sides, and that is when the fighting starts.

The step-by-step-towards-peace policy of power politics is no such thing. It is a sleigh ride to disaster devised by coffee-house pinheads and politicians.

I am aware that somebody may point out an apparent flaw in this argument, stating that my diagnosis reveals the cure. These people will hold that a safeguard against any runaway tendency in power politics lies in the continued freedom of the American people to criticize the policy of the administration. This is true, but the Jeffersonian argument has one basic condition, which is that the will of the people shall be freely heard and shall not be distorted by the efforts of special interests. A corollary of this is that the people shall be so alive to their interests and their responsibilities, all the time and not merely on individual occasions, that special interests have no opportunity to seize control. The power of the pressure groups is no secret in Washington, nor is the fact that certain special interests were behind the 1946 strikes and agitations to bring the troops back from overseas.

The future policy of the communists in America is already clear. It is they who will inspire, support, and direct the future isolationist movement in this country in order to undermine America's responsibilities overseas. They will be abetted, perhaps ignorantly, by those financial and manufacturing interests which are so hypnotized by the devastation in Russia that they see nothing but a flock of business orders for a generation to come, a fact of which the Soviet rulers are well aware. (And watch how they will use this carrot to increase rivalry between the surviving democracies!)

The cycle is being completed. The extreme Right and the extreme Left are at last discovering that they have nothing immediately to fear from each other. It may come to a struggle in the end, but in the meantime both are concerned with dealing with the mass in the middle!

This, I know, is heresy to all those members of the moderate Right, as well as to those members of the Left who have not yet wakened to the dynamics of Soviet history. For—and this is a cause for intense despair—nothing that I have written so far in this book about Soviet policy, none of the utterances of the Russian radio or its subsidiaries in the Soviet sphere, none of the Russian actions outside their frontiers, will seem to the Left in any way incompatible with their conception of Soviet Russia as the fountainhead of socialism. Contradictions between Russian statements and Russian actions, ruthless tactics, broken pledges, imprisonments, purges, assassinations . . . all are reconcilable under the theory that the ends justify the means.

In the eyes of the Left, these ends stand out clearly as the ultimate achievement of world socialism. Their picture of Soviet Russia is that of a state so handling herself in her conduct vis-à-vis the nefarious capitalist democracies as to insure that these ends are achieved.

Once a person subscribes to this theory, logic and illogic become one. It becomes possible to retreat from one line of argument to another without any apparent contradiction. For example, in the case of a specific country such as Jugoslavia, the Left will maintain at the outset that the new system installed by Marshal Tito is fully democratic in all respects. Subsequently an overwhelming body of evidence becomes available to demonstrate that Tito's system is not only not democratic but the reverse. Compelled to retreat, the Left then takes up the line that Tito's repressive measures are justified in order to stamp out the activities of the Jugoslav "fascists," to quell the "collaborators," and to subordinate industry and agriculture to the all-important needs of reconstruction. If American opinion becomes thoroughly aroused over the persecutions in Jugoslavia, a subsidiary line is then adopted in order to persuade the public to lay aside its fears. By now this line is fairly familiar and runs somewhat as follows: "These Balkan countries! They are always having fights over something or other. It all goes to show that they are not yet ready for democracy. The Serbs kill the Croats, then the Croats turn round and start killing the Serbs. There's always somebody killing somebody else in the Balkans. Nothing to worry about!"

There is only one way to uproot these arguments, and that is to expose the falsity of the original conception of Soviet Russia as a state working towards world socialism. For those who care to take the trouble, there is a wealth of material on this point, but I shall try to summarize the main arguments of the Left and to show the facts as they exist in the light of the latest evidence.

1. *That the men who took part in the Russian Revolution have never forsaken their original idea of achieving a socialist state.*

This argument is fallacious for the simple reason that most of the men who took part in the Russian Revolution, leaders and workers alike, no longer exist; they were wiped out in Stalin's purges.

The following facts are quoted by Gregory Bienstock, Solomon M. Schwarz, and Aaron Yugow in their admirable survey of Russian industry and agriculture.*

At the time of the 17th Congress of the Russian Communist Party (the all-Soviet Bolshevik Party, as it is called in Russia)

* *Management in Russian Industry and Agriculture* (1944).

held in January-February, 1934, before the purges, the Party had 1,872,488 members.

At the time of the 18th Congress, held five years later, after the purges, this membership total had dropped to 1,588,852. Nearly three hundred thousand members had disappeared in the purges.

Who were these victims? At the beginning of 1918, the Party had numbered between 260,000 to 270,000, mostly young people. Allowing for deaths during the Civil War that followed the Revolution and for subsequent deaths from natural causes, at least two hundred thousand of these would have survived until 1939. But only twenty thousand were listed as still belonging to the Party. Nine-tenths of them had disappeared.

2. *That although the Communist Party is the real ruling body of Russia and no other political party is allowed to exist, this is tantamount to rule by the proletariat, since the workers in industry and agriculture can exercise their influence through membership in the Party.*

Not only were Stalin's purges directed primarily against those Russian political leaders, writers, workers, and peasants who had taken part in the Revolution, but the Communist Party ceased to be the party of the workers and became the party of a new elite class.

Of the delegates to the 17th Congress, 9.3 per cent were members of the proletariat—not people who had risen from the working classes, but actual manual workers from production. This was a point which had always been examined by each congress.

Five years later, at the 18th Congress, the Credentials Commission made no mention of this point. And at this congress, no representatives of the workers—not even representatives of the Stakhanovites, the elite of Russian workers—were elected to membership of the Central Committee of the Party.

From which class, then, came the other delegates who formed more than nine-tenths of those present? Soviet Russia recognizes only one other class besides the workers—its intelligentsia, comprising bureaucrats, technocrats, scientists, and the like. According to Molotov, this class totals nearly ten million people, or only one-seventeenth of the total population.*

3. *That the Russian workers, through their trade unions, can secure decent wages and working conditions.*

The spirit of the Russian trade-union movement was shattered in 1929 when almost all its leaders were purged and replaced by new men. Almost the entire leadership of the Central Trade Union Council was removed.

During the thirties, the triangular control of factories by managers, the Party, and the trade unions was scrapped. The manager was placed in sole control. He alone could select, promote, and remove administrative personnel. Trade unions were allowed to participate in discussing fundamental questions of production but could not make or even share in decisions.†

In 1931 plant managers were given the right to hire directly without applying to the employment offices, and when it later became necessary to stimulate the flow of manpower to the factories by organizing recruiting drives throughout the country, the trade unions were allowed no influence on hiring decisions in or outside the plants. Nor could they take part in these recruiting activities.

In fixing wages and working conditions, the trade unions have ceased to be an instrument of policy. In the early days of the Soviet Union, collective contracts were renewed annually through an organized drive conducted by the trade unions and the economic authorities. Since 1935 no collective

* V. Molotov, "The Third Five Year Plan," Address to the 18th Party Congress (Moscow, 1939), pp. 44–45.
† *Management in Russian Industry and Agriculture.*

contracts have been written or renewed. The fixing of wage rates is now a function of industrial management. Piece rates are also determined, in effect, by plant management.

4. *That, although the idea of equal wages has been abandoned by the Soviet Union, the Russian wage differential is still less than in any other country.*

Leaving aside the steadily increasing cost of living in the Soviet Union *before* the war and the fact that the Soviet Union is the only great state which for years has published no standard-of-living index, there are certain facts which show the falsity of this conception.

The 1921 schedule defining rates of pay for all workers was scrapped in 1929 and replaced by new schedules, which placed managers, directors, and engineers in a different category from the workers. To take an example, the average monthly salary for technical personnel in a Donetz coal mine for the third quarter of 1940 was 1,200 rubles. On top of this the upper-salaried elite class may receive bonuses many times the annual salary. The average monthly earnings of coal-mining manual workers for the same year were 132.60 rubles. The salaries of directors, chief engineers, and administrators in the top class are up to one hundred times higher than the average wage and three hundred times higher than the minimum wage.

5. *That there is equal opportunity for all, enabling manual workers and their children to rise out of the working class.*

Far from this being the case, there is increasing inequality of education. Up to 1932 a minimum of sixty-five per cent of the students in engineering colleges and technical schools, the prerequisite for future managerial positions, had to be manual workers or their children. A decree of September, 1932, abolished this principle.*

A decree of October 2, 1940, reintroduced fees for higher education, one hundred and fifty to two hundred rubles a year

* Arthur Koestler, *The Yogi and the Commissar* (1945).

for high schools, three hundred to five hundred rubles a year for colleges. Compare these fees with the average monthly earnings of a coal miner, quoted earlier, and it will be seen how few manual workers are able to afford to send their children to high school or college.

For those who are able to afford the high-school fees, scholarships for colleges were made more difficult by the same decree. A student now has to obtain examination marks of "excellent" in at least one-third of all subjects and no marks below the level of "good," in order to win a scholarship.

No scholarships at all are granted for high schools.

When the decree was announced, it stipulated that the new fees must be paid within one month from its promulgation; six hundred thousand students of poor parents who could not afford the new fees had to leave school.*

A simultaneous decree introduced four years' compulsory labor service for those children whose parents can not afford to send them to high school or colleges. Between eight hundred thousand and one million children are mobilized annually for this labor service, with the inevitable result that the students from high schools and colleges grow up with a feeling of social superiority.†

The final result is seen in the attendance figures at Russian high schools and colleges. The proportion of manual workers or their children at these institutions began to decrease from the introduction of these decrees and, by 1938, was lower than at any time since 1928.

Enough! This should be sufficient to demonstrate that for some years *before* the war Russia was swinging away from the idea of a socialist state and was introducing a new elite class whose wealth and power far exceed that of any ruling class in the Western democracies.

* *Ibid.*
† *Management in Russian Industry and Agriculture.*

And if this is so, it is equally clear that the expansionist aims of Soviet Russia are not with the ultimate idea of introducing world socialism but are solely concerned with extending the frontiers of a Russia turned imperialist.

The apologists for Russia have no grounds for what they believe is the final proof of the healthiness of the Russian system—that if the Russian people were really oppressed by their rulers they would not have fought so magnificently in the war. For if the tenacity with which a nation fights is proof of the benefits conferred upon it by its social and economic systems, then the National-Socialist regime in Germany was at least as good as the Socialist-National regime in Russia. All that this argument amounts to is that the means of mass control have become so powerful that it is possible to hoodwink any nation into taking castor oil and believing it to be orange juice.

Not until we realize that Russia has ceased to become the home of the Revolution and has become the seat of Reaction shall we begin to understand the apparently confusing methods of Russian diplomacy and propaganda which are now causing us and our statesmen such embarrassment.

It is only against this background that the restoration to their pedestals of pre-revolutionary Russian heroes makes any sense. The new heroes of Russia are not the men who fought for the Revolution, but Peter the Great, Alexander Nevsky, conqueror of the German knights seven centuries ago, Catherine the Great, and Ivan the Terrible, to name but a few. "For Soviet patriots," said Molotov, "homeland and communism are fused into one inseparable whole." This explanation carries as little conviction as a Yankee trying to eulogize Benedict Arnold.

All the old tactics of pre-revolutionary Russian imperialism have been brought out of their cupboard, dusted off, and stood on their feet again. Pan-Slavism has been revived under the new name of All-Slavism as a means of uniting all Slav countries under the control of Russia. The Orthodox Church has been given a new lease on life and its dignitaries sent out to organize Orthodox communities in the Balkans, the Middle East, and the United States.

And to all nations not directly under her control, the Soviet Union poses as both the cavalier and crusader. And, not content with this contradiction, as the only cavalier and the only crusader. Indeed by her own account, she is not merely the only true democracy, but the only really great empire, the only true socialist state, and the only efficient one. All others are frauds, shams, shadows, substitutes, and fakes.

Here is a specimen of the technique, as displayed by the Moscow radio since the end of the war:

"The Soviet man has checked the barbarian's invasion, has routed fascism, and has liberated the peoples of oppressed Europe. Had it not been for him, the fascists would long ago have shot down children and women somewhere in India and would have bombed New York skyscrapers. England, hiding in ruins, could not sleep even one night in peace, while Maidanek and Oswiecim would commence their work in the East in Iran and Egypt, with the same heartlessness as they did in Europe. Europe has been saved by the Russian people, saved by the very Soviet Union whose destruction, exploitation, and dismemberment for decades had been wished for, prophesied, and worked for by so many in this same Europe. The Soviet Union and only the Soviet Union, has made possible the final victory of civilization over Nazi barbarism. There cannot be the slightest dispute as to who has saved Europe from the rule of the German bandits. The war is finished. The Soviet Union has smashed two aggressors, in the West as well as in the East, and provides guarantees against a repetition of aggression. . . ."

Or this:

"With the destruction of the Japanese source of aggression

330

ended that abnormal situation which allowed this imperialist
State to try to turn the Great Pacific Ocean into its own closed
sea. Gone forever are the grim times when the problems of
the Pacific were solved without the participation of the Soviet
Union, a great Pacific State."

Or this:

"By doing away with private ownership of the means of
production, we have eliminated unemployment (which is a
terrible whiplash held over the workers of the capitalist countries) once and for all. In our own time, for instance, there are
close to seven million unemployed in a most advanced capitalist country like the U.S., which has not even had time to de-
mobilize its main Army contingents."

Or Anglo-American material aid to the Red Army is minimized. This:

"The U.S.S.R. realized the transfer of civilian branches of
economy, to war production, several times quicker than England and the U.S. Many American and British firms were afraid
of a decrease in profits, of losing former markets. A number
of capitalist firms tried at all costs to preserve their former
civilian production. Thus motor car firms in the U.S. for two
years challenged State decrees and produced millions of civilian
cars. Sometimes stores of vital products were even destroyed
during the war with the aim of raising their prices. . . .

"Both in the U.S. and England the production of war materials was hindered by monopolies for commercial reasons.
. . . In the bourgeois countries the interests of private capital-
ists clashed with those of national defense. . . . The war did
not reduce the part played by the capitalist monopolies. On
the contrary, they used the conditions of wartime to strengthen
their positions and to increase their profits considerably. Only
in the U.S.S.R. is planning carried out in the economy
which proved so vital in the Fatherland War of the Soviet
Union." (Sic.)

Now there is only one way of extricating ourselves from this rat race of power politics before we go pumping ourselves into another war.

First of all, it must begin with the realization that somewhere during what was at one time called the Peoples' War we began to travel down the wrong road. Indeed, the very fact that the name chosen by the late President Roosevelt after canvassing American opinion was since discarded and replaced by that of World War II is a sign that the essence of the Peoples' War has been forgotten.

Not only have we missed the right road, but we have travelled a long way down the wrong one. We shall never find the right road until we retrace our steps with our eyes open and our minds clear. So far we have been willing to use only our own signposts and our own standards of distance, and it is about time we began to admit that we have about as much idea where we are going, or how far we have gone, as Paddy's pig.

Nobody can help us except ourselves. There are no winds to blow away the political fog except those we ourselves create.

We must concern ourselves more and more with peoples and not with their governments. We must learn to add up what Tolstoy calls the infinitesimals of history, the events that influence peoples. We must reject the comforting but deadly temptation to accept oversimplifications.

We must decide which are the important essentials of democracy, and no matter how we change the system to cope with technological problems, we must see to it that the political structure is not changed in such a way that these essentials are lost. Some of the aspects of totalitarianism have too much logic in them to be brushed aside. Whatever we may say about their methods, it is a fact that the National-Socialist system in Germany and the Socialist-National system in Russia abolished unemployment. Democracy must meet this deep urge for se-

332

curity and must still preserve its political freedom—or else, either way, it will cease to exist.

We must know what we mean by democracy.

To the uninitiated, Tito says it is his system in Jugoslavia. He says that the right of habeas corpus is protected even though any pedestrian in Belgrade can see for himself the secret police prisons where people are incarcerated without charge or trial. Is this what we mean by habeas corpus, or by democracy? If not, then Tito is damned as an international criminal, not merely because of his victims but because, by helping to increase public confusion about what democracy really means, he is contributing materially to that public cynicism regarding the benefits of democracy which is the most serious crisis that democracy faces today. It is possible for a democracy to undergo the various crises of industry and to pass through succeeding cycles of unemployment, and still to survive. But once the people of a democracy become apathetic or cynical, then the system is really in danger of its life.

We must not allow ourselves to be confused. We must not be tricked by the extreme Left into damning all its opponents as "fascists;" nor must we allow the extreme Right to damn all its critics as "communists." Yet this is what is happening every day.

In the great post-war tasks that confront us, we must steadily remember that it is people who really matter, and not merely those people who are marked with the blue stamp of approval from the Left. All too many people have been hounded by the Left as "collaborationists," which is another of those simplifications passed on to the American public by ill-advised and uncritical war correspondents. For there were many more people who opposed the Nazis and fascists than the extreme Left would now have us believe.

There were those who opposed openly and refused to keep silent, the Pastor Niemoellers and Cardinal Faulhabers. These

333

people, the extreme Left now denounces as "collaboration-ists," "neo-fascists," and the like.

There were those who used their positions to give secret aid to the underground resistance movements. Those who have since refused to resign themselves to the equally totalitarian methods of the Left are also now denounced as "collabora-tionists" and the like.

There were those who fought actively with the under-ground. If they subsequently allowed themselves to be ab-sorbed by the Left, they are praised. If they turned against the Left, as did the Chetniks in Jugoslavia, they are now termed "fascists."

Finally, there were those great masses of people who were so placed that they could resist only secretly, in their hearts, waiting for the time when the Allies would come to liberate them.

If we learn to put ourselves in the other man's place, most of these generalizations will lose their effect. But every time we regard ourselves as remote observers we suffer a defeat, and a little bit of democracy dies whenever we shrug off troubles in another country as proof that that country is not yet ready for democracy. For if there is only one kind of de-mocracy in the essentials it guarantees to men and women the world over, then the only way of preserving democracy in this shrinking world of ours is to see that it exists every-where. In other words, the world cannot endure half slave and half free.

In the whole world today, America is the only surviving democratic state which is sufficiently powerful to propound this idea and to carry it through to realization. At first sight, it seems to entail great sacrifices, but all these are minute com-pared to the sacrifices that the world will make—and no country more than America—if the idea of national sovereignty is maintained.

Of what use is the United Nations Organization if national sovereignty is maintained? The only way in which the UNO can take any effective action against a nation committing aggression is by using force. And what is force against a sovereign nation but war?

Every kind of device has been used in the past to prevent war between sovereign states, and all have failed.

It was not until kings established their authority that wars between feudal barons were brought to a standstill.

Wars between England, Scotland, and Wales were frequent until all three countries were brought under one government.

Wars between the separate German states were frequent until all were united into one state.

We have reached the stage when a larger fusing is necessary. National sovereignty must go; a World Government must arise to put international bickerings into their proper place.

There are dozens of pressure groups in this country who would oppose such a scheme with all the means in their power. There are the industrial and farm groups who regard the prospect of a tariff-less world with terror, not seeing the boundless horizons that such a world would open. There are the labor groups who fear that cancellation of immigration quotas would kill their monopoly of the labor market. There are the politicians who are still concerned with minor rackets and are not yet ready for larger affairs.

All of these nightmares are unreal, because they are based on conceptions of national frontiers, national currencies, national wage scales, and so forth, all of which would disappear or be levelled out in a world state. There would remain inequalities, of course—just as there remain inequalities between the North and the South ninety years after the Civil War.

335

But the national ambitions that lead to war . . . these would not remain, because there would be no soil in which they could flourish.

The way ahead is littered with formidable obstacles, many of which seem unsurmountable. For on top of the difficulties of rousing the American public from its apathy towards outside affairs and its preoccupation with its own domestic future, there is the opposition which the Soviet Union would undoubtedly offer to such a proposal. If the American pressure groups think they have worries, they should take a look at Soviet Russia and see what a World State would do to the system that presently exists there. If the Soviet rulers are so unsure of themselves that they have had to impose an internal passport system, how much more unsure they would be if there were a tangible realization of the Four Freedoms, including the freedom for all to come and go across any frontier, guaranteed by a World Government.

This is why Soviet emissaries everywhere oppose any attempt to convert the United Nations Organization into a World State.

And lest this seem too biased a diatribe against the Soviet Union, let me say that I for one would be happy to accept the authority of a Russian as World President. Or a Chinese President. Or anybody else whom the consensus of world opinion elects to office. For, in cutting out power politics, our only hope is to appeal over the heads of those officials at present conducting mercenary national politics and to appeal to the hearts and aspirations of people. If we do this, there is a possibility that Russia may dominate the consequent World Assembly. It is a mathematical certainty that the cowed and crushed Russian people would vote down the line for Russian candidates and that the votes in democratic countries would be split.

But this is a chance we must take. If we do not take this chance, we condemn ourselves to the perpetuation of national sovereignty which means the certainty of ultimate war. And if there should be any survivors of such a war, there will assuredly be a World State—but not one necessarily corresponding to the will of all concerned.

This, I know, may be condemned as visionary or as "warmongering." It has been my experience that the visionary politics of one decade become the practical politics of another, and that the voices of the Cassandras are soon drowned out by the roar of the cannon.

A World State by choice or by ultimate imposition—this is the alternative confronting America now.

Until this idea is accepted, I would like to suggest the attachment of some safety devices to the present machine which is running away with us. They may at least give us time to open our eyes to the speed with which we are travelling towards another explosion.

I would like to see the press devote more space to the propaganda methods of other nations. Psychological warfare did not end with the dismemberment of the United States Office of War Information. The ether is filled with it, while we render ourselves mentally disarmed. The potentialities of "black" propaganda are only now being realized.

We are entering an era when "stooge" newspapers and "stooge" political parties in dozens of different countries will be used in the nefarious battles to influence the unprotected minds of people in the democratic countries. It is not enough that the American administration through the State Department should know the real interests behind these newspapers and parties. That information must be made available also to the American people.

It is no secret that communists are hard at work everywhere, creating fronts behind which they can work—just as, for example, they created the organization known as America Peace Mobilization which continued to agitate against American intervention right up to the day when Germany attacked Russia, and which then agitated just as raucously in favor of American intervention.

We need to know who are behind these fronts. We need to know who is financing this newspaper in Stockholm, that one in Lisbon, this other in Istambul. We shall have to run fast because these shadowy figures are skilled at their work. As fast as one agency is exposed and outlives its usefulness, another is created.

But if we fail in this task of keeping ourselves informed, there will be more and more confusion on that vital task of creating the World Creed for which the world is so desperately hungry. And we shall pass through a succession of stormy battles in that war of nerves which is the prelude to the real thing.

For this is the danger of an aggressively expanding power: like a millionaire who is driven to make his second million in order to protect his first, then a third to insure the two he already has, each conquest not only whets the appetite for another but creates the necessity for it. Like men in modern business, such powers believe they know when they will be content to stop—and, like men, they never do.

This is a time when America is at the pinnacle of her power. Her armies demobilized, the weapons of war tossed onto the scrap heap, and the specialized agencies designed to deal with the intricacies of a totalitarian war dissolved, America's immediate physical power has vanished. But there remains the enormous prestige which America still enjoys among the peoples overseas.

It is a prestige which the British might have had if the people who controlled British policy had not been so influenced by archaic ideas of empire and world influence.

It is a prestige which the Russians seemed at one time to be on the verge of inheriting but which they decided to forego in favor of more tangible possessions.

It is now for America to decide whether she will inherit that prestige, with all its responsibilities and obligations, or whether she will allow history, with its inscrutable laws, to pass it to another.